Colorado Restaurants
Off The Beaten Path
with Recipes

Benjamin
Benjamin James Bennis

Edited by: Linda P. Viray

Small Town Publications
Denver, Colorado

Cover by: Susan Foppé,
              Foppé Johnson Communications, Inc., Denver, CO

Published by:
Small Town Publications
PO Box 621275
Littleton, CO 80162
(303)329-8283

Printed by:
Transcontinental Printing and Graphics
Peterborough, Ontario
Canada

Copyright 1998 by Benjamin James Bennis and Small Town Publications. All rights reserved. Except for brief quotations by a reviewer, no part of this book may be reproduced of transmitted in any form or by any means without the written permission of the author and publisher.

ISBN 0-9629799-3-7

Dedicated to my lovely wife Linda, for all her patient support in helping me produce another book. Thanks, Sweetie!

Linda at the Cliff Palace, Mesa Verde National Park

INTRODUCTION

This book is for people who love to dine out, for people who love to cook and for people who just love to eat! It is the fourth book that I have written since 1991 on Colorado's small-town restaurants and the first to offer color photography of the restaurants and their recipes. All the restaurants selected in this guide are NEW. That is, they have not appeared in any of my previous three books.

When I go to a town in Colorado, I select restaurants based on quality and variety. My goal is to provide not only the best places to dine but also to supply the reader with options in choosing a cuisine that will be tempting to the palate.

The format of this restaurant guide/cookbook is alphabetical by town. Within each town you will find the restaurants in alphabetical order with my reviews. I personally dined at each of the restaurants in all of my books. You will also find one of the chef's favorite recipes from each restaurant and, in some cases, a special one-time offer that will save you money if you bring the book into the restaurant. The following outline follows the format used for each town and each restaurant. It should help you enjoy this book more, and, hopefully, answer questions that you may have.

TOWN HISTORY, RESTAURANT SUMMARY, TOWN LOCATION AND STATISTICS

At the beginning of each town chapter is a brief history of the town and a summary of the restaurants that follow. The location of the town is given next to help you find it on a Colorado state map. The zip code, area code, population and elevation are provided for the town. The population figures are from 1990. While the census bureau updates population figures for zip code areas and counties with annual estimates, such figures are only available once a decade for cities and towns.

RESTAURANT NAME, ADDRESS, TELEPHONE AND DIRECTIONS

This section is provided to assist you in finding the restaurant and, if necessary, making a reservation. The directions are from major highways, like I-70, and are detailed down to a tenth of a mile.

ESSENTIALS

This section provides you with the basics behind each restaurant. It gives the type of food or cuisine; the hours they are opened; the price range of entrées for each meal; whether the restaurant offers a nonsmoking section (Yes), does not have a nonsmoking section (No) or is all nonsmoking (All); whether take-out service is provided; whether alcohol is served, or not, or just beer and wine; which major credit cards are accepted; the policy with regard to accepting a personal check; the policy on taking reservations; how wheelchair accessible the restaurant is; the way most people dress when they dine at the restaurant and other important information on restaurant policies or services offered.

HISTORY, PERSONALITY AND CHARACTER

There is a story behind each restaurant. Each restaurant has a history as do the people who operate the restaurant. The building occupied by the restaurant has a background as well. Many restaurants are located in structures that date back to the 19th century. A fundamental understanding of who is preparing your meal, managing the place and the place itself should enhance your dining pleasure.

Food, Service and Ambiance

Here is where I talk about the meal or meals that I had. I attempt to order an entrée that is special, unique or interesting. Besides giving my impression of their food first hand, I will cater a sampling of what the rest of the menu has to offer. After briefly commenting on the service and music, I will describe the restaurant's look, its feel, its ambiance. The intent is to provide an impression, a preview of the experience that awaits you.

Special One-Time Offer

The restaurants had the option of making a special offer in the book to attract diners. Of the 71 restaurants, 45 elected to give an offer. **The offer is only valid if you bring the book into the restaurant.** Simply mentioning that you have the book or that you saw the offer will not work. You must present the offer, and the book to your server and have the owner or manager sign the book. Once an offer has been signed, it cannot be used again. When the offer states "receive 50% off one entrée up to $6", it means you can save up to $6 by purchasing one entrée.

The Recipes

All the recipes in the book are from the restaurants that I visited and, in the majority of cases, they were written by one of the chefs at the restaurant. Recipes that have no credit for who wrote the recipe are restaurant or "house" recipes.

Wine Recommendations

For the majority of recipes, there is a wine recommendation provided by the owner or chef of the restaurant. Some recipes do not go well with wine, so there is no recommendation for those. In a few instances, beer was a better choice than wine. For all but a few of restaurants, the wine recommended is available at the restaurant.

Color Photos of Restaurants and Recipes

Color photos are provided for 57 restaurants. In all, 24 restaurants, about 1/3 of all restaurants, have both a restaurant and recipe photo; 33 restaurants, almost half, have either a restaurant or recipe picture.

Back Cover

The twelve Colorado top towns are Aspen, Beaver Creek, Breckenridge, Crested Butte, Durango, Glenwood Springs, Grand Lake, Keystone, Snowmass Village, Steamboat Springs, Vail and Winter Park. The seven front range towns are Berthoud, Allenspark, Castle Rock, Evergreen, Golden, Manitou Springs and Woodland Park. The remaining seventeen towns are one-restaurant towns in this book.

TABLE OF CONTENTS

Allenpark	The Fawn Brook Inn (Classic French)	1
Aspen	Cache Cache (French Bistro/Gourmet Vegetarian)	5
Aspen	Caffé Amici (Italian)	9
Aspen	The Mother Lode (Italian)	12
Aspen	Renaissance (Modern French)	16
Basalt	Chefy's (Eclectic)	21
Beaver Creek	The Golden Eagle Inn (Creative American)	24
Beaver Creek	Grouse Mountain Grill (Progressive American)	28
Berthoud	Wayside Inn (Family American)	32
	COLOR PHOTOS OF RESTAURANTS AND RECIPES	37
Breckenridge	Adams Street Grill (American with a Southwest Flair)	53
Breckenridge	Blue River Bistro (Modern Italian and American)	57
Breckenridge	Hearthstone (Regional)	60

TABLE OF CONTENTS

Breckenridge	Mi Casa (California Mexican)	64	
Breckenridge	The Mountain Sage Cafe (Innovative Health Food with a Pacific Rim Flair)	68	
Breckenridge	Rasta Pasta (Jamaican Pasta)	70	
Breckenridge	Swan Mountain Inn (Continental/Colorado)	73	
Breckenridge	Top of the World (Regional American)	78	
Breckenridge	The Wellington Inn (Continental/German)	82	
Castle Rock	Augustine Grill (Pasta, Grill Specialties, Seafood)	86	
Castle Rock	Pino's Place (Italian Trattoria)	90	
Copper Mountain	Double Diamond Restaurant (Steaks, Ribs, Pasta, Seafood, Pizza)	93	
Crested Butte	Backcountry Gourmet (Global Fusion)	96	
Crested Butte	The Brick Oven Pizza (Pizza, Pasta, Subs)	100	
Crested Butte	The Forest Queen (American)	103	

TABLE OF CONTENTS

Crested Butte	Soupçon (French/Continental)	105
Durango	Cyprus Café (Mediterranean)	109
Durango	Le Rendezvous (Swiss, American, Mexican)	113
Durango	Mama's Boy (Italian)	115
Durango	Seasons Grill (Modern American)	118
El Jebel	Blue Creek Grill (American Provincial)	122
Evergreen	The Columbine (International)	125
Evergreen	Keys on the Green (Steaks, Seafood, Prime Rib)	128
Fairplay	The Historic Fairplay Hotel Restaurant (Country-Style American)	131
Frisco	Uptown Bistro (Contemporary)	135
Glenwood Springs	Daily Bread (Café/Bakery)	139
Glenwood Springs	Dos Hombres (Sonoran-Style Mexican)	142

TABLE OF CONTENTS

Glenwood Springs	Los Desperados (Mexican)	145
	COLOR PHOTOS OF RESTAURANTS AND RECIPES	149
Golden	Table Mountain Inn (Southwestern)	165
Grand Lake	Back Street Steakhouse (Classic American)	170
Grand Lake	E. G.'s Garden Grill (Eclectic with a Southwest Flair)	174
Granite	Country Peddler (Country-Home)	177
Keystone	Great Northern Tavern (Contemporary American)	180
Keystone	Su Casa (California Mexican)	183
La Junta	Café Grand'mere (American Regional/European Countryside Style)	187
Limon	J. C.'s Deli and Bakery (Fresh Pastries, Salads, Pastas, Sandwiches)	191
Manitou Springs	European Café and Deli (Polish, German, Russian)	194
Manitou Springs	The Loop (Baja Mexican)	197
Manitou Springs	Stagecoach (Colorado/Western)	200

TABLE OF CONTENTS

Marble	Crystal River Way Station (Home-Cooked American)	204
Minturn	Chili Willy's (Casual Tex-Mex)	208
Penrose	The Goose Berry Patch (Family/American Country)	212
San Luis	Emma's Hacienda (Southwest/Mexican)	215
Silverton	The Pickle Barrel (American with a Southwest Flair)	219
Snowmass Village	The Brother's Grille (Casual American Bistro)	223
Snowmass Village	Butch's Lobster Bar (Seafood)	227
Snowmass Village	The Stew Pot (American Country)	230
Snowmass Village	Village Steakhouse (Family Steakhouse Offering Vegetarian/Seafood)	233
South Fork	The Mother Lode (Texas-Style Barbecue/Pizza)	237
Steamboat Springs	Alpine Bistro (Multi-National)	240
Steamboat Springs	The Cantina (Mexican)	243

TABLE OF CONTENTS

Steamboat Springs	L'Apogée (Contemporary French)	247
Steamboat Springs	Steamboat Brewery and Tavern (New American)	250
Steamboat Springs	Steamboat Smokehouse (Texas-Style, Hickory-Smoked Pit Barbecue)	253
Sterling	T. J. Bummer's (Family)	256
	COLOR PHOTOS OF RESTAURANTS AND RECIPES	261
Vail	The Tyrolean (Creative European/American)	277
Walsenburg	Alys' Fireside Café (International Eclectic)	282
Westcliff	Alpine Lodge Restaurant (Colorado High Country Meat and Potatoes)	286
Winter Park	The Hideaway (Mountain Eclectic/International)	290
Winter Park	La Taquería (Mexican)	294
Winter Park	Smokin´ Moe's (Hickory Smoked Barbecue)	296
Woodland Park	Grandmother's Kitchen (Country Family)	300
	RECIPE INDEX	302

ALLENSPARK

Allenspark was named for an early settler and prospector, Alonzo Allen, who homesteaded here in 1859. The first post office in Allenspark, built in the 1870s was destroyed by fire in 1894. Nestled next to Rocky Mountain National Park, the Indian Peaks Wilderness and the Ironclads surround this tiny town.

The Fawn Brook Inn is a classic French restaurant of high quality that has been going strong since 1978.

Location of Town: Northwest of Denver
Zip Code: 80510. Area Code: 303. Population: 400. Elevation: 8,520ft.

The Fawn Brook Inn

357 Business Loop Highway 7. PO Box 387. 747-2556.
Directions: From Lyons, take Highway 7 to the northwest for 18 miles. Exit to the left for Ferncliff/Allenspark onto Business Loop Highway 7. Continue for one mile into Allenspark. The restaurant is on the right. From Estes Park, go south on Highway 7 for 15 miles. Turn right onto Business Loop Highway 7. Continue for ¼ mile into Allenspark. The restaurant is on the left.

ESSENTIALS
Cuisine: Classic French
Hours: Mid-MAY through AUG: Tue-Sun 5PM-8:30PM. Closed Mon. SEP: Wed-Sun 5PM-8:30PM. Closed Mon/Tue. OCT to Mid-JAN: Please call for serving hours. Mid-Feb to Mid-MAY: FRI-SUN 5PM-8PM. Closed Mon-Thu. Closed Mid-JAN to Mid-FEB.
Meals and Prices: Dinner $27-$32.
Nonsmoking: All
Take-out: No
Alcohol: Full Bar
Credit Cards: MC, Visa, Amx
Personal Check: Yes, with I.D.
Reservations: Required OCT to Mid-MAY. Highly recommended, otherwise.
Wheelchair Access: Yes, with help from staff.
Dress: A combination of casual and dressed up.
Other: Available for company dinners, holiday parties and family gatherings from OCT through APR.

ALLENSPARK

HISTORY, PERSONALITY AND CHARACTER

The site of The Fawn Brook Inn was originally a bathhouse. John and Lee McAllister constructed the building in 1922 as a general store. Augusta Mengedoht purchased the store in 1935 and converted it into a hunting lodge and restaurant with its current name. Augusta, known as the "The Gun Woman" for always carrying two guns and hunting mountain lions in the middle of the night, sold the place to Charles Wettig in 1946. During the 1950s, 1960s and 1970s, other owners (the Reinholds, Richards and Alfords) operated various restaurants.

In 1978, current owners Hermann and Mieke Groicher purchased the property with their friends Jim and Lucile Morehouse. The Morehouses assisted the Groichers with much renovating and remodeling before selling their interest. Hermann, from Austria, received basic chef training in Europe but is otherwise self-taught. He came to the United States in 1962 and worked as a chef in Texas for 7 years before moving to Colorado. He cooked at The Greenbriar in Boulder for 11 years, then took over The Fawn Brook. Mieke, from Holland, manages the front of the restaurant.

Hermann and Mieke have continued to expand and enrich the restaurant, developing its well-deserved reputation. The Fawn Brook Inn was given five stars in Mobil's Restaurant Guide.

FOOD, SERVICE AND AMBIANCE

I had a marvelous dining experience at The Fawn Brook Inn. Both their hot and cold soups are exceptional. The apple/blueberry is yogurt based with apple cream and tiny blueberries. It is refreshing and unique. The cream of shiitake mushroom made with wine is warm and appetizing. A salad of greens, tomatoes, fresh basil, balsamic vinaigrette dressing, Roquefort bits, red peppers and canola seeds on the side, is a delectable prelude to lobster curry prepared tableside. Chef Hermann melts butter; adds shallots, coconut, pineapple and raisins; deglazes with Chardonnay; and finishes with crème fraîche, a béchamel cream-based white sauce and grated coconut. He then adds poached rock lobster medallions. This scrumptious dish is mildly seasoned with Madras curry powder and fresh ginger and served with fruit chutney on the side — what a delight for the taste senses!

Five-course daily specials are featured at the Fawn Brook Inn. Some of the other hot soups presented are vegetable with cheese puffs and oxtail soup with meatballs while whole cranberry/apple cream is another yogurt-based chilled soup. Other highlights on the dinner menu are roast duckling, pheasant souwaroff, a casserole of sautéed veal sweetbreads (a very popular entrée), a vegetarian entrée, free-range veal loin or medallions, filet of red deer forestière, various tenderloin and filet dishes and shrimp provençal. For those who like to share, they have gourmet dinners for two: beef Wellington, Châteaubriand 'escoffier' and lamb medallions 'shepherd style' served on medieval skewers with five side dishes and finished tableside.

Service is gracious, proficient and impeccable. There are four dining areas in the restaurant. You enter into the main dining room replete with hanging ferns and philodendrons, blue and white decorator plates, two fish tanks, a print of a woman baking, pencil sketches of forest animals by local artist Tom Blaue and a photograph of the Gothic-style town hall in Gouda. Off to the left is the Garden Room with one small round table, books, a black-iron stove and a crystal cabinet. To the rear is a small service bar with a fireplace and a one-table lounge used for waiting diners and diners looking for a cozy place. Just beyond the bar is the Wine Room, a small private room with white linen.

I sat in the fourth dining area, the Swiss-Austrian Room to the right. This is an enchanting, rustic environment with polished pinewood logs and vigas. The walls are adorned with photos from Austria, wooden skis, snowshoes and a deer head with antlers. White table cloths and napkins, oil lamps, an antique cash register, a black-iron wood-burning stove and two fish tanks add to the bucolic allure. Relaxing classical music creates an almost mystic mood. This is a place to speak in soft whispers and quiet tones. The Fawn Brook Inn blends a delightful escape for the mind and a tranquil setting for the soul with classic French cuisine.

See bottom of page 37 for restaurant photo.

Sweetbreads "Fawn Brook"
(Serves 2)

14 ounces lightly poached sweetbread, cleaned and deveined
1 small shallot, about 3/4 oz, diced
2 small cloves garlic, chopped fine
2 tablespoons black truffle oil
1/2 cup Madeira
1 teaspoon pink peppercorns

2 slivers of black truffle, coarsely chopped
2 sprigs chopped Italian parsley
1/2 cup demi-glace
2 tablespoons creme fraîche
A pinch of kosher salt, if needed
3 tablespoons olive oil

ALLENSPARK

4 medium-sized shiitake mushrooms, about 3 ounces, 2 sliced, 2 whole
4 ounces mousse de foie gras (goose liver puree)
1 pinch lavender flowers
2 to 4 ounces baked puff pastry shells

<u>To poach the sweetbreads</u>: Season water with salt, a quarter of a lemon, and bay leaf. Bring to a boil and plunge the raw sweetbreads into it. Reduce the heat and simmer them for 15-20 minutes. Check for doneness. They should be slightly pink outside but not bloody. Immediately place them in iced water, cool them, and peel them while still warm. Gently break them in pieces removing all fat, tissues, and skin. Keep them refrigerated until ready for use.

1. <u>Sauce</u>: Lightly glaze the shallots and garlic in the truffle oil. Add the Madeira and pink peppercorns, and with low heat, reduce the liquid to about 2 tablespoons.
2. Add the chopped truffles, the parsley, and the demi-glace. Keep the sauce at simmering point for about 10 minutes.
3. Add the creme fraiche and combine well. Taste the sauce for correct seasoning. Add a little salt, if needed. Remove from heat.
4. In a separate skillet, heat the olive oil, add the mushrooms, sliced and whole, and lightly sauté them. Remove the whole mushroom for garnish, add the foie gras mousse and mix well.
5. Add the sweetbreads and the lavender flowers. Combine all ingredients as soon as the sweetbreads are warm.
6. Add the sauce to it, cover the skillet with a lid and simmer the dish just enough until the sweetbreads are heated through.
7. Fill the preheated pastry shells with the sweetbreads and garnish with mushroom caps.

<u>Caution</u>: Do not overcook the sweetbreads as they have a tendency to become rubbery, chewy, and quite tough.

<u>Wine Recommendations</u>: A Light Merlot or Gewürztraminer

<u>Recipe by</u>: Hermann Groicher, owner and chef.

See top of page 37 for recipe photo.

ASPEN

The post-Ute Indian history of Aspen falls into three eras. The first began in 1879 with the discovery of silver in the Roaring Fork Valley. It was during this era that mining promoter B. Clark Wheeler renamed the town from Ute City to Aspen for the abundance of the appealing trees. With the demonetization of silver in 1893, Aspen's population diminished by 90% and the town reverted to ranching for its survival. Aspen had entered its second era, a sleepy cow-town.

In the 1930s, the town began to stir with the prospects of skiing. However, it wasn't until World War II brought the 10th Mountain Division to the area that the movement for skiing in Aspen began to take off. This, combined with cultural and music festivals in the late 1940s, launched Aspen into its current, modern era. Aspen today is a world-renown resort attracting celebrities from all parts for skiing in the winter and festivals in the summer.

My sampling of four Aspen dining establishments gives you two very different Italian restaurants, one that believes in simplicity, the other offering candlelit dining in an historic building; a highly-rated French bistro with gourmet vegetarian cuisine and an elegant modern French restaurant earning a world-class reputation.

Location of Town: Central Colorado, southeast of Glenwood Springs
Zip Code: 81611. Area Code: 970. Population: 5,049. Elevation: 7,907ft.

Cache Cache

205 South Mill Street (in the Mill Street Plaza, Garden Level). 925-3835.
Directions: From the northwest (Glenwood Springs), stay on Highway 82 as you enter town. Make a right on 7th Street and a left on Main Street. Go 10 blocks to Mill Street (1 block past Monarch Street) and turn right. Go 1 block. The Mill Street Plaza is on the right and the restaurant is on the lower level in the southwest corner.

ESSENTIALS
Cuisine: French Bistro/Gourmet Vegetarian
Hours: 7 days 5:30PM-10:30PM.
Closed NOV and Easter to Mid-MAY
Meals and Prices: Dinner $14-$26.

Nonsmoking: All including bar
Take-out: Yes, unless busy
Alcohol: Full Bar
Credit Cards: MC, Visa, Amx
Personal Check: Local only

ASPEN

Reservations: Highly recommended
Wheelchair Access: No
Dress: Casual to dressy

Other: Private parties welcomed. Split charge of $2 for appetizers and $5 for entrées.

HISTORY, PERSONALITY AND CHARACTER

Cache Cache, which means "hide and seek" in French, was established by French nationals Philippe Mollicchi and Marie Casanova in 1987. Originally named for the small, difficult to find, 14-seat restaurant in the corner of Mill Street Plaza, it has grown into one of Aspen's favorite dining spots seating over 150 indoors and outdoors.

Jodi Larner joined Cache Cache in 1990 as maitre d', became general manager in 1991 and partner in 1992. Rick Hession, Canadian-born entrepreneur with a background as a multi-unit McDonald's licensee, restaurant consultant and venture investor, bought out Mollicchi and Casanova and joined long-time friend, Jodi, as partner in 1996. In the spring of 1996, Rick and Jodi completely renovated the dining room and bar bringing in soft lighting, gentle hues of cream and ochre, leather banquettes and beveled mirrors to recreate the feel of a hip, French bistro. Michael Berry was appointed chef in 1992 and presents the true flavors of the French countryside in his menu.

FOOD, SERVICE AND AMBIANCE

Chef Michael Beary has a love for the rural fare of French provinces. He finds the food "honest, healthy and incredibly tasty" and "is the kind of cooking that [he] wants to provide [his] guests". Instead of adding fat, butter or cream, Chef Michael will use a little extra virgin olive oil, herbs and spices. He slow roasts duck, pheasant and chicken for more than an hour using a non-piercing rotisserie that seals in juices and flavors and results in succulent meat.

For dinner, I went somewhat on the lighter side and ordered a salad. The zucchini potato cake would appeal to any potato pancake lover, including myself, as it was a tasty, shredded, crisp, fried, primarily potato cake with zucchini flavor. It was topped with red pepper and sour cream and came with Boursin cheese and field greens of arugula, spinach, red oak and red and green romaine lettuces. Cache Cache's signature dishes and favorites that come highly recommended, especially if this is your first time dining here, include the tian of lamb with ratatouille, spinach and a candied garlic sauce; grilled tenderloin of pork with apple-raisin-cabbage compote; grilled Chilean sea bass over basmati rice served with artichoke and roasted pepper vinaigrette; and osso bucco in Marsala sauce.

Your evening at Cache Cache can start with an appetizer like prosciutto di Parma with grilled eggplant, an onion tart strudel or Marseilles seafood stew. If salads are to your liking, try some of Chef Michael's innovative selections like warm chèvre in nuts, fresh Roma tomatoes tossed with a balsamic caper vinaigrette or the warm spinach salad with marinated chicken. The entrées were creative and varied offering pasta, risotto, vegetarian, seafood, meat and roasted fowl. Some of the more notable dishes were honey curry couscous, grilled salmon with spinach, diver-caught scallops and fresh pheasant split-roasted slowly. To accompany your fine dining, Cache Cache boasts 400 different wines to choose from and as a sweet ending, the desserts include d'Anjou pear crisp, fresh berry tart, sorbets, gelatos and homemade biscotti.

I found the service at Cache Cache to be courteous, helpful and, in the words of partner Jodi Larner, "professional yet relaxed". Spanish guitar, jazz and blues showcased the eclectic election of music. The ochre and cream-color walls were decked with black and white photos of French village streets and the Seine River. On the opposite side of the restaurant, windows face the courtyard and patio dining.

Cache Cache was rated one of Aspen's top three restaurants by Gourmet Magazine in October 1996 and has been raved about from Aspen Magazine to Britain's Tatler. It advances provençal cuisine sans the stuffy attitude in a true French bistro style.

Grilled Pork Tenderloin
with Apple Brandy Mustard Sauce
(Serves 6)

Veal Stock:
5 pounds veal bones
1 bunch celery, without leaves
10 large yellow onions
8 large carrots
10 very ripe tomatoes
15 black peppercorns
4 bay leaves
2 gallons tomato juice, preferably fresh

Apple Brandy Mustard Sauce:
1 1/2 cups brandy
2 Granny Smith apples, peeled, cored, and finely chopped
1 bay leaf
6 black peppercorns
2/3 cup honey
1 1/2 cups veal stock
1 1/2 cups whipping cream, warmed slightly to prevent curdling
1/4 cup whole grain mustard

ASPEN

Pork Tenderloin:
3 pounds pork tenderloin
Peanut oil
Salt and pepper

1. Veal stock: Stock should be made at least 72 hours prior to serving. Roast bones in pan at 300 degrees until browned, then place bones in 3 to 5 gallon stock pot.
2. Roughly cut vegetables, leaving skins on. Roast vegetables in same pan until soft and transfer to stock pot. Add peppercorns and bay leaves.
3. The size of the stock pot will determine how much tomato juice to add initially. The tomato juice should comprise 1/2 to 2/3 of total liquid. The remaining amount should be cold water. Fill pot with liquid, but not so much that it will spill over when heated. Cook uncovered over very low heat for 72 hours. As separation takes place, add remaining tomato juice or cold water. Skim grease from top, especially during first 24 hours or stock will become bitter.
4. After 72 hours, pour through very fine mesh strainer or cheese cloth. Return to pot and cook over medium-high heat. Place pot slightly off center on burner, allowing impurities to collect on side for easy extraction. Cook until liquid is reduced by 2/3. The end product should be a sweet, rich, brown glaze.
5. Apple Brandy Mustard Sauce: In saucepan combine brandy, apples, bay leaf, peppercorns, and honey. Bring to a boil, reduce heat to low and simmer until reduced by 1/3. Add veal stock and reduce by 1/3. Add whipping cream and mustard and reduce by 1/3 again. Remove bay leaf and puree thoroughly.
6. Pork Tenderloin: Lightly brush pork with peanut oil, season with salt and pepper, and grill slowly until medium-rare to medium. Slice tenderloin.
7. Serving: Cover plates with sauce and place tenderloin slices in center of each plate.

Notes: Veal stock may be purchased from many local restaurants if you do not have the time to make your own. Veal stock can be frozen for future use.

Wine Recommendation: David Bruce Russian River Pinot Noir, 1995

Recipe by: Michael W. Beary, chef

Caffé Amici

525 East Cooper Avenue (in the Aspen Grove Mall). 925-6162.
Directions: From the northwest (Glenwood Springs), stay on Highway 82 as you enter town. Make a right on 7th Street and a left on Main Street. Go 11 blocks to Galena Street (one block past Mill Street) and turn right. Go 3 blocks and turn left onto Cooper Avenue. The restaurant is ½ block down on the right behind the Aspen Grove Chocolate Factory.

ESSENTIALS

Cuisine: Italian
Hours: 7 days 7:30AM-10PM (breakfast until 10:30AM, lunch from 11AM-3PM, dinner from 5PM).
Meals and Prices: Breakfast $5-$9. Lunch $8-$9. Dinner $11.
Nonsmoking: All
Take-out: Yes
Alcohol: Beer, wine and Italian cocktails

Credit Cards: MC, Visa, Amx, Disc
Personal Check: Local only with I.D.
Reservations: Recommended for parties of 6 or more
Wheelchair Access: Yes
Dress: Casual
Other: Available for catering and private parties. The entire restaurant can be rented.

HISTORY, PERSONALITY AND CHARACTER

Caffé Amici was originally the Aspen Grove Café built in the 1970s. In September 1997, Richard Sultani and Michel Wahaltere converted the restaurant into Caffé Amici. Richard has been in the restaurant business since 1975 and previously owned Les Champs in the Watergate Complex in Washington, D.C. He also owns Mirabella in Aspen. Michel is the general manager and chef. He comes from a restaurant family, graduated from the Culinary School of Liege in Belgium and has been cooking in restaurants since 1980. Michel previously opened Campo De Fiori and Farfalla, both in Aspen.

FOOD, SERVICE AND AMBIANCE

"Simplicity is the key to this restaurant" says Chef Michel who uses homemade soups, sauces, pizza dough and gnocchi and lasagna noodles. I started my lunch with a soup that had a not-so-simple name, straciatella. It consisted of spinach and egg drop in a chicken broth with parmesan cheese. It was served "hot, hot" with plenty of fresh spinach, just the right amount of Parmesan, enough egg for flavor and a healthy chicken broth. Perfect medicine for my cold at the time. My pick of the pastas was homemade ravioli stuffed with ricotta and spinach in a light, spicy, flavorful tomato sauce. Ricotta cheese and fresh parsley were sprinkled on top and

ASPEN

my server added some fresh Parmesan. Extra-virgin olive oil seasoned with sun-dried tomato, rosemary and garlic for dipping bread accompanied the meal. This was a very tasty and delicious dish.

Breakfast features egg specialties like two eggs with Italian sausage, pancetta or prosciutto; an English muffin smothered with fresh spinach topped with poached eggs and a light, mascarpone creamy sauce; or scrambled eggs with baked Italian ham and fresh asparagus. Highlighting the lunch and dinner menus are soups, salads, anitpasti, pizza and pasta. Sandwiches like a smoked salmon club, grilled vegetables and Fontina cheese and grilled mild Italian sausage are also served for lunch. For a first course, choose from vegetable soup with basil pesto, an assortment of fresh seafood, lightly fried calamari, cured beef tenderloin with zucchini, tossed seasonal vegetables and greens, or Colorado organic tomatoes and sweet Maui onions marinated in a fresh herb vinaigrette.

Caffé Amici's pizzas are topped with fresh basil, chicken, creamy herb goat cheese, fontina cheese artichoke and many of your favorite items. For a second course, you can select from egg ribbon pasta with veal and beef Bolognese sauce, spaghettini, cannelloni stuffed with spinach and cheese, gnocchi, thin ribbon spinach pasta with smoked salmon, linguini with shellfish and lasagna. There are about 44 red and white wines, many Italian, to enhance your meal. Pastry chef Joe Munoz at Mirabella Restaurant prepares homemade desserts for Caffé Amici that include Italian cannoli, white and dark chocolate mousse, tiramisu, sorbet and ice cream.

Service was very friendly and courteous. Rhythm and blues played in this one-room restaurant. The walls, which were sponge-painted an antique gold color, were adorned with beautiful color photographs and paintings from Europe that include Portofino, Lake Osta, Toscana, the Alps and Venice in Italy; Santorini, Greece; Alsace, France; England and Ireland. The pictures present seashores, villages, brick streets, narrow alleys, Spanish arches, houses and old buildings. For a taste of Italy and a nostalgic look at the best of Europe, dine at Caffé Amici.

<u>Special One-Time Offer</u>: Buy one entrée and receive a second entrée of equal or lesser value free (up to $11.00) OR receive 50% off one entrée (up to $5.50). Please present to server at time of ordering.

_____ Owner/Manager. _____ Date.

Zuppa di Carote "Macro Polo"
Carrot Ginger Soup (Hot or Cold)
(Serves 6)

1 tablespoon canola oil	Ground white pepper
1 medium onion, chopped	1 teaspoon honey
2 pounds carrots, sliced	Fresh Italian parsley
4 quarter-size slices of peeled fresh ginger, lightly smashed	
	For cold soup only:
2 1/2 cups chicken stock or canned low-sodium broth	Dash of hot sauce
	2 teaspoons of fresh lemon juice
Salt	

1. Heat the oil in a large saucepan. Add the onion and cook over moderately low heat, stirring occasionally, until softened, about 5 minutes. Add the carrots and ginger and cook for 5 minutes stirring occasionally.
2. Add 2 1/2 cups of stock, season with salt and pepper to taste, and bring to a boil. Cover and simmer over low heat until the carrots are tender, about 40 minutes.
3. Strain the cooking liquid into a heat-proof bowl. Discard half of the ginger.
4. In a blender, puree the vegetables with 1 cup of cooking liquid until smooth. Stir the puree into the cooking liquid in the bowl and add 1 teaspoon of honey.
5. You can serve this soup hot or cold. If you serve it cold, season the soup with a dash of hot sauce and 2 teaspoons of fresh lemon juice, refrigerate until chilled or for up to 1 day.

Wine Recommendation: Sauvignon Blanc, "Costello Della Sala" Antinori

Recipe by: Michel Wahaltere, general manager and chef

See page 38 for recipe photo.

The Mother Lode
314 East Hyman Avenue. 925-7700.
Directions: From the northwest (Glenwood Springs), stay on Highway 82 as you enter town. Make a right on 7th Street and a left on Main Street. Go 9 blocks to Monarch Street (one block past Aspen Street) and turn right. Go 2 blocks and turn left onto Hyman Avenue. The restaurant is ½ block down on the left.

ESSENTIALS
Cuisine: Italian
Hours: Mid-JUN thru OCT and Mid-NOV thru Mid-APR: 7 days 5:30PM-10:30PM. Closed Mid-APR to Mid-JUN and first two weeks of NOV.
Meals and Prices: Dinner $13-$27.
Nonsmoking: All, except at the bar
Take-out: Yes
Alcohol: Full Bar
Credit Cards: All 5
Personal Check: Yes, with I. D.
Reservations: Recommended
Wheelchair Access: Yes
Dress: Casual
Other: Large parties welcome

HISTORY, PERSONALITY AND CHARACTER
The Mother Lode is in a building dating back to the 1880s, Aspen's silver mining boom days. Over the years, the structure was used as a coal and grain store and a bookstore. Judge Dorothy Shaw filled the property with antiques in the early 1900s. Current owner Howard Ross purchased the restaurant in 1980. Howard has been in the restaurant business since 1964. From 1955 to 1959, the Crystal Palace occupied this space and was immediately followed by The Mother Lode.

Head chef Shane Stark is a graduate of the Culinary Institute of America in Hyde Park, New York, and has been with the restaurant since 1996. He has been cooking since a teenager in the mid-1980s and worked previously as a head chef at Kenichi and the Ritz-Carlton in Aspen and a private resort in Canada.

FOOD, SERVICE AND AMBIANCE
Their soup du jour, roast red pepper puree with a few sprinkles of parsley, was flavorsome, lightly peppery and warmed me up on a rainy night in late summer. The pan-roasted sea bass wrapped in prosciutto sounded interestingly different and I was not disappointed. The prosciutto is seared keeping in all of the bass's juices and resulting in an incredibly moist fish. It is served on a bed of julienne carrots, yellow squash and zucchini in a lemon broth with fresh sage and diced tomatoes, topped with roasted shallots. The soup and sea bass were a most delectable meal.

For an appetizer, you can treat yourself to roasted garlic or basil pesto spread on Tuscan bread, calamari, mussels, carpaccio and, depending on the season, crab cakes, mushroom rave or roasted asparagus. There are also several worthwhile salads on the menu: a classic Caesar, arugula with julienne beets and roasted walnuts, organic wild greens with goat cheese and toasted pinenuts, and hot smoked salmon and orange with Asiago cheese.

The pasta dishes — capellini, penne, fettuccini, farfalle, ravioli, spaghetti and linguini — are prepared with a variety of wonderful foods: baby spinach, roasted peppers and garlic, asparagus, porcini and shiitake mushrooms, prosciutto, rock shrimp, chicken breasts and jumbo prawns. Fresh herbs, like thyme, basil and rosemary are used in some savory sauces: classic Italian meat, roasted garlic cream and sundried tomato pesto. In addition to Chilean sea bass, The Mother Lode's specialties include risotto with smoked sea scallops, seared tenderloin of beef, grilled pork tenderloin, roasted free range chicken, peppered ahi tuna, veal chop and grilled filet of Sterling salmon. For dessert, settle back for bread pudding with white chocolate, cheesecake with pear sauce, tiramisu, warm walnut fudge cake, rice pudding, gelatos and sorbets in assorted flavors: double espresso bean, pistachio, black cherry, vanilla, mango, lemon and raspberry.

Service was very efficient, courteous and helpful. Light jazz played in this historic building with pastel walls adorned with paintings of nineteenth century Victorian belles. When you enter The Mother Lode, there is an old safe at the entrance used for a host's stand, a small dining area with a gas fireplace and black pipe exhaust, hanging ferns and a small bar to the right. This is candlelight dining with ceiling fans and white tablecloths and napkins. The paintings of the ladies of the night, some nude, are displayed in idyllic settings, playing music in a meadow, floating in a canoe, wading in water and placed in an ocean grotto by the seashore. A stained-glass window in front of the restaurant depicts two miners on either side of one of Colorado's finest working girls with black coal in the foreground and gold in the background. Exceptional Italian cuisine served with caring hands in an antiquated environment awaits you at The Mother Lode.

Special One-Time Offer: One free crostino appetizer with the purchase of one dinner. Valid for every member of your party. Please present to server at time of ordering. _____ Owner/Manager. _____ Date.

Peppered Ahi Tuna with Tomato Risotto and Brown Butter-Balsamic Vinaigrette
(Serves 6)

4 ounces brown butter*
1 1/2 ounces balsamic vinaigrette
6 cups vegetable stock
1/4 cup tomato paste
Kosher salt and fresh ground black pepper as needed
6 6-ounce pieces #1 Tuna, cut into small "loins"
1/2 cup canola oil

2 medium shallots, minced
2 cups Aborio rice
1/3 cup grated Parmesan cheese
1/4 cup chopped chives
2 tablespoons whole butter
1 pound spinach, stemmed and cleaned
2 Roma tomatoes (peeled, seeded, and diced small)

1. Preheat oven to 400 degrees. Combine the brown butter* and balsamic vinegar in a blender and process until the mixture is emulsified. Set aside at room temperature.
2. In a medium saucepan, whisk together the vegetable stock and the tomato paste, season with salt and pepper, and bring to a simmer. Lower the heat so that it remains hot, but not simmering.
3. Season the tuna with salt and a liberal amount of fresh ground black pepper.
4. In a large skillet, heat half of the canola oil until it begins to smoke from the pan, place on a baking sheet, and set aside.
5. In another saucepan, heat the remainder of the canola oil and sauté the shallots until translucent. Add the rice and cook, stirring constantly, for 5 to 6 minutes.
6. Add 1/3 of the stock mixture and lower the heat. Cook slowly, stirring occasionally, until the liquid has absorbed. Repeat this process two more times until all of the liquid has been absorbed.
7. Stir in Parmesan, chives, and half of the butter into the risotto and keep warm.
8. Place the tuna in the oven for about 5 to 8 minutes according to desired doneness.
9. In a large skillet, heat the remainder of the butter, add the spinach, season with salt and pepper, and cook until wilted.

<u>Presentation</u>: Spoon equal amounts of the risotto into the middle of 6 warm dinner plates. Place equal portions of the spinach on top of the risotto. Slice each of the tuna "loins" in half on an angle, and arrange on top of the spinach. Drizzle with the vinaigrette, diced tomatoes, and serve.

*Brown butter is made by taking a pound of whole butter and slowly burning over low heat. Then skimming off the foam and straining the solids out through a fine sieve or coffee filter. The remaining fat is what you want to reserve.

<u>Wine Recommendations</u>: Morgan Sauvignon Blanc (California) or Pinot Noir King Estate (Oregon)

<u>Recipe by</u>: Shane Stark, head chef

See page 39 for recipe photo.

ASPEN

Renaissance

304 East Hopkins Avenue. 925-2402.
Directions: From the northwest (Glenwood Springs), stay on Highway 82 as you enter town. Make a right on 7th Street and a left on Main Street. Go 9 blocks to Monarch Street (one block past Aspen Street) and turn right. Go 1 block and turn left onto East Hopkins Avenue. The restaurant is one door down on the left.

ESSENTIALS
Cuisine: Modern French
Hours: 7 days 6PM-10:30PM. Closed Mid-APR to Early JUN and Mid-OCT thru NOV.
Meals and Prices: Dinner: á la carte $30-$36, chef's tasting menu $85, vegetarian menu $65, matching wines $40.
Nonsmoking: All
Take-out: Yes
Alcohol: Full Bar

Credit Cards: MC, Visa, Amx, DC
Personal Check: Yes, with I. D.
Reservations: Strongly recommended
Wheelchair Access: Yes, including restrooms
Dress: Casual elegance
Other: Available for catering. Available for private parties, receptions and other special occasions.

HISTORY, PERSONALITY AND CHARACTER

Chef, owner and culinary alchemist, Charles Dale opened Renaissance, The Alchemy of Food, in June 1990 in a location formerly occupied by a fish market. Charles' extensive and dynamic career was inspired by his experiences growing up in the palace of Monaco with Prince Rainier, Crown Prince Albert and Princess Caroline. He attributes his success to an early appreciation for refinement in food and service.

After graduating from Princeton University in 1978, Charles apprenticed himself in 1982 to Alain Sailhac, then chef at New York's celebrated Le Cirque. His metier led to Georges Masraff's restaurant in Paris before he returned to New York to work for Daniel Boulud at the Plaza Athenée Hotel. Charles then traveled to the kitchens of Jean-Paul Lacombe, a disciple of Paul Bocuse, in Lyon, France. He followed this stint by coming full circle back to Le Cirque as chef saucier. After three years at Le Cirque, Charles left New York to join the staff of the Hotel Jerome in Aspen.

Charles was the recipient of Food and Wine Magazine's "Best New Chefs in America" award for 1995. He has been featured in Bon Appetit, The New York Times and Travel and Leisure and is a regularly featured guest chef on Crystal Cruises. Charles is also an entrepreneur releasing his own line of food products, St. Dalfour All-Natural Marinades — One Minute To Use. In June 1997, he and his wife Aimée co-authored "The Chef's Guide to America's Best Restaurants", a compilation of 170 of the country's best chefs' choices of the 482 best restaurants nationwide. In their "spare time", Dale and Aimée hold cooking classes in their home on Monday evenings throughout the winter.

General manger and Aspen native Pamela McLain has been in the restaurant business since 1986 and at Renaissance beginning in 1995. She helped to open the Border Grill in southern California and previously managed at Bix and Bizou, both in San Francisco. Chef de cuisine C. Barclay Dodge self-trained in San Francisco. He has traveled extensively and has a passion for food. Barclay worked at Bix with Pamela, at Roti in San Francisco and helped open Stoke's Adobe in Carmel, California.

Pastry chef Amanda Atchley is a Colorado native and graduate of the San Francisco Culinary School. She began cooking in 1992 and worked at the Broadmoor in Colorado Springs and Sweet Basil in Vail, Colorado, before coming to Renaissance in 1997. Sommelier Steve Humble has been working in restaurants since 1989 and was formerly at the Caribou Club in Aspen. He joined Charles in 1993 as a bartender in the R Bistro, upstairs from Renaissance. He apprenticed under then sommelier Jeff Walker and advanced from assistant sommelier to sommelier in 1997. Assisting in the Renaissance kitchen are Jason Tostrup, Hector Rivas, Bryan Nelson, Gregorio Rivas, Hector Gomez, and Alex Castillo.

FOOD, SERVICE AND AMBIANCE

Renaissance, a restaurant in a class of its own, presents classic fine dining with renewed spirit and perpetual innovation. Culinary artistes Charles Dale and Barclay Dodge infuse global influences derived from their worldly travel and their own personal creativity into a cuisine that is constantly experiencing rebirth.

My evening in this graceful establishment began with the chef's welcome, a ceviche of sea bass with lime, lemon, cilantro, salt, black pepper, orange juice, red pepper, onion and julienne carrots on crackers. Ceviche is a popular Latin American appetizer whereby the acid in the citrus juices "cooks" the raw fish. White bread rolls were served with butter on a granite-marble slab.

A sampling from their à la carte menu introduced me to the butternut squash soup with duck hash and the marinated and grilled loin of venison. My server poured the soup from a pitcher into a bowl at my table. The soup consisted of vegetable stock with a puree of butternut squash, potato, apple, banana, onion and cumin. It had a fine consistency and excellent flavor. A dollop of duck hash in the middle of the plate with a mint leaf comprised duck confit, red pepper and onion. It provided just the right tincture to complement the puree. The venison was five sweet and tender, medium-rare slices seared on the edges with light but rich in taste poivrerad sauce. The sauce was made from venison stock added to orange juice, cinnamon, ginger seed, brown sugar and cherry vinaigrette, reduced and joined with a multitude of spices including cloves and peppercorns. Accompanying this very savory dish were honey-roasted chestnuts, Morbier cheese polenta and a butternut squash chutney.

Besides ordering à la carte, Renaissance offers a skillfully arranged nightly Tasting Menu. It is a five-course meal that includes two appetizers, salad, entrée and dessert. There is also a five-course Vegetarian Menu. Matching wines could be added to either five-course menu to take you on a remarkable culinary odyssey. Smokey pea soup with Maine lobster and brandy syrup, spinach and Dungeness crab tart, and fresh foie gras with caramelized pears and maple pecans are examples of Chef Barclay's appetizers. The salad on the Tasting Menu was slow-roasted salmon "brushetta" with hot-house tomato jam, arugula and Parmesan.

Accentuating the entrées are crispy Chilean sea bass with artichoke, shiitakes and foie gras; duck two ways: crisp confit and smoked breast; and expresso-blackened tenderloin of beef. Wine is almost a necessity with this kind of dining experience and sommelier Steve Humble will be glad to assist in your decision. Renaissance boasts a treasure-trove of 550 exquisite wine selections and has been the recipient of the Wine Spectator Award of Excellence every year since 1993. As a sweet finis to the extraordinary evening that you are sure to have at Renaissance, the chefs give you Belgian chocolate soufflé, mini crème brûlée, homemade sorbets and fresh fruit.

An evening at Renaissance is one of relaxed elegance. The servers are professional, very helpful and first-rate. Light instrumental music provides the ideal backdrop for this romantic setting. The softly lit dining room in peach and green tones is reminiscent of a Provençal sunset. An engrossing array of watercolors from the Huntsman Gallery in Aspen emblazoned the walls. Highlighting this collection were pictures describing light shining through clouds on a rural house at the end of a road, a man lighting a cigarette and a boy who fell asleep at his studies. A table right-center in the dining room was covered with huge wine bottles. Charles Dale and his talented and energetic troupe are culinary artists performing at their highest levels. Few Colorado restaurants shine as brightly as Renaissance and none cast shadows upon this Mecca of dining establishments.

ASPEN

See bottom of page 40 for restaurant photo.

Espresso-Blackened Tenderloin of Beef, Au Poivre, with Rich Mashed Potatoes and Yam Frites
(Serves 4)

Mashed Potatoes:
3 large Idaho potatoes, not peeled
1/2 cup heavy cream
4 tablespoons sweet butter
1/4 cup 2% milk
1 tablespoon salt

Yams:
1/2 cup all purpose flour
1/4 teaspoons cayenne pepper
1 yam, peeled and julienne (optional -- very fine)
1 cup oil for frying, canola or vegetable

1/4 pound fresh watercress

Sauce:
2 shallots, finely diced
1/4 cup green peppercorns in brine, or substitute 2 tablespoons dried green peppercorns, soaked in warm water for 1/2 hour
1/2 cup cognac or good quality brandy
1/2 cup veal demi-glace or 2 cups chicken stock, reduced to 1/2 cup

Beef:
1/3 cup decaffeinated espresso, finely ground
1 chipotle chile, finely ground in a spice grinder, or substitute 1/2 teaspoon cayenne pepper
4 8-ounce beef tournedos, cut from the tenderloin
Salt to taste

1. Place the potatoes in a saucepan and cover with salted water. Boil, skins on, until the tip of a knife passes easily into the middle of the potato.
2. Meanwhile, bring the cream, butter, milk, and salt to a boil, and keep warm.
3. When the potatoes are cooked, peel off the skins with the back of a paring knife; you can hold the hot potatoes with a towel, and put them through a "potato ricer" (this is preferable to a food processor). Or you may mash them by hand. Immediately add the cream mixture, stirring until smooth, then set aside, cover, and keep warm.

ASPEN

4. Meanwhile, in a 12-inch stainless steel bowl, mix the flour and the cayenne.
5. Cut the yams into julienne strips, by hand or with the aid of a mandolin.
6. Heat the oil in a 10-inch, straight sided sauté pan (or a deep fryer if you have one) until just smoking gently.
7. Gently toss the yams in the flour mixture, until they are evenly but sparingly coated. Fry the yams in the oil until just golden in color. Remove to a paper towel. They should stay crisp for several hours, depending on the humidity and climate.
8. For the sauce: In a non-reactive sauce pot, combine the shallots, peppercorns, and the cognac. Reduce to a syrup (do not worry if it flames; it will go out by itself); add the veal demi-glace. Simmer for 1/2 hour, skimming, and keep warm. Do not strain.
9. To finish: Preheat the oven to 450 degrees. Mix the espresso and ground chipotle. Heat a 12-inch cash iron sauté pan (or a similar heavy-duty pan) over a medium high flame. When the pan is hot, season the beef with salt on both sides, then dredge the beef on all sides in the espresso mixture. Place each tournedos of beef in the dry sauté pan, and allow to sear for 3 minutes.
10. Turn the beef and place the entire pan in the oven for 5 minutes. Remove from the oven, turn the beef once more, and serve with the mash potatoes at 12 o'clock, the fried yam julienne on top and garnish with the fresh watercress.
11. Cut the beef in two, and place the two halves opened up on the plate at 6 o'clock. They should be medium rare.
12. Place a ladle of the sauce on the plate and serve.

Wine Recommendations: Rosenblum "Old Vines" Zinfandel or Robert Mondavi Cabernet Sauvignon Reserve

Recipe by: Charles Dale, owner

See top of page 40 for recipe photo.

BASALT

Basalt was named after Basalt Peak, a basaltic lava formation in the area. The town was founded when the Colorado Midland Railroad was built through here. Basalt is best known for its world-class fly-fishing on the Frying Pan River. The town's chamber of commerce office is located in an old train car in the town park.

An eclectic restaurant in a former house is described here for your enjoyment.

Location of Town: Southeast of Glenwood Springs on the way to Aspen
Zip Code: 81621. Area Code: 970. Population: 1,128. Elevation: 6,620ft.

Chefy's

166 Midland Avenue, 927-4034.
Directions: Take Exit 114 from I-70 and go north to the signal. Turn right onto Highways 6 and 24 and go to the next signal. Turn right onto Highway 82, go over I-70 and continue on this road for 11.7 miles to the intersection with Highway 133. Continue straight on Highway 82 for 11½ miles to the fourth signal and turn left onto Basalt Avenue. Go .2 miles and turn left onto Two Rivers Road. Go .2 miles to the stop sign and turn right onto Midland Avenue. The restaurant is .1 miles down on the left.

ESSENTIALS
Cuisine: Eclectic
Hours: SUN-THU 5:30PM-9:30PM. FRI/SAT 5:30PM-10PM.
Meals and Prices: Dinner $9-$23.
Nonsmoking: Yes
Take-out: Yes
Alcohol: Full Bar
Credit Cards: MC, Visa
Personal Check: From the Roaring Fork Valley with I.D.
Reservations: Recommended
Wheelchair Access: Yes
Dress: Casual
Other: Split plate charge $5. Service charge of 15% may be added to parties of 6 or more.

HISTORY, PERSONALITY AND CHARACTER

Chefy's was originally built as a private residence in the 1920s and remained a private residence until 1988 when Claude van Horton leased the property and opened Chefy's on March 4th. He added a patio in the summer and enclosed a portion of it in the winter into what is now the main dining room. Claude started out in the restaurant business in 1972 at the Golden Horn in Aspen. He became the chef at DiMaggio's at

BASALT

the Frying Pan in Basalt in 1976. Claude moved to Sedona, Arizona, in 1979 where he worked as a chef at the Oak Creek Owl from 1981 to 1984 and was owner and chef at Fiddler's from 1984 to 1987. Today, he is owner, chef and manager at Chefy's. Susan, his wife, has been actively involved with the restaurant since its inception and is co-manager.

FOOD, SERVICE AND AMBIANCE

For dinner, I ordered an à la carte cup of warm, creamy asparagus soup with shaved carrots and parsley. They have since replaced the asparagus soup with wild mushroom soup, roasted garlic soup and, in the summer, gazpacho. My entrée, blackened salmon with brown-butter, was a high-quality filet, black and crisp on the outside and moist and pink on the inside. It came with fresh, sautéed vegetables, rice pilaf with scallions, parsley and pimentos. Homemade mashed potatoes are available as an alternative to the rice pilaf. Their soups, sauces, salad dressings, some spices and most desserts — crème brûlée, Grand Marnier chocolate mousse, and key lime and apple pies — are homemade.

Steak tartare, oysters Rockefeller or crab cakes will get your dinner started. As a second course, you can order gazpacho with shrimp and avocado, wild mushroom soup or a Caesar salad. Their diverse selection of entrées includes Rocky Mountain trout amondine, broiled salmon and shrimp scampi, cioppino, steaks, veal dishes, paprika pork schnitzel, chicken, barbecued Korean pork loin, orange-glazed roast duckling and New York strip scorpion steak (pepper steak with shrimp). Alcohol-free beer is included at their full bar.

Service was attentive and courteous. I listened to some new age vocal music while I gazed onto the patio. In the wintertime, they have a Christmas tree outside. The inside has a small bar at the entrance and three small dining rooms with white lace curtains, flower-pattern tablecloths over white cloths, paintings by local artists, pictures of fish and wire fishes hanging from the ceiling. There is summer dining "al fresco" on either of the two patios under pine and aspen trees. Chefy's is cozy and homey. Just the perfect place to be for great food in a relaxed atmosphere.

See bottom of page 41 for restaurant photo.

Cioppino
(Serves 8)

1/2 cup olive oil
1 medium/large onion, finely diced
1 tablespoon chopped garlic
3 cups fish stock or clam juice
2 cups red wine
1 25-ounce can crushed or diced tomatoes
2 pounds (approximately 6 to 8) fresh tomatoes, cored, seeded and diced

2 stalks celery, finely diced
1 to 2 bell peppers, diced
1/2 teaspoon thyme leaf
1 teaspoon fennel seed
1/4 teaspoon crushed saffron

1. Sauté onion and garlic in olive oil over medium heat for 3 to 4 minutes
2. To removed seeds from tomatoes, cut in half and squeeze.
3. Add the rest of the ingredients and bring to a boil. Simmer for 20 minutes.
4. Add salt and pepper to taste.
5. Sauce may be prepared days ahead of serving.
6. Add pieces of various fish to hot cioppino mixture. For example, salmon, sole, grouper, snapper, mahi, etc. and shellfish: mussels, scallops, shrimp, crab claws, crab meat, etc. If adding fresh clams, simmer clams for about 5 minutes before adding rest of fish. For best results, simmer fish covered for 3 to 4 minutes, remove from heat and let stand covered 4 to 5 minutes.
7. <u>Optional</u>: Just before serving, add 2 to 3 cloves of garlic with 2 minced anchovies. Gently stir thoroughly into cioppino.

<u>Wine Recommendation</u>: Calera Pinot Noir

<u>Recipe by</u>: Claude van Horton, owner and chef

See top of page 41 for recipe photo.

BEAVER CREEK

Created in 1982, Beaver Creek has much to offer skiers and other visitors. In addition to world-class skiing, Beaver Creek boasts a Center for the Arts, a small-world play school for children, a year-around ice rink, a multi-use 550-seat theater and a visual arts gallery. In 1999, Beaver Creek will host the World Ski Championships.

Beaver Creek shares the same zip code as Avon and the population statistic below is for Avon, which includes Beaver Creek.

I found two elegant yet casual and comfortable restaurants in Beaver Creek. One serving creative American cuisine with international touches. The other a progressive American restaurant with majestic mountain views.

Location of Town: West of Denver between Vail and Glenwood Springs
Zip Code: 81620. Area Code: 970. Population: 1,798. Elevation: 8,200ft.

The Golden Eagle Inn
Village Hall on Bear Creek Plaza. 949-1940.
Directions: Take Exit 167 from I-70 and go south ½ mile to the roundabout at Highway 6. Continue south and go 2 miles past the Beaver Creek Welcome Station. Turn left onto Offerson Road. Go .4 miles and turn right on East Thomas Place (at the Hyatt), then make an immediate second right to the down ramp for underground public parking. Upon exiting the parking garage on foot, go downstairs past the water fountain to the plaza (lowest) level. Turn left and proceed about 100 feet. The restaurant will be on your left. Or, you can stop at the Welcome Station to ask for directions to parking and the restaurant.

ESSENTIALS
Cuisine: Creative American
Hours: 7 days 11:30AM-4PM and 5:30PM-10PM. Bar stays open 4PM-5:30PM. MAY and OCT: Closed Mon. Meals and Prices: Lunch $8-$10. Dinner $16-$32
Nonsmoking: Smoking only at the bar
Take-out: Yes
Alcohol: Full Bar

Credit Cards: MC, Visa, Amx
Personal Check: Yes, with I.D.
Reservations: Recommended for dinner. Not necessary for lunch.
Wheelchair Access: Yes
Dress: Nice Casual
Other: Available for business lunches, banquets and special parties.

HISTORY, PERSONALITY AND CHARACTER

The Golden Eagle Inn was built in the early 1980s in a space previously occupied by Zambini's, an Italian restaurant. Zambini's imported and restored wood arches and a back bar from Old Town Dillon before the construction of the reservoir. The arches and back bar have remained with The Golden Eagle Inn.

Owner Pepi Langegger is from Austria and has been in the restaurant business for 40 years. In the early 1970s, he took over the Tyrolean restaurant in Vail, which he still owns. He is also the former owner of the Lancelot and Lord Gore restaurants, also in Vail. Pepi organically raises elk on his Twin Creek Game Ranch in Silt, Colorado, 100 miles west of Beaver Creek. General manager Don Bird started at the Tyrolean in 1980 where he remained until opening The Golden Eagle Inn in 1987.

Head chef Michael S. Joersz, who grew up in the Vail Valley, started in the restaurant business in 1981. He worked as a line cook at Mirabelle in Beaver Creek and the Left Bank and Blu's in Vail. He is a graduate of Western State College in Gunnison where he also worked as a sous chef at Josef's. He has been with The Golden Eagle Inn since June 1991. The sous chefs are Terry Kerouac and Ryan Parks.

FOOD, SERVICE AND AMBIANCE

When I order off a menu, I will instinctively go directly to any unusual item or one that I have never tried before. Antelope is one of those meats that I never had. This antelope is from Nepal and raised in West Texas. It comes as an appetizer barbecued with pineapple on skewers and served over quinoa tabbouleh. It is a most interesting and different dish that I recommend you try once. I found the lightly charbroiled antelope had a beef and liver flavor. Onions and yellow, red and green bell peppers enhanced this Middle Eastern dish.

For my entrée, I delved into an artful presentation of shrimp sautéed with papaya and scallions served over linguini, in a lime-coconut broth. Topping this plate was deep-fried oriental noodles that reminded me of the crystalline entity from the "Silicon Avitar" episode of Star Trek — The Next Generation. Also accompanying the five gargantuan prawns were shrimp crisps: tapioca-floured crackers with a shrimp flavor that were dipped in oil; diced pineapple, tomatoes, julienne cucumbers and onions, all sprinkled with cayenne and diced bell peppers. This unique meal is sweet, citrus and flavorsome.

Dessert is no less a special treat: an espresso cup made of chocolate, filled with white chocolate mousse served on a plate with a layer of caramel and skillfully designed vanilla syrup in a scallop pattern with

BEAVER CREEK

cherry syrup red hearts. I hesitated demolishing this work of culinary art, but then I wouldn't be able to tell you how scrumptious it was. The five flavors complement each other well, creating the illusion that I wasn't stuffing myself with too much of a good thing.

Their creative American cuisine imports sensations from the Gulf of Mexico, the Mediterranean and the Pacific. If you stop here for lunch, you can get started with soup or salad like black bean-tequila soup, smoked crawfish gazpacho or traditional Caesar with jerk-spiced ahi tuna. Forest mushrooms, farfalle and applewood smoked chicken are used in their pastas. Try the spicy soft-shelled crab tortilla roll for an Oriental-Mexican mix. The elk burger is their house specialty and they offer several sandwiches like balsamic-marinated grilled chicken breast and grilled salmon with curried aïoli.

Dinner appetizers feature crabcakes, red deer and hazelnut-bacon crusted scallops. For the pastas, entrées and game specialties, Chef Joersz takes common main courses like lamb chops, ginger beef, rack of lamb and roast duckling and distinguishes them with outlandish mushrooms, fanciful flavors and exotic tastes like hearts of palm, basil, capers, feta, eggplant, wonton, peanut, blackberry-bourbon jus and armagnac cream. Other decadent desserts include hazelnut-Tuaca cheese torte, blackberry-rhubarb crisp à la mode and cinnamon mocha ice cream pie with Oreo cookie crumb crust. Choose from over 80 wines, mostly Californian, some French, Australian and Chilean, to go with your meal. Seafood lovers should visit on Sundays when they display a seafood chalkboard highlighted by fresh oysters, whole Maine lobster and Atlantic salmon. You'll challenge your taste buds to a real treat when you dine here.

Service was helpful, professional and congenial from my server, who found answers to all my questions, to the managers and chef. The decor inside would please a hunter because of all the hunter greens, teal blues, maroons, turquoises, blond-color wood panels, stuffed mallards and pictures of buffalo, grouse, Indians with head dresses, deer, horses and hunters with their dogs. Classical music like Ravel's Bolero played quietly in the background. Beds of wild flowers out front border the patio: lobelia, pansies, aster, verbena and alyssum. The flowers are an attractive welcome for passers-by on the street and you may just find Don Bird proudly tending the foliage. If the bouquets don't lure you in, the exquisitely prepared food served by their fine staff will entice you to dine at The Golden Eagle Inn.

See page 42 for restaurant photo.

Pan-Seared Medallions of Australian Kangaroo with Sugar Plum Kiwi Compote
(Serves 4)

1/3 cup water
1/3 cup sugar
6 kiwi fruits
8 sugar plums
1 tablespoon red wine vinegar
2 to 3 tablespoons chopped fresh cilantro

Salt and pepper
2 tablespoons whole butter
1 1/2 pounds kangaroo loin (can be purchased through most game meat vendors and at some specialty markets)

1. Trim all sinew from kangaroo loin very carefully (go slowly, meat is ultra tender and will tear easily).
2. Cut against grain into 2-ounce medallions. Use meat mallet and plastic wrap and pound loin very lightly into 1/4-inch thickness. Set aside.
3. Compote: Combine water and sugar and reduce to make simple syrup. Peel kiwi fruit and cut into halved slices. Julienne plum. When syrup has reduced to medium thickness, add fruit and vinegar. Pull from heat and add cilantro, salt and pepper to taste.
4. Heat sauté pan to medium high and add whole butter. Do not burn (whole butter will give the meat a lightly nutty flavor).
5. Flash fry kangaroo in pan, just to rare and set aside to rest for 3 to 5 minutes.
6. Fan meat out on plate and spoon compote over liberally. Makes 4 6-ounce portions.
7. Serve with favorite starch.

Wine Recommendation: 1995 Archery Summit Pinot Noir

Recipe by: Michael S. Joersz, chef

See top of page 43 for recipe photo.

BEAVER CREEK

Grouse Mountain Grill

141 Scott Hill Road (in the Pines Lodge). 949-0600.
Directions: Take Exit 167 from I-70 and go south ½ mile to the roundabout at Highway 6. Continue south and go 2.2 miles past the Beaver Creek Welcome Station. Turn right onto Scott Hill Road and go ¼ mile. The restaurant is in the Pines Lodge on the left. There is complimentary valet parking.

ESSENTIALS
Cuisine: Progressive American
Hours: 7 days 6PM-10PM. Closed late-APR thru Memorial Day Weekend.
Meals and Prices: Dinner $26-$34.
Nonsmoking: All. Smoking only permitted on patio and lobby.
Take-out: Yes
Alcohol: Full Bar
Credit Cards: MC, Visa, Amx

Personal Check: Yes
Reservations: Highly recommended in winter. Recommended in summer.
Wheelchair Access: Yes
Dress: Casual elegance
Other: Children's Menu. Service charge of 18% for parties of 9 or more. Split plate charge $7.50/entrée.

HISTORY, PERSONALITY AND CHARACTER

Nancy Dowell and Joan Jaffe who lease the property from Vail Resorts operate the Grouse Mountain Grill. The Pines Lodge was constructed in 1990 and the original name of the restaurant was The Camberly Club. Nancy has been in the restaurant business since 1974 and was the former owner of Cyrano's Restaurant in Vail until 1993 when she opened the Grouse Mountain Grill. Joan owns the Double J Ranch, a cattle-working ranch that raises all of the limousin beef used in the restaurant. She also owns the Beacon Grill in Denver.

Dining room manager Tony McNally has been at the Grouse Mountain Grill since 1993 and was with Cyrano's between 1983 and 1993. Executive chef Rick Kangas has also been with the Grouse Mountain Grill since 1993 after owning and managing three restaurants in Billings, Montana, working in Winter Park for 2 years and cooking at Blu's in Vail from 1990 to 1993. He hails from a restaurant family and has been working in restaurants since 1974. Entertainer Tony Gulizia has been at the restaurant since 1993 where he plays the piano and sings six nights a week in the summer and almost every night in the winter.

FOOD, SERVICE AND AMBIANCE

I could not resist ordering the Grouse Mountain Grill's own signature dish, the grilled limousin tenderloin from cattle that they raise on their own ranch. The entrée consisted of two five-ounce filets that were virtually fat free, very tender and "melted in my mouth". They were served with herb white mushrooms with basil and onion and sprinkled with black pepper. My choice of a side dish was a generous portion of 23 full-length spears of asparagus. Slices of homemade multi-grain bread similar in texture to rye with caraway seeds and a relish tray were served. The tray included several tasty treats like sweet red onion marmalade to put on sweet jalapeño glaze and Asiago-gorgonzola homemade crackers; pickles, red peppers, carrots, onion and cauliflower. I preceded the entrée with a Caesar salad with romaine lettuce, roasted garlic Caesar dressing, two anchovies on top, two Parmesan toasts on the side and the side of the bowl dusted with Parmesan cheese. This was a smart presentation that allowed me to decide how much Parmesan to include with the salad.

Chef Kangas tries to keep the meals at the Grouse Mountain Grill rustic and simple but makes seasonal changes to the menu to keep it innovative and new. Dinner starters include fried portobello mushrooms and crispy soft-shell crab for appetizers and salads with lobster and mascarpone cheese or spinach , mushrooms and bacon. Your other side dish selections are horseradish mashed potatoes; carrots and pea shoots; roasted corn, sweet red pepper and chayote (a gourdlike, bland tasting fruit); and fried white cheddar grit cakes. You will be encouraged to have every member of your dining party choose a different side dish as they are served family style and you can pass the bowls around and share.

For entrées, select from dry-aged New York steak, grilled lamb T-bones on roasted tomato and garlic, double cut pork chop on tomato-apple chutney with pickled fig, pine-nut crusted Alaskan halibut, Ritz crusted walleye fillet, pan-fried breast of chicken and five-spiced duck. To complement your meal, call for a glass or bottle from their list of about 365 domestic wines that were given the Wine Spectator Award of Excellence in 1996. For dessert, try the stir-fried strawberry sundae, amaretto crème brûlée, apple bread pudding or port wine with a chocolate truffle trio. Ice cream drinks, dessert wines, grappas, and fruit brandies are also available to complete your dining experience.

My server was prompt, attentive with water refills, helpful with my questions and knowledgeable. Lively jazz emanates from Tony singing and playing the piano in the lounge. The enormous dining room has high ceilings, polished pinewood columns and beams and white stucco walls

BEAVER CREEK

with colossal paintings of flowers, fruits and a flower garden. The centerpiece to the room, however, is the floor to ceiling adobe-style, wood-burning, three-sided fireplace that also opens up to the lobby and the lounge. There is a wide-arched opening to the bar and lounge with a shelf filled with a basket of dried flowers, wrought-iron deer-shaped candleholders and candles. Four pairs of window doors provide majestic views of the mountains and lead to patio dining, through long red, gold and green-color drapes. The Grouse Mountain Grill offers a complete dining experience accomplished by serving high-quality food with style in a fresh, friendly atmosphere presenting a pleasing panorama.

Double Cut Pork Chops on Tomato-Apple Chutney with Pickled Figs
(Serves 8)

8 double-cut pork chops

Chutney:
1 2/3 cups sundried tomatoes (yellow), chopped
1 each Granny Smith apple, peeled and cored
1/4 cup red bell pepper, chopped
1/4 cup yellow onion, chopped
1/3 cup cucumber, peeled, seeded, chopped
2 2/3 tablespoons dried currants
1/2 cup brown sugar, packed
1 1/3 dashes crushed ice
1/4 teaspoon crushed red pepper
1/4 teaspoon garlic, chopped
1/2 teaspoon ground ginger
1 1/3 dashes salt
1 1/3 dashes ground cinnamon
1/2 cup cider vinegar

Pickled Fresh Figs:
1 flat fresh figs
Boiling water to cover figs, as needed
3/4 cup white sugar
1/2 quart water
1/2 cup white sugar
1/2 each whole cinnamon stick spice
1/4 tablespoon whole allspice
1/4 tablespoon whole cloves spice
3/4 cup cider vinegar

1. Marinate pork chops in lime juice and Jamaican jerk seasoning or use any seasoned pork chops.
2. <u>Two methods for cooking the pork</u>: Soup pan sear and finish in oven or sear over hot grill and finish in oven.
3. Roast pork in 400 degree oven for 20 minutes for a medium finish.
4. If you prefer your meat rarer, leave it in the oven for less time. If you prefer a more well-done cut, leave the pork in the oven for more than 20 minutes.
5. <u>Chutney</u>: Combine all the ingredients above and cook slowly until thick. Refrigerate.
6. <u>Pickled Figs</u>: Place figs in boiling water. Remove from heat and allow to cool. Drain. Discard water. Bring the 1/2 quart water and sugar to a boil. Add figs. Simmer for 30 minutes. Tie the spices into a cheese cloth bag. Add the remaining sugar and the bag of spices to the simmering figs. Slowly cook the figs until they are clear. Remove the spice bag.

<u>Wine Recommendation</u>: Acacia 1994 St. Clair Pinot or Qupé 1995 Bien Nacido Syrah

<u>Recipe by</u>: Rich Kangas, executive chef

See bottom of page 43 for recipe photo.

BERTHOUD

Berthoud was first called Little Thompson. It was later named for Captain Edward L. Berthoud, an early explorer and chief civil engineer of the Colorado Central Railroad. Berthoud Pass, which he discovered, was also named for him.

The family American restaurant below has been an institution in these parts for three-fourths of a century, serving country, home-cooked, family-style dinners.

Location of Town: North of Denver
Zip Code: 80513. Area Code: 970. Population: 2,990. Elevation: 5,030ft.

The Wayside Inn
505 Mountain Avenue. 532-2013.
Directions: Take Exit 250 from I-25 and go west for five miles to the first stop sign. Turn left onto Highway 287 (Mountain Avenue) and go .3 miles. The restaurant is on the left one block past the signal on the southwest corner of Mountain Avenue and 5th Street.

ESSENTIALS
Cuisine: Family American
Hours: Tue-Sun 7AM-9:30PM. Closed Mon. Breakfast until 11AM. Lunch/Dinner from 11AM.
Meals and Prices: Breakfast $4-$5, Lunch $4-$6, Dinner $7-$13.
Nonsmoking: Yes
Take-out: Yes
Alcohol: Full Bar
Credit Cards: MC, Visa, Amx, Disc
Personal Check: Yes
Reservations: Recommended for parties of 7 or more. Not necessary otherwise.
Wheelchair Access: Yes
Dress: Casual
Other: Service charge of 15% for tables of 8 or more. Catering and banquet rooms for receptions available.

HISTORY, PERSONALITY AND CHARACTER
The Wayside Inn, "the inn with family tradition", has been family-owned and operated since 1922. Steeped in history and family tradition, this restaurant was originally opened by the Eickels in 1922 as a cottage in the tradition of English wayside inns. It consisted of a dining room serving family-style meals, a kitchen and six small bedrooms for rent. In 1924, the Inn was sold to Wilbur (Bill) and Helen Griffin who operated the Inn until Bill's

death in 1932. Neil and Esther Nielson then operated the Inn until 1950 when it was sold to Stanford Williams.

The first major expansion of the Inn occurred in 1960 when the American Legion building next door was purchased and converted into a small banquet room. At the same time, overnight lodging was discontinued. The second major remodeling was done in the spring of 1973 when a pub was added, the front entrance was moved to the west side, the dining room was enlarged and the kitchen was modernized.

Fred and Annely Peterson purchased The Wayside Inn in May 1978 and transformed the banquet room to house "Ye Olde Wayside Inn Dinner Theater" for live plays and musicals. On Christmas Eve 1993, when the Inn was empty, a faulty furnace burned the restaurant to the ground. Fortunately, in the spirit of "It's a Wonderful Life", the Petersons received an enormous outpouring of support from community members and long-time customers urging them to rebuild. Combining their Swedish heritage along with some furnishings from the old building, the Petersons were able to reopen in the same location in May 1995. I think there is a little of Bedford Falls in Berthoud.

Fred hails from a restaurant family in Chicago and has a Hotel and Restaurant Management Degree from Denver University. He has been in the restaurant business since the mid-1960s and previously co-owned the Aspen Buffet in Longmont from 1972 to 1978 with wife Annely. Son Jon has worked in the restaurant business since he was a kid and has managed The Wayside Inn since May 1995. Head cook Pete Krauss has been there since 1995 and previously cooked in Pennsylvania and at "This Old House", now Marie's, during the 1980s. Donny Olander, Jon's aunt, prepares many of the salads and desserts.

FOOD, SERVICE AND AMBIANCE

Linda and I both took pleasure in the country, home-cooking, family-style dinners served at The Wayside Inn. She ordered the two piece pan-fried chicken while I had the two center-cut pork chops. Both meals came with two side dishes. The chicken was tender with a light, brown breading. The pork chops were well done with a thin layer of barbecue sauce on top. Complementing Linda's dinner were a hearty bowl of vegetable soup filled with cauliflower, broccoli, green beans, peas and carrots and pasta Alfredo made from scratch with al dente noodles in a light Alfredo sauce. My very creamy, cream of chicken soup and mashed potatoes were hot and delicious. Condiments served before dinner included applesauce sprinkled with cinnamon, bread and butter pickles and fresh bread with honey butter.

BERTHOUD

Good, wholesome food and ample portions is what you will find at The Wayside Inn.

Highlighting the breakfast menu are fluffy and light pancakes with a hint of vanilla, thin and rich Swedish pancakes, several skillet dishes and many omelets. Lunch offers lots of sandwiches from chicken bacon melt and burgers to roast beef and grilled ham and cheese. Chicken potpie, fried chicken, salads and baked potatoes are also featured for lunch. Additional dinner entrées include steaks, prime rib on weekends only, Swedish meatballs, rainbow trout, jumbo shrimp and salmon with your choice of two or four side dishes or desserts. The rice pudding is one of Grandma Peterson's recipes. Other options are pies, like coconut meringue or banana cream, ice cream, carrot or cheesecake and bread pudding.

Service was amiable and courteous. This is a spotlessly clean restaurant with numerous paintings by Swedish artist, Carl Larson, portraying families at picnics and children in homey settings. As you enter the restaurant, you will notice an old church pew in the front hallway. Inside you will find high, vaulted plaster ceilings and walls with half-moon shaped sconces and paintings high on the walls by Ann Marie Kaspersen. There was a huge quilt on one wall and baskets of dried flowers on a wall ledge separating rooms. At the entrance to the dining room was a large plant with artificial aspen trees and pumpkins. This is an outstanding family destination that has garnished much deserved respect from scores of people in the area.

See top of page 44 for restaurant photo.

<u>Special One-Time Offer</u>: Buy one entrée and receive a second entrée of equal or lesser value free (up to $15.00) OR receive 50% off one entrée (up to $7.50). Please present to server at time of ordering.

_____ Owner/Manager. _____ Date.

Rice Pudding
(Makes one 9" x 13" pan)

1 1/2 cups rice, regular
1/2 gallon milk

2 cups evaporated milk
6 whole eggs
2 cups sugar
1/2 teaspoons nutmeg

1. Cook rice in milk, over medium heat until tender.
2. In a separate bowl, mix together the other ingredients.
3. Slowly add cooked rice to the cold mixture (add slowly to prevent curdling).
4. Pour into a buttered 9" x 13" pan. Put small pats of butter on top of mixture.
5. Bake at 350 degrees for 30 to 45 minutes, until knife comes out clean.

This is an old family recipe created by Grandma Anna Peterson.

Sweetbreads from The Fawn Brook Inn in Allenspark.
Photo by Hermann and Mieke Groicher.

The Fawn Brook Inn in Allenspark.
Photo by Hermann and Mieke Groicher.

Zuppa di Carote "Marco Polo," Carrot Ginger Soup (hot or cold) from Caffé Amici in Aspen.

Peppered Ahi Tuna with Tomato Risotto and Brown Butter-Balsamic Vinaigrette from The Mother Lode in Aspen.
Photo by David J. Gruber.

Espresso-Blackened Tenderloin of Beef, Au Poivre with Rich Mashed Potatoes and Yam Frites from Renaissance in Aspen.
Photo by Jason Dewey.

Renaissance in Aspen.
Photo by Jason Dewey.

Cioppino from Chefy's in Basalt.
Photo by David J. Gruber.

Chefy's in Basalt.
Photo by David J. Gruber.

The Golden Eagle Inn in Beaver Creek.

Pan-Seared Medallions of Australian Kangaroo with Sugar Plum Kiwi Compote from The Golden Eagle Inn in Beaver Creek.
Photo by Vino Anthony.

Double Cut Pork Chop on Tomato-Apple Chutney with Pickled Figs from the Grouse Mountain Grill in Beaver Creek.
Photo by David J. Gruber.

The Wayside Inn in Berthoud.
Photo by Fred Peterson.

Caribou from the Adams Street Grill in Breckenridge.
Photo by David J. Gruber.

*The Adams Street Grill in Breckenridge.
Photo by David J. Gruber.*

*Feta Fettuccine from the Blue River Bistro in Breckenridge.
Photo by David J. Gruber.*

*Chipotle Barbecue Tuna with Caramelized Onion
from the Hearthstone in Breckenridge.
Photo by David J. Gruber.*

*The Hearthstone in Breckenridge.
Photo by Bruce Carlton.*

Cinnamon Spice Rubbed Sea Bass with Pico de Gallo from Mi Casa in Breckenridge. Photo by David J. Gruber.

Cornish Game Hen from The Mountain Sage Café in Breckenridge. Photo by David J. Gruber.

*Rasta Pasta from Rasta Pasta in Breckenridge.
Photo by David J. Gruber.*

*Crawfish Chili Rellenos with Tabasco Buerre Blanc on top of a Roasted Corn and Black Bean Relish from the Swan Mountain Inn in Breckenridge.
Photo by Stacy Anderson.*

The Swan Mountain Inn in Breckenridge.

*Beef Wellington from The Wellington Inn in Breckenridge.
Photo by Hollie van der Hoeven.*

*Spinach Walnut Fettuccini from the Double Diamond in Copper Mountain.
Photo by David Luthi.*

*The Augustine Grill in Castle Rock.
Photo by Anna Linney.*

BRECKENRIDGE

Breckenridge was originally named Fort Meribeh after the only woman, a Mary B., in the original party of settlers led by General George E. Spencer in 1859. The town was later renamed after former U. S. Vice President, John Cabell Breckinridge. Angered by Breckinridge's sympathy for the Confederacy during the Civil War, the town's citizens, ardent Unionists, changed the spelling. The first 'i' was changed to 'e' to disassociate the town of Breckenridge from Vice President Breckinridge. On July 23, 1887, the largest single gold nugget ever found in Colorado was discovered by miner Tom Groves at nearby Farncomb Hill. It weighed in at 13 pounds, 7 ounces! Today, Breckenridge has over 350 buildings on the National Register of Historic Places.

Breckenridge provides the largest selection of restaurants of any town in this book. The eclectic collection of 9 restaurants that I visited includes a Victorian landmark serving regional cuisine, an American grill with a southwest flair, a regional American restaurant in a lodge and spa, a modern Italian and American bistro, a Continental/German restaurant, a Continental/Colorado eatery, a Jamaican pasta place, a California/Mexican dining establishment and an innovative health food café with a Pacific rim flair. Go choose!

Location of Town: Central Colorado on Highway 9 between Frisco and Fairplay
Zip Code: 80424. Area Code: 970. Population: 1,285. Elevation: 9,602ft.

Adams Street Grill
10 West Adams Street. 453-4700
Directions: From the north on Highway 9 (Main Street), proceed 2 blocks past the signal at Lincoln/Ski Hill Road. The restaurant is on the right on the northwest corner of Main Street and Adams Street. From the south on Highway 9 (Main Street), proceed 2 blocks past the signal at Park Avenue. The restaurant is on the left on the northwest corner of Main Street and Adams Street.

BRECKENRIDGE

ESSENTIALS

Cuisine: American with a Southwest Flair
Hours: 7 days 11AM-4PM and 5PM-10PM. Closed late-OCT to Mid-NOV and Mid-APR to Late-MAY.
Meals and Prices: Lunch $6-$9. Dinner $9-$28.
Nonsmoking: All. Smoking only permitted at bar.
Take-out: Yes

Alcohol: Full Bar
Credit Cards: MC, Visa, Amx
Personal Check: Yes, with I.D.
Reservations: Accepted
Wheelchair Access: Yes, including bathrooms
Dress: Casual, dressier at night
Other: Children's Menu. Wedding and banquet facilities available.

HISTORY, PERSONALITY AND CHARACTER

The Adams Street Grill was originally a residence built in the early 1950s. Between 1969 and 1975, it was the Adams Street Café under different owners before converting to the Adams Street Grill. In 1990, the restaurant was redesigned and expanded to three times its original size. The current owners are Reginald and Pamela Gray, Warren and Annette Kesselring and Steven and Sheila Jagentenfl. Reggie, a graduate of Cornell Hotel and Restaurant Management School, also owns the Horseshoe II, which Steve and Sheila manage, the Gold Pan and Mountain Sage Café, all in Breckenridge.

Dining room manager Dave McCrae has been with Adams Street Grill since 1997 and previously worked in restaurants in Minnesota. Head chef Chris Hayashi also came in 1997 after cooking in Hawaii and attending the culinary arts program at Keystone Management School.

FOOD, SERVICE AND AMBIANCE

The Adams Street Grill serves some "healthy-size" lunches as I discovered when I ordered the blue corn chicken enchiladas. The tasty enchiladas were stuffed with grilled chicken breasts, cheddar and Monterey Jack cheeses, tomato and onion, topped with their savory green chili and big dollops of sour cream and served with Anasazi wild rice and black beans. The beans were different, mixed with corn, onion, tomato and green pepper, and excellent. The rice was also something special: white, wild grain and brown rice with shaved carrots. Great side dishes made for a great combination.

Burgers and hot and cold sandwiches make up the lunch menu which is highlighted by a Copenhagen club, hot vegetable sandwich and Reuben sandwich. For an evening appetizer, you can try Rocky Mountain oysters, house smoked trout, a spring roll or gravlox. As a second course or light meal, choose the New Mexico style black bean roasted soup, the goat cheese salad or deluxe chicken sandwich. Headlining the pastas, entrées and wild game selections are ahi tuna fusilli, ultimate ravioli, Colorado prime rib (on weekends only), chicken Marsala, salmon Napoleon, caribou and elk. The delightful dessert selections feature the chef's daily cheesecake, a Hawaiian snowball — vanilla ice cream rolled in coconut with pineapple, guava and raspberry sauce — Pam's homemade bread pudding and a Colorado apple sensation — cinnamon baked apples and walnut puff pastry with muscat butter cream.

    Service was pleasant, courteous, efficient and very helpful. The Adams Street Grill has much southwest warmth with maroons, peaches, mauves and turquoise tile sconces. The New Mexico cross pattern can be found with paintings of the southwest, cactus and potted plants. Two red brick fireplaces are the centerpieces of the restaurant. A deer's head with antlers is mounted over one fireplace while two comical wood sculptures of bears greet you at the entrance. Bay windows add another touch of character to the place.

    The dining room upstairs emphasizes a more tropical theme with paintings of palm trees, Spanish arches, steps and beaches. Joining this look are paintings of marshes and Columbines in splashes of blue, pink and maroon imparting the look of the southwest wilderness. A stain-glass picture of a mountain with the symbol "9,600'" supplements this scene very well. A bar at the end of the second floor leads to an upper level balcony overlooking the Blue River below and offering a view of the ten-mile range to the west. A patio on ground level in front of the restaurant is the perfect place to watch Main Street walkers in summer. Whatever season you visit the Adams Street Grill, you will be treated to some fine American and southwest cuisine in an ideal setting with picturesque scenery.

See page 45 for restaurant photo.

SPECIAL ONE-TIME OFFER: Buy one entrée at the regular price and receive a complimentary beverage of your choice. Valid for every member of your party. Please present to server at time of ordering.

_____ Owner/ Manager. _____ Date.

BRECKENRIDGE

Caribou
(Serves 1)

3 2-ounce caribou medallions, marinated for at least 12 hours

Marinade:
1 shallot, diced
1 clove garlic, minced
1/2 teaspoon pepper
3 ounces corn oil
1/2 teaspoon thyme
1 bay leaf

Sauce:
1 ounce tamarind (tamarind water is made by dissolving tamarind candy in water and then straining out fibers)
2 ounces demi-glace
1/2 teaspoon raspberry vinegar
1/2 teaspoon sugar
1/4 teaspoon salt
1 ounce guava puree

1. Mix ingredients for marinade. Coat medallions with marinade and let sit overnight.
2. Grill caribou to medium rare.
3. Sauce: Mix and reduce by 1/2, thicken with a cornstarch and water.
4. Place medallions on plate and pour sauce on top. Serve with steamed vegetables sautéed in butter seasoned with fresh basil, salt, and pepper.

Wine Recommendation: Far Niente 1990 Cabernet Sauvignon

Recipe by: Chris Hayashi, head chef

See bottom of page 44 for recipe photo.

Blue River Bistro

305 North Main Street. 453-6974.
Directions: From the south on Highway 9 (Main Street) the restaurant is ½ block past the Watson Avenue on the left.

ESSENTIALS

Cuisine: Modern Italian and American
Hours: 7 days 11AM-10PM. 9PM in MAY/JUNE and SEP/OCT. Lunch to 4:30PM. Dinner from 4:30PM.
Meals and Prices: Lunch $6-$9. Dinner $12-$18.
Nonsmoking: All. Smoking only permitted in bar area.
Take-out: Yes

Alcohol: Full Bar
Credit Cards: All 5
Personal Check: Summit County only
Reservations: Recommended
Wheelchair Access: Yes
Dress: Nice casual
Other: Service charge of 15% may be added to parties of 7 or more.

HISTORY, PERSONALITY AND CHARACTER

Wayne and Cindy Spaulding opened the Blue River Bistro in 1991 in a new building constructed in 1990. They met in California in 1985 while they were working at a Houlihan's Restaurant in the San Francisco Bay area. Wayne and Cindy also own the Uptown Bistro in Frisco, Colorado. Wayne is the chef and Cindy is the floor manager and hostess. Assisting Wayne in the kitchen is Pete Shields who began at the restaurant in 1997. He has been in the restaurant business since 1980 having previously worked for Hearthstone Catering and the Breckenridge Barbecue. Sous chef Timothy Milonzi has been in the restaurant business since the mid-1980s and came to the Blue River Bistro in 1996.

FOOD, SERVICE AND AMBIANCE

I wanted to see why the Blue River Bistro's fried calamari was an award-winning recipe at the Taste of Breckenridge so I ordered them as an appetizer. The answer was easy to find. They were a generous portion of about two dozen rings and a half-dozen tentacles, lightly breaded, flavorful, very tender, chewy and too good for the cocktail sauce that came with them. Shaved parmesan cheese and parsley were sprinkled on top. For the entrée, I chose ravioli alla Veneziana, another hearty measure of 10 raviolis stuffed with veal and spinach with prosciutto, fresh tomato, mushrooms and green onions in cream sauce. This was a rich, filling and delicious dish. A small loaf of warm, Italian bread with a crispy crust and soft dough, brought down from their sister restaurant, the Uptown Bistro in Frisco,

BRECKENRIDGE

was served with the meal. The focaccia served for the dinner bread is made at the Blue River Bistro.

Lunch and dinner offer some tantalizing appetizers, salads, soups and pasta dishes. For starters, you might try crab cakes, baked brie, lobster strudel or onion straws. The soup and salad selections feature grilled seafood, cashew chicken, cobb, niçoise and baked French onion soup. The pasta favorites include four winners at the Taste of Breckenridge: tortellini carbonara prepared with turkey, linguini Leonardo with sautéed chicken breast, seafood primavera and shellfish cioppino. Some of the sandwich choices for lunch are crab melt, vegetarian, grilled chicken gyro, chicken walnut and burgers with blue cheese or Thousand Island dressing and cheddar cheese. Special entrées are also available for dinner like stuffed chicken breast or pork chop, veal picatta, New York peppercorn, herb encrusted ahi tuna and potato wrapped salmon. Select one of their 50 varieties of wine to augment your meal. For a sweet finish, treat yourself to one of their homemade desserts such as chocolate mousse cake, apple-blueberry cobbler, espresso flan, almond or mango cheesecake or key lime pie.

Service was quick, informative and helpful. The Blue River Bistro has a high vaulted ceiling with exposed red and blue heat pipes, ceiling fans, white plaster walls with red trim and several hanging and potted plants. Straight back to the right is a bar and in the rear are wine cabinets. Adorning the walls are mountain photos of streams and flowers taken by Jeff Ryan; pictures of aspen trees, cactus and Italian villas; and mixed media art works by Leona Sophocles depicting highways with sharp 90° right turns. Most of the pictures change about once a month. Enhancing this decor are posters of the Taste of Breckenridge '97 and a Willy Ronis poster of skiers. The Blue River Bistro was a first-place winner at the Taste of Breckenridge every year from 1994 to 1997. It is an innovative and fun dining establishment with exceptional cuisine in an ever-changing environment.

SPECIAL ONE-TIME OFFER: Purchase two entrées and receive one complimentary appetizer. Please present to server at time of ordering. _____ Owner/Manager. _____ Date.

BRECKENRIDGE

Feta Fettuccine
(Serves 1)

4 extra large shrimps (16u to 20u per pound, i.e., extra large shrimps come 16 to 20 shrimps per pound)	1 tablespoon lemon juice
	1/2 cup white wine
1/2 teaspoon fresh ground garlic	3 ounces feta cheese, crumbled
4 scallions, cut into 1/4-inch long pieces	Salt and pepper to taste
	8 ounces cooked fettuccine
6 artichoke hearts, quartered	Parmesan cheese
4 medium-sized mushrooms, sliced	Fresh parsley

1. Heat up medium-sized skillet.
2. Coat shrimp in flour; cook shrimp for one minute in skillet. Flip over and cook the other side for another minute.
3. Add garlic. Cook until it sweats (about 10 to 20 seconds). Add scallions, mushrooms and artichoke hearts. Cook for one minute.
4. Add lemon juice and wine. Let reduce for 2 minutes. Add feta cheese. Cook for 1 more minute. Season with salt and pepper.
5. Add cooked fettuccine to skillet and flip to coat the pasta. Pour into plate. Garnish with Parmesan cheese and fresh parsley.

Wine Recommendation: Cake Bread Sauvignon Blanc

Recipe by: Wayne Spaulding, owner and chef

See top of page 46 for recipe photo.

BRECKENRIDGE

Hearthstone

130 South Ridge Street. 453-1148.
Directions: From the north on Highway 9, proceed 1 block past the signal at Lincoln/Ski Hill Road. Turn left on Washington. Go 1 block. The restaurant is on the northeast corner of South Ridge Street and Washington. From the south on Highway 9, proceed 3 blocks past the signal at South Park Avenue. Turn right on Washington. Go 1 block. The restaurant is on the northeast corner of S. Ridge Street and Washington.

ESSENTIALS

Cuisine: Regional
Hours: SEP to Mid-APR: 7 nights 5PM-10PM. Mid-APR to Late MAY: 7 nights 6PM-10PM. Memorial Day Weekend to Early SEP: 7 days 11AM-3PM and 6PM-10PM.
Meals and Prices: Lunch $6-$10. Dinner $12-$20.
Nonsmoking: All. Smoking only permitted in the lounge upstairs.
Take-out: Yes
Alcohol: Full Bar
Credit Cards: MC, Visa, Amx
Personal Check: Local only with I.D.
Reservations: Recommended
Wheelchair Access: Yes
Dress: Casual
Other: Full service catering available in your home or at one of three restaurants in Summit County. Private dining room for special parties, banquets and receptions. Service charge of 15% added to parties of six or more.

HISTORY, PERSONALITY AND CHARACTER

  The Hearthstone, a Victorian landmark, began in 1886 as a small log cabin. In the early 1900s, Christ Kaiser purchased the property and extensively remodeled it. His daughter, who currently lives in Denver, still dines at the restaurant. While the Hearthstone remained a residence until 1978, it has been rumored to also have been Summit County's first brothel. There have been three restaurants in this building since 1978: Andrea's Pleasure Palace from 1978 to 1984, Whitney's from 1986 to 1989 and the Hearthstone from 1989 to the present. The original home occupied the back of the front dining room and the kitchen.
  The Hearthstone is locally owned and operated by Dick Carleton and Jane Storm, who also own and operate Mi Casa Mexican Restaurant and Cantina in Breckenridge and Su Casa Mexican Restaurant and Cantina which opened in Keystone in 1997. Jane began in the restaurant business in 1971. Dick joined Jane at Mi Casa shortly after she purchased it in 1981 and advanced quickly from waiter to general operating partner.

Jane and Dick both share a commitment to Summit County and are active in supporting various non-profit organizations such as the Breckenridge Outdoor Education Center, the Summit Foundation, Summit Recycling, the Breckenridge Music Festival and many other fund-raising efforts. Their contributions are frequently noted with awards and recognition such as the Summit Foundation Philanthropist of the Year and Breckenridge Resort Chamber Business of the Year.

The Hearthstone Mission Statement reads, "A guest-driven company with a commitment to consistency of quality, we strive to offer a value-based experience through staff development and community service." General manager Tracey Hill and assistant manager Peter Bakken take this statement very seriously and apply it to every aspect of the day-to-day operation of the restaurant. Corporate chef Bruce Carlton and chef de cuisine Chris Cawley are constantly refining and changing the menu to offer a variety of new and tasty cuisine. The Hearthstone was given the 1997 Wine Spectator Award of Excellence for the 100+ selection wine list combined with the varied menu offerings. The restaurant also received honors from The Taste of Breckenridge placing second overall in 1990, 1994, 1996 and 1997 and third best appetizer in 1997.

FOOD, SERVICE AND AMBIANCE

The Hearthstone's menu is seasonal, changing two or three times a year. Their fish is flown in fresh three times a week, never frozen. Sauces are made from scratch. I had the pleasure of dining at the Hearthstone on two occasions. I sampled their jalapeño wrapped shrimp stuffed with jalapeño and cream cheese, dipped in beer batter and deep fried: my kind of appetizer (also available as an entrée). I also tried the New England clam chowder — a thick soup with big pieces of potatoes and a few vegetables and spices. The Caesar salad with very crisp fresh croutons, field greens, Parmesan cheese and ground black pepper was refreshing. Onion rolls were served on one visit; a combination of four bread rolls, chipotle-Asiago cheese, multi-grain, sesame and sun-dried tomato, were served on the other visit.

For an entrée, I recommend the filet au poivre, a seared, custom-aged, medium-rare tenderloin encrusted in cracked black pepper that is offset by a smooth, rich, brandy-Dijon cream sauce. Also of high quality was the grilled fresh ahi tuna with homemade barbecue sauce seasoned with smoked jalapeño and regional spices, then finished with caramelized Bermuda onion and crispy cilantro. The barbecue sauce was light and mild with tomato taste. I ordered this dish rare. It was a toothsome medley of flavors. Two specials that are also excellent are the trout in asparagus dill

BRECKENRIDGE

sauce and Colorado lamb in an orange stout glaze with brown sugar. The trout has an uncooked split asparagus spear on top and chopped asparagus cooked into the sauce. The rack of lamb is a tasty morsel of white meat with a delectable sweet sauce. They now serve a crab-stuffed trout and New Zealand lamb rack as regular menu items. New red potatoes soft enough to gently pass a knife through and side vegetables of lightly sautéed broccoli, cauliflower and yellow squash are served.

Some of their other appetizers are grilled quail, ale-steamed mussels and pan-seared crab cakes. Their eclectic menu features meat specialties (slow-roasted prime rib, charbroiled filet topped with crab meat and a grilled or stuffed New York strip), seafood (charbroiled Atlantic salmon, jumbo gulf shrimp, Maine lobster tail and Alaskan king crab legs), chicken (with macadamia nuts and coconut or lemon and julienne vegetables) and vegetarian dishes (portobello strudel and grilled eggplant Napoleon). End your evening of fine dining with white chocolate raspberry bread pudding, double chocolate truffle fudge torte, crème brûlée, or peach linzer torte. For summertime lunch, the Hearthstone offers appetizers of salmon cakes and portobello strudel, fresh salads like Thai noodle and tarragon chicken, homemade soups, sandwiches such as turkey avocado and veggie, and char-grilled burgers.

I found their service to be pleasant, helpful, accommodating and very informative. Their servers are "on the spot", exhibit a pleasant smile and enjoy their jobs. The staff is pleased to prepare an entrée combination of your own choosing upon request, so don't be shy if you're in a creative mood. They play some low volume rock and blues music one evening, big band and snappy jazz the other.

The building is a National Historic Landmark with most of the original wood. The very authentic-looking natural wood walls decorated with Victorian-style paintings combined naturally with a very attractive red floral carpet. Stained-glass and homey-looking needlework pieces added some nice touches as did old photos of girls in Victorian dresses and white-laced curtains and tablecloths. A large bay window in front with a table for five is a superb place to dine. Even the hallway between restrooms is worth a few minutes of your time. There are 12 photos of original needlework showing flower arrangements for each month of the year. They are from a collection by Rob Furber, Gardner at Kensington 1730.

The Victorian lounge upstairs showcases an old mahogany bar, an old dresser, a wall shelf with polished brass pots, pitchers, plates and kitchen utilities, brass chandeliers, an arched ceiling, and Victorian era photos. The Hearthstone displays a class and elegance all its own. The people present an exquisite cuisine with a down-to-earth, comfortable attitude.

BRECKENRIDGE

See page 47 for restaurant photo.

Chipotle Barbecue Tuna with Caramelized Onion
(Serves 4)

For Barbecue Sauce:
1/2 cup onion, diced
2 tablespoons vegetable oil
2 cups ketchup
2 tablespoons pureed chipotle peppers (canned)
1/4 cup brown sugar
2 tablespoons Worcestershire sauce
2 tablespoons garlic, minced
2 tablespoons balsamic vinegar
1/4 cup orange juice concentrate
1/2 teaspoon salt
1/2 teaspoon black pepper
1/2 teaspoon chili powder

For Caramelized Onion:
1 large red onion, sliced thin
4 tablespoons butter

For Tuna:
4 6-ounce yellowfin tuna steaks

1. For Caramelized Onions: In a large sauté pan, cook onion in butter over very low heat 2 to 3 hours, stirring occasionally. Onions will take on a dark color and give a sweet aroma when done. (Can be prepared 1 to 2 days in advance; cooled, then reheated when needed.)
2. For Sauce: In a medium sauce pan, sauté diced onion in oil until clear. Add all remaining ingredients and cook over low heat for 45 minutes, stirring often. Remove from stove and cool. Keep refrigerated until needed.
3. For Tuna: Grill steaks to desired doneness. About 5 minutes per side for medium rare. After turning tuna onto second side, baste liberally with barbecue sauce.
4. Transfer tuna to serving dish and top each steak with hot caramelized onions.

Wine Recommendation: 1996 Caymus Sauvignon Blanc

See bottom of page 46 for recipe photo.

BRECKENRIDGE

Mi Casa

600 Park Street. 453-2071.
Directions: From the north on Highway 9 (Main Street), proceed 4 blocks past the signal at Lincoln/Ski Hill Road. Turn right on Park Avenue. Go ½ block. The restaurant is on the right in the Der Steiermark Condo Building next to Blue River Sports. From the south on Highway 9 (Main Street), turn left on Park Avenue. Go ½ block. The restaurant is on the right in the Der Steiermark Condo Building next to Blue River Sports.

ESSENTIALS
Cuisine: California Mexican
Hours: 7 days 11:30AM-3PM and 5PM-10PM. 4:30PM NOV to Mid-APR.
Meals and Prices: Lunch $5-$9. Dinner $6-$14.
Nonsmoking: All. Smoking only permitted in the cantina.
Take-out: Yes
Alcohol: Full Bar
Credit Cards: MC, Visa, Amx
Personal Check: Local only with I.D.
Reservations: Recommended

Wheelchair Access: Yes
Dress: Casual
Other: Full service catering available in your home or at 1 of 3 restaurants in Summit County. Private dining room for special parties, banquets and receptions. Service charge of 15% added to parties of 6 or more. Spicy items and "good heart" items identified on menu.

HISTORY, PERSONALITY AND CHARACTER

The building housing Mi Casa dates back to the 1970s when it was another Mexican Restaurant. Mi Casa Mexican Restaurant and Cantina, a local's favorite for fresh, homemade Mexican food, began operation in 1981. The restaurant expanded in 1994 to offer a festive cantina for happy hour and sports viewing as well as a large, cozy hacienda-style dining room.

Mi Casa is locally owned and operated by Dick Carleton and Jane Storm, who also own and operate Hearthstone Casual Dining in Breckenridge and Su Casa Mexican Restaurant and Cantina which opened in Keystone in 1997. Jane began in the restaurant business in 1971 supervising her family chain of seven El Paso Cantinas in California. Dick joined Jane at Mi Casa shortly after she purchased it in 1981 and advanced quickly from waiter to General Operating Partner.

Jane and Dick both share a commitment to Summit County and are active in supporting various non-profit organizations such as Summit Recycling and The Breckenridge Music Festival and many other fund-raising efforts. Their contributions are frequently noted with awards and recognition such as the Breckenridge Resort Chamber Business of the Year.

Mi Casa's general manager Brian Pietsch has been with the restaurant since 1990. He is assisted by two floor managers, Julie Mattos and Tracy Hammond. The three of them are committed to "consistency of quality" and "strive to offer a value based experience through staff development and community service", a goal of the Mi Casa Mission Statement. Bar manager Sean Damon is dedicated to customers having a fun, yet safe time in his cantina. The head chef is Phil Dilks, formerly the chef at Pasta J's in Breckenridge. He has been with Mi Casa since 1995. Phil and corporate chef Bruce Carlton have traveled to Mexico for special training in a constant effort at refining and changing the menu to offer a variety of new and up-to-date cuisine. Snow Country Magazine readers recently voted Mi Casa one of the Top 10 Resort Restaurants in the country.

FOOD, SERVICE AND AMBIANCE

Mi Casa offers some authentic and unique Mexican dishes. Fresh, homemade chips and salsa are brought to your table. There are two kinds of salsa; one, mild and thick with tomato, green pepper, onion and cilantro; the other a spicier version with serrano peppers. Keep the ice water handy!

I ordered a delicious platter of Yucatan chicken enchiladas with Spanish rice and refried beans. The enchiladas were stuffed with chicken and pico de gallo and topped with diced tomatoes and chipotle mushroom sauce that I found flavorful but not very spicy. The Spanish rice with green pepper and onion were loose and fluffy. The refried beans topped with Monterey Jack and cheddar cheeses were thick and tasty. For dessert, I could not resist trying their deep-fried ice cream. They use hard, frozen ice cream, dip it into a mixture of corn flakes with cinnamon, sugar and egg whites, then deep fry it for 30 seconds. Strawberries, whipped cream and cherry are placed on top. It was crispy, cold and tantalizing!

Their lunch and dinner menus feature appetizers, soups, salads, enchiladas, combinations, burritos, chimichangas and house specialties. Showcasing the lunch items are strawberry serrano chicken breast salad, fish tacos, mango duck quesadilla, steak fajita chimichanga and a Cancun sandwich with burger or chicken breast. The Mi Casa combos offer you a choice of taco, tostado, tamale, chili relleno, enchilada or burrito with chicken, beef or veggies. The dinner headliners include sizzling fajitas, fresh seafood burrito, American dishes and squash enchiladas. They also serve several tempting specialties like a fire roasted poblano chili filled with rock shrimp, charbroiled sea bass rolled in a spinach wrap and baby-back ribs with homemade chipotle barbecue sauce. Specialty coffees and liquors are available and for dessert you can delve into flan made with Kahlúa, sopapillas served with honey or French vanilla ice cream.

BRECKENRIDGE

Service was quick, pleasant and accommodating. They brought me some cilantro on the side when I told them how much I liked it. Mexican vocal music could be heard throughout the restaurant. This is a large place that can seat almost 200 in two major dining areas. The restaurant has a definite Mexican look presenting sponge-painted, peach-color stucco walls with turquoise-color window frames dividing the two dining rooms; hand-painted, turquoise-color iron chandeliers and warm-color seating with maroons, browns and dark greens. Enhancing this setting are an artificial cactus at the entrance, aspen wood ceilings and paintings of a Spanish villa and a still life depicting guacamole, lime and clay jars. A long stretch of windows facing north and extending to both the west and east overlooks Dredge Pond leading into the Blue River and offers a magnificent view of the Ten-Mile Range of mountains.

The adjacent cantina complements the dining areas with paintings of cowboys and buffaloes, matadors and bulls, and Dick Carleton and company dressed and posed as western outlaws. There are seven televisions for viewing football, hockey and other sports; a trophy case with softball, bowling and skiing trophies from the many teams that Dick sponsors and a chili poster. In the warmer months, you can dine outside on their patio just above the water with the same great view as the dining room. Mi Casa is a Breckenridge tradition providing authentic Mexican cuisine with the look and feel of Mexico and a genuine Colorado vista.

Cinnamon Spice Rubbed Sea Bass with Pico de Gallo
(Serves 4)

For Pico de Gallo:
2 cups tomatoes, diced
1 cup onion, diced
1/4 cup cilantro, minced
1 tablespoon garlic, minced
1 tablespoon fresh lemon juice

For Fish:
4 6-ounce fillets of Chilean sea bass
4 tablespoons butter

For Spice Rub:
1/2 cup dark chili powder
1/2 cup achiote (crushed anatto seed)
1/2 cup paprika
1/2 cup cinnamon
1 cup coriander
1 tablespoon salt
1 tablespoon white pepper

1. For Pico de Gallo: In a plastic or glass bowl, combine all ingredients and toss well. This salsa is at its best when it is just made. However, it will hold adequately for one day.
2. For Spice Rub: Combine all spices in a bowl and whisk together thoroughly. This recipe will make more than you need so store it with your spices in a well-sealed jar.
3. For Fish: Place fillets in a pie pan or large shallow bowl. Coat fillets completely with spice rub.
4. Melt butter in a large sauté pan and heat until it just stops bubbling.
5. Carefully place fillets in the sauté pan and sear about 3 to 4 minutes on each side. Be sure to have adequate ventilation in your kitchen as this does create a bit of smoke. (Pull battery out of smoke detector.)
6. Reduce heat and continue to cook fish, turning fillets every 4 to 5 minutes until fillets are white and flaky throughout.
7. Transfer fillets to a serving dish and serve with Pico de Gallo on top.

Wine Recommendation: A fruity Chardonnay or a dry 1996 Bauchaine Gewürztraminer

See top of page 48 for recipe photo.

BRECKENRIDGE

The Mountain Sage Cafe
103 North Main Street. 547-4628.
Directions: From the North on Highway 9 (Main Street), proceed past the first signal for North Park Avenue, French Street and Watson Avenue. The restaurant is on the right just before the second signal for Lincoln Avenue and Ski Hill Road.

ESSENTIALS
Cuisine: Innovative Health Food with a Pacific Rim Flair
Hours: Late MAY to late OCT: 7 days 7:30AM-3PM. Fri/Sat 5PM-9PM. Mid-DEC to late APR: Fri-Sun 7:30AM-3PM. 7 days 5PM-9PM. (Breakfast until 12PM, lunch 12-3PM). Closed late-OCT to Mid-NOV and Mid-APR to Late-MAY.
Meals and Prices: Breakfast $4-$6. Lunch $5-$8. Dinner $6-$18.
Nonsmoking: All

Take-out: Yes
Credit Cards: MC, Visa, Amx
Personal Check: Yes, with I. D.
Reservations: Recommended for weekend evenings. Accepted otherwise.
Wheelchair Access: Yes
Dress: Casual
Other: Service charge of 15% added for parties of 5 or more. No separate checks. Available for large groups.

HISTORY, PERSONALITY AND CHARACTER

The Mountain Sage Café opened in June 1997 in a building dating back to 1879. It was formerly part of the Gold Pan Saloon next door, the oldest saloon west of the Mississippi. Before that it was a bowling alley.

The restaurant is owned by Reginald and Pamela Gray, Warren and Annette Kesselring and Steven and Sheila Jagentenfl. Reggie, a graduate of Cornell Hotel and Restaurant Management School, also owns the Horseshoe II, which Steve and Sheila manage, the Gold Pan and the Adams Street Grill, all in Breckenridge. Sous chef Daniel Hodges started at The Mountain Sage Café in April 1998 after spending four years learning the trade from Reggie at the Adams Street Grill. He has been in the restaurant business since 1991.

FOOD, SERVICE AND AMBIANCE

The Mountain Sage Café has a variety of offerings from vegetarian to wild game using items like jasmine rice and buffalo sausage. Everything is made from scratch. Soups and desserts are all homemade. Specialty wraps, salad wraps and sandwiches are served for lunch and dinner. I ordered the Greek salad wrap — a huge stuffed spinach tortilla that I estimated was 9" long, 4" wide and 2" high. It was filled with yummy grilled chicken, feta cheese, black olives, Roma tomatoes and red bell peppers; tossed with an olive oil and white wine and loaded with orzo pasta. This was very filling, a meal by itself and was topped with a delicious tomato pesto salsa. Other specialty wraps include a goat cheese and veggie, a Thai beef or chicken, and a Caribbean with black beans and brown rice. The sandwich selections feature grilled eggplant, black bean burger and wild game sausage.

Highlighting the breakfast fare are rice cereal with dried mango and toasted coconut, specialty pancakes with banana-walnut or whole wheat apple cinnamon, and banana-stuffed French toast with a streusel topping. Distinctive omelets are also available with goat cheese or Camembert cheese and bacon as are frittatas, breakfast wraps in sundried tomato tortillas and traditional eggs benedict.

Assorted dinner entrées present something for just about everyone. There is grilled polenta and vegetables for the vegetarian, cannelloni with fresh homemade pasta for the Italian in each of us, pesto chicken for those fowl of heart, Colorado rainbow pecan trout for seafood lovers, pork tenderloin with a black bean sauce for those who like to "pig-out" and New York strip for meat eaters. One of their homemade desserts like blueberry white chocolate cheesecake, raspberry Grand Marnier and chocolate sauce over ice cream, or a cobbler will put a smile on your face.

My server was very accommodating bringing extra tomato pesto salsa to my table. Oldies rock music played in this one-room restaurant with wagon-wheel chandeliers. There is a natural wood log coat hanger at the entrance with a green door frame and matching window frames. A piece of old railroad track and horse harnesses deck the painted white wood walls. Also adorning the walls are blown-up old photographs of antique autos on the Pikes Peak Hill Climb, a rodeo, children on a toboggan, a bridge over a river with mountains in the background, and a horse drawn carriage with five men on board and the caption "Not Fishing". Adding to this milieu are old photos of the barge wreck in the Blue River, James Dean, and two men next to a log cabin. The Mountain Sage Café has an eclectic choice of creative dishes for your enjoyment in a setting that accentuates the history of Breckenridge.

SPECIAL ONE-TIME OFFER: Buy one entrée at the regular price and receive a complimentary beverage of your choice. Valid for every member of your party. Please present to server at time of ordering.
_____ Owner/ Manager. _____ Date.

BRECKENRIDGE

Cornish Game Hens
(Serves 4)

1 teaspoons fresh chopped garlic
2 tablespoons canola oil
1 teaspoons rosemary
1 teaspoons thyme
1/2 cup chicken stock

2 cups 1-inch cubed white bread, toasted
4 18-ounce Cornish game hens
Soy sauce
1 teaspoons fresh parsley, chopped

1. Sauté garlic in oil. Add rosemary, thyme, and chicken stock. Reduce by 1/2 and add bread cubes.
2. Bake hens for 30 minutes at 350 degrees. Pull from oven and stuff with bread stuffing. Heat an additional 20 minutes in oven and splash top of hens with soy sauce and chopped parsley. Remove from oven and serve.

Wine Recommendation: Sonoma Loeb Cabernet Sauvignon 1991 or Clos du Bois Chardonnay 1996

Recipe by: Daniel Hodges, sous chef
See bottom of page 48 for recipe photo.

Rasta Pasta

411 South Main Street (in the Four Seasons Plaza). 453-7467.
Directions: From the north on Highway 9 (Main Street), proceed 3¾ blocks past the signal at Lincoln/Ski Hill Road. The restaurant is on the right before the signal for Park Avenue. From the south on Highway 9 (Main Street), go ¼ block past Park Avenue. The restaurant is on the left.

ESSENTIALS
Cuisine: Jamaican Pasta
Hours: 7 days 11AM-9PM (10PM Fri/Sat). Closed 1st 3 weeks of MAY.
Meals and Prices: Lunch $3-$6. Dinner $6-$10.
Nonsmoking: All
Take-out: Yes
Alcohol: Full Bar
Credit Cards: MC, Visa, Amx, Disc

Personal Check: Yes, with I.D.
Reservations: No
Wheelchair Access: Yes
Dress: Casual/ski attire
Other: No separate checks. Service charge of 15% added to parties of 5 or more. Any menu item can be made strictly vegetarian.

BRECKENRIDGE

HISTORY, PERSONALITY AND CHARACTER

Rasta Pasta occupies three spaces built in the late 1980s for Remington's Restaurant, Subway Sandwiches and an ice cream shop. New York Pizza moved in for a couple of seasons before Dan Gnos opened Rasta Pasta in the summer of 1993 with his own healthy alternative recipes. Dan is a cordon bleu graduate Swiss chef with experience dating back to 1974. Current owner Scott Lias purchased the restaurant in November 1993. He has been working in restaurants since then and opened a second Rasta Pasta in Fort Collins, Colorado, in June 1998.

Manager and chef Chris Simoni worked for Dan for two years and has previous experience in seafood restaurants in Connecticut. Assisting Chris in the management of the restaurant are Noel Schlicht who previously worked at Downstairs at Eric's in Breckenridge and Kristy Thompson, formerly at Beaver Run, also in Breckenridge. Both Noel and Kristy started at Rasta Pasta in 1995. Rasta Pasta employs various chefs to cook their unique pasta recipes.

FOOD, SERVICE AND AMBIANCE

Rasta Pasta serves some savory Jamaican pastas that are both interesting and creative. I chose the tortellini Jamaica 'Mon, a truly unique pasta dish with fruit. It consisted of tender tortellini made from ricotta cheese, secret spices, pineapples, bananas and grapes, simmered to a sweet, delectable flavor. This was a luscious bowl with scallions, parsley and herbs in a broth that must be eaten with a spoon. It was quite different from anything I had experienced before. Accompanying the meal were garlic bread and a house salad with tangy homemade sundried tomato vinaigrette.

Highlighting Rasta Pasta's menu are several spaghetti dishes featuring traditional tomato sauce, garlic and herb sauce, light beef broth and garlic tomato sauce. Specialties include seafood marinara, primavera, rotini with sundried tomatoes or baby shrimp, jerk chicken and pasta in a pineapple curry sauce, ricotta cheese ravioli with chopped clams or spicy sausage, and the Rasta Pasta — jerk chicken, green onions, basil and diced tomatoes in garlic tomato sauce. Lovers of exotic food, Italian food, curry, seafood or the unconventional will not want to pass by Rasta Pasta when visiting Summit County.

Servers dressed in T-shirts and jeans were quick and casual. Music from the Caribbean played in this extremely colorful place with wall murals covering both sides of the restaurant. The murals depict tropical ocean scenes with palm trees, a Jamaican band, white-capped waves, yellow billowing clouds and the Lion of Judah, a prominent figure in Rastafarism,

BRECKENRIDGE

the Jamaican religion. Bright color tablecloths displayed an underwater scene with yellow, red, blue and green-color fish. There is a photograph of Ras Pidow signed to Scott on one of the tables and a signed poster of Jamaican entertainer, Bob Marley.

Further enhancing this vibrant setting were solid-color ceiling lights in red, yellow and green; a red, yellow, green and black flag with the words "One World, One People"; multi-hued plastic toucans; several head masks and a small fish tank. There is a counter in the middle of the dining room with an open kitchen directly behind. The windows in front face Main Street. Come to Rasta Pasta and experience a chromatic environment with some of the most unusual and delicious dishes found in Colorado.

SPECIAL ONE-TIME OFFER: Receive 20% off your total food bill. Please present to server at time of ordering. _____ Owner/Manager. _____ Date.

Rasta Pasta
(Serves 1)

1 tablespoon garlic oil
1/2 tablespoon Jamaican jerk seasoning (more for a spicier dish, less for a milder one)
1/2 cup green onions, diced
4 ounces beef broth
4 ounces tomato sauce
1/3 cup tomatoes, diced

1/2 cup cooked chicken breast, diced
2 cups penne pasta
Pinch of oregano
Pinch of basil

Garnish:
Parsley
Fresh Parmesan cheese, grated
Garlic bread

1. Cook penne pasta.
2. Combine all ingredients (except pasta, beef broth, tomato sauce and garnish) in pan. Heat over medium-high heat to sizzle.
3. Add beef broth and toss. Bring to a rapid boil for 1 minute.
4. Add tomato sauce and toss. Return to a boil. Add pasta, toss and return to boil.
5. Serve in a deep dish bowl. Garnish with parsley. Sprinkle with cheese. Serve with garlic bread on the side.

Wine Recommendation: Your favorite Merlot
Recipe by: Dan Gnos
See top of page 49 for recipe photo.

Swan Mountain Inn

16172 Highway 9 (Farmers' Korner). 453-7903. 800-578-3687.
Directions: Take Exit 203 from I-70 and go south for 4 miles. Turn left at the signal for Swan Mountain Road (just past Lake Dillon on your left), an immediate right onto the frontage road then your first left into the restaurant parking lot.

ESSENTIALS

Cuisine: Continental/Colorado
Hours: Mid-JUN thru SEP: Mon-Fri 11:30AM-2PM. Sat/Sun 8AM-2PM. 7 days 5:30PM-9:30PM. OCT to Mid-JUN: Mon-Sat 8AM-10AM. Sun 8AM-2PM. 7 days 5:30PM-9:30PM.
Meals and Prices: Breakfast $6-$9. Lunch $7-$8. Dinner $15-$21. Four-course dinner $28.
Nonsmoking: All. Smoking only permitted on patio.
Take-out: No

Alcohol: Full Bar
Credit Cards: MC, Visa, Disc
Personal Check: Yes, with I.D.
Reservations: Suggested
Wheelchair Access: Yes
Dress: Casual
Other: Available for weddings and private parties up to 50 people. Smaller breakfast portions for children under 12 for a $2 discount. Smaller dinner portions for seniors over 65 for a $3 discount.

HISTORY, PERSONALITY AND CHARACTER

The Swan Mountain Inn, built in 1985, was originally a model show home and real estate office. The oil crash in Colorado and the real estate bust in Summit County forced the real estate company to close the show home and office shortly after it opened. It remained empty for several years before Steve Gessner and his wife, Robin Robson, purchased the building, did an extensive remodeling job and opened the Swan Mountain Inn on Thanksgiving 1991.

Steve has been in the restaurant business since 1978 and was previously the kitchen manager at Pug Ryan's in Dillon and Charities in Frisco. Robin started working in restaurants in the late 1970s and used to wait tables at the Ski Tip Lodge in Keystone. Steve heads the kitchen staff that includes Stacy Anderson and Jason Brown. Stacy trained at the Greenbriar in West Virginia and Balsams in New Hampshire before coming to the Swan Mountain Inn in 1996. She does most of the baking and breakfast preparation. Jason has been with the restaurant since 1995 fixing dinners. He started cooking in 1985 and worked at Charities in Frisco from 1988 to 1995.

BRECKENRIDGE

FOOD, SERVICE AND AMBIANCE

I arrived at the Swan Mountain Inn on a Sunday morning and ordered their vegetable and cheddar cheese omelet. The green and red peppers, mushrooms, tomatoes and onions were crisp and lightly sautéed. The omelet was topped with a sprig of cilantro and great-tasting fire-roasted tomato and cilantro salsa that added just the right flavor to all the fresh ingredients. Home fries, big round slices of lightly seasoned potatoes with skins; a fresh fruit garnish of strawberries, orange, pineapple and grapes and toast came on the plate. Fresh baked goods, blueberry coffeecake and banana and cranberry bread, along with coffee and orange juice were served before the entrée. This was a plentiful meal that I could not finish.

Other options for breakfast are raisin bread French toast, buttermilk pancakes topped with champagne mountain berry sauce and homemade granola. Headlining the summer lunches are gourmet pita pizza including a Grecian and an Italian, salads such as cobb and Mediterranean, and sizzlers, oven baked open-face sandwiches featuring roast beef, Reuben or vegetarian lasagna.

The chef's choice of dinner appetizers may include open-face mussels, deviled oysters Rockefeller, stuffed artichoke hearts or Louisiana crab cakes. The menu offers regular dinner specialties like Alaskan king crab legs, étouffée, a spicy Cajun stew prepared with chicken and/or shrimp rather than the traditional crayfish, marinated pork tenderloin and vegetarian pasta. There are nightly selections of poultry, meat, fish and seafood pasta such as chicken Oscar, New York strip, sea bass and a shrimp, scallop and fish pasta dish. A variety of vegetables accompanies these dishes, from sweet to garlic-tasting. For dessert, try a piece of chocolate mousse pie, cheesecake, bread pudding or apple pie.

Service was courteous and attentive. A 1970s tape of Cat Stevens was played in the dining room followed later by country-rock music. The Swan Mountain Inn is a ponderosa pinewood log cabin with a cedar wood front and a high vaulted ceiling. At the entrance to the main dining room is a stain-glass artwork in a walnut frame displaying hummingbirds and flowers. Straight overhead in the dining room are wooden skis, poles and a rifle hanging from the pinewood walls. Fresh flowers are set at antique, carved tables with flower-pattern cloth place mats and people sit on antique, carved chairs. Finches feed on birdfeeders outside the windows that face the pine trees and hills to the east. Wreaths and several artificial pine and acorn garlands adorn the restaurant including the rock fireplace with rock hearth and chimney.

Two separate series of artworks prevail throughout the dining areas, the lounge downstairs and the connecting stairway. One is an array of framed prints from original watercolors by Ann Weaver and Jack Simmonds that reveal various aspects of Breckenridge and the surrounding mountain area. The other is a rather unique collection of black and white photographs taken by Gary Adler who then enhanced them with his own paint colors.

There are two smaller dining areas in the front of the restaurant to either side of the entrance. These two rooms unveil white-lace curtains over windows facing the Ten-Mile Range of mountains to the west, crawling philodendrons, paintings of aspen trees and willow chairs for seating. Down below, on the lower level, is a lounge and bar with more willow chairs, a couch, a red brick fireplace with decorator plates on the mantel, photographs of Natural Bridges and the Goosenecks in Utah and an antique medicine cabinet with an old sign for "Munyon's homeopathic remedies". In the summertime, a patio in the back is decked with tables, umbrellas and flowers for outdoor dining. The Swan Mountain Inn serves a diverse and changing menu in a secluded and romantic environment with picturesque landscapes.

See page 50 for restaurant photo.

BRECKENRIDGE

Crawfish Chili Rellenos with Tabasco Buerre Blanc on top of a Roasted Corn and Black Bean Relish
(Makes 12 appetizers or 6 main dishes)

Chili Rellenos:
1 tablespoon butter
2/3 cup scallions, minced
2 teaspoons garlic, chopped
12 each green chilies, canned
1 cup cooked shelled crawfish tails, chopped
1/2 cup cream cheese
1 cup grated Jack cheese
1 cup cooked white rice
1/2 teaspoon salt
1 tablespoon Tabasco
6 eggs, beaten
4 cups seasoned bread crumbs
Canola oil, for frying

1. Heat butter in 10-inch frying pan.
2. Add scallions and garlic. Cook for 4 minutes over medium high heat.
3. In a bowl, combine Tabasco, crawfish, cream cheese, Jack cheese, rice, and salt. Add scallions and garlic. Mix well.
4. Fill chili rellenos with crawfish mixture by using a pastry bag.
5. Dip into egg mixture, then bread crumbs, then repeat to double the breading.
6. Heat in 3/4 inch of oil in a shallow large fry pan until hot.
7. Fry chili rellenos until golden brown, turning as needed. Remove from pan and finish in oven at 375 degrees for 10 to 12 minutes.
8. To Assemble: Place 1/2 cup of corn bean relish on a plate, top with sliced chili rellenos and then surround with Tabasco Buerre Blanc.

Roasted Corn and Black Bean Relish:
6 ears fresh corn
1/3 cup Tabasco Jalapeño Sauce
1/2 cup chopped cilantro
1 1/2 cups small diced red bell pepper
1/2 cup fresh lime juice
2 teaspoons fresh minced garlic
1 1/3 cup small diced red onion
2 teaspoons salt
2 cups cooked black beans

1. Preheat oven to 400 degrees. Roast corn in husks for 30 minutes. Remove from oven and cut away kernels.
2. Combine remaining ingredients with corn.

BRECKENRIDGE

<u>Tabasco Buerre Blanc:</u>
1/2 cup + 1 tablespoon butter
1/4 cup shallots
1 tablespoon garlic
1 1/2 cups white wine
2 bay leaves
3 2-inch springs of thyme
1 1/2 cups heavy cream
1 1/2 tablespoons Tabasco
3/4 teaspoon paprika
1 1/2 tablespoons fresh lemon juice
1/4 teaspoon salt

1. Heat a small sauce pan with 1 tablespoon of butter in it. Add shallots and garlic then sauté for 4 minutes over medium high heat.
2. Add wine, bay leaves, and thyme.
3. Reduce wine by 3/4.
4. Add cream, reduce mixture again by half.
5. Add Tabasco, paprika, lemon, and salt. Whisk in remaining 1/2 cup of cold butter, cut into small pieces a little at a time to incorporate. Strain.

<u>Wine Recommendation:</u> Kendall Jackson Chardonnay

<u>Recipe by:</u> Stacy Anderson, National Grand Winner in Tabasco's 1997 Hottest Chef Contest

See bottom of page 49 for recipe photo.

BRECKENRIDGE

Top of the World

112 Overlook Drive (in The Lodge and Spa at Breckenridge). 453-9300. 800-736-1607. Fax 453-0625

Directions: Take Exit 203 from I-70 and go south on Highway 9 for 10 miles to Breckenridge. Continue through the town on Main Street (Highway 9). Go ¼ mile past the signal for South Park Avenue. Turn left at the next (flashing) signal for Boreas Pass Road. Go 2 miles. The entrance for The Lodge and Spa at Breckenridge is on the right, 200 feet past Baldy Road. Park, enter the lodge, then pass through the lobby and take the stairway down to Top of the World.

ESSENTIALS
Cuisine: Regional American
Hours: 7 days 7AM-10AM, 11:30AM-2PM and 6PM-10PM (5PM from DEC thru APR)
Meals and Prices: Breakfast $9-$13. Lunch $8-$16. Dinner $18-$35.
Nonsmoking: All. Smoking only permitted at the bar.
Take-out: Yes, at certain times. Room service for The Lodge.
Alcohol: Full Bar
Credit Cards: All 5
Personal Check: Yes, with I.D.
Reservations: Preferred
Wheelchair Access: Yes
Dress: Casual to nice
Other: Banquet room available for wedding ceremonies and special parties up to 150 people. Foyer available for cocktail receptions. Room service available during restaurant hours.

HISTORY, PERSONALITY AND CHARACTER

Top of the World started out as "The Top of the Rock" in 1968 before the lodge and spa existed. In the 1970s, the name was changed to "Aristocrat Inn". The Athletic Club was added in 1982 and the restaurant was renamed to "Choices". In 1987, the restaurant was remodeled and converted into a comedy club called "Final Run". The comedy club was short-lived. The restaurant was closed from 1988 until Christmas 1990 when, after another remodeling, it reopened as Top of the World. Rooms were added during the 1990s and the property became know as The Lodge at Breckenridge. The Lancaster Group of Houston, Texas, took over the lodge in 1997, initiated a process of numerous improvements and changed the name to The Lodge and Spa at Breckenridge. Today, the award-winning Top of the World restaurant was a winner at the 1994 through 1997 'A Taste of Breckenridge'. Their latest success was 1st prize for best dessert.

Executive chef Ken Hughes, who began working in restaurants in 1979, has been with Top of the World since May 1997. He was classically trained by master French chefs in the Napa Valley in California between 1983 and 1987 and attended the California Culinary Academy in San Francisco between 1986 and 1987. Ken believes in using traditional recipes with keen attention to appearance, color, texture and taste to present honest food where each dish stands alone.

FOOD, SERVICE AND AMBIANCE

Top of the World serves a noteworthy variety of regional American dishes on menus that change from summer to winter. Chef Hughes consistently strives to maintain quality and freshness by introducing new items. On the evening that I visited, I dined on oven-roasted, double-cut pork chops with a cracked mustard and caramelized onion sauce. The chops were seared first then roasted to keep in all the juices. The result was savory pork that was sweet, tender and juicy. It was served with soft polenta, a mush made from corn meal with the texture of mashed potatoes, the flavor of corn and a taste of garlic. Other vegetables accompanying the dish were fresh, sweet and flavorsome brandy-glazed baby carrots with tops still on, Chinese long beans and tasty crispy fried leaks.

For dessert, I delighted in their award-winning white chocolate sun-dried cherry bread pudding with berry sauce and vanilla bean cream. It was in the shape of an English muffin, the center filled with sun-dried cherries. It was sweet with a soft texture and served on a large plate sprinkled with powdered sugar, dollops of whipped cream, fresh-tasting strawberries and raspberries and a fresh mint sprig on top. Vanilla bean, raspberry and mango sauces were drizzled on the plate. This was as good as it sounds. The dessert's visual presentation and taste sensation made it easy to see why it won 1st prize.

Starters on the Top of the World restaurant include Sonoma foie gras on crisp potato cake, roasted quail salad, smoked salmon 'igloo' and red deer carpaccio. Seafood and regional game dishes highlight the entrées that feature grilled filet of Atlantic salmon, filet mignon of Colorado beef, roasted herb-crusted Colorado rack of lamb, oven-roasted Boursin and basil-stuffed natural breast of chicken, and red bell pepper and smoked mozzarella raviolis. For dessert, you can choose from fresh seasonal fruit, homemade ice cream with chocolate sauce, Belgium dark chocolate decadence torte, crème brûlée and a tropical fruit tartlette.

Breakfast offers an expanded continental buffet of assorted breads and pastries, sliced seasonal fruit, cereals, cheeses and fresh squeezed

BRECKENRIDGE

juices. For a full, hot breakfast, your choices are smoked salmon, eggs, breakfast meats, and Belgian waffles. Headlining lunch, which is served in the adjacent library during the winter and in the main dining room and on the deck in the summer, are an imaginative mixture of salads and sandwiches. Favorites include house made turkey or red deer salad with black bean vinaigrette, and grilled vegetables batons on croissant with smoked gouda.

Top of the World is a very people-oriented restaurant with servers and managers that are always there to provide attentive, courteous and proficient service. A combination of new age, jazz and easy listening music with flute and guitar provided the right mood for a charming evening. The southwest flavor of the decor inside is an ideal supplement to the impressive alpine setting outside. There were rows of poinsettias in rock flower boxes with pinewood borders. Red rocks, blue mountains and flowers were predominant in the paintings as were Indian women and villages. The sconces were in the shape of antlers and in the middle of the dining room was an upright piano. Seating was on log wood chairs with cushion seats in a Southwest-style pattern. The tables were set with navy blue tablecloths and candles. A red brick, wood-burning fireplace stood opposite a row of windows facing south with majestic views of the ski runs on Peak 10 and the surrounding Rocky Mountains. Top of the World serves classic cuisine with professional flair and personal touches in an environment of rustic elegance.

SPECIAL ONE-TIME OFFER: Buy one entrée and receive 25% off a room at The Lodge and Spa at Breckenridge. Please present to server at time of ordering. _____ Owner/Manager. _____ Date.

White Chocolate Sundried Cherry Bread Putting with Berry Sauce and Vanilla Bean Cream
(Serves 6 to 8)

Bread Pudding:
2 3/4 cups 2% milk
2 3/4 cups heavy whipping cream
2 1/4 cups white sugar
4 1/4 ounces sweet butter, melted
5 egg yolks
2 fresh sourdough baguettes
1 pound sundried tart cherries, no pits
1 pound white chocolate chunks

Vanilla Bean Cream:
5 egg yolks
1/3 cup white sugar
6 ounces half and half
1 vanilla bean

Raspberry Sauce:
1 pint fresh raspberries
Juice of 1 lemon
1/2 cup white sugar

Garnish:
Mint leaves
Fresh raspberries

1. Bread: Slice bread on an angle. Layer sliced bread in a ceramic casserole dish. Add layer of cherries and chocolate chunks. Top with bread layer.
2. Pudding. Combine milk, cream, sugar, and butter and scald over hot stove. Temper hot cream over eggs and carefully combine. Pour custard mixture over bread mass.
3. Vanilla Bean Cream: Over a double boiler, combine egg yolks and sugar. Be careful not to overcook eggs. Scald half and half with split vanilla bean and carefully combine with egg and sugar mixture. Cook carefully to a sauce-like consistency and strain through a fine sieve.
4. Raspberry Sauce: Blend ingredients in a food processor. Strain and chill.
5. Baking Instructions: Preheat oven to 300 degrees. Cover casserole dish with aluminum foil and bake for 50 minutes. Remove aluminum foil and bake for 10 minutes or until center is done.
6. To Assemble: Spoon a generous amount of bread pudding onto a plate, surround with vanilla cream and raspberry sauce. Garnish with fresh berries and mint leaf.

Wine Recommendation: 1992 Cowra Estate Botrytis Sauvignon Blanc

Recipe by: Ken Hughes, executive chef

BRECKENRIDGE

The Wellington Inn

200 North Main Street. 453-9464. 800-655-7557. Fax 453-0149.
Directions: From the north on Highway 9 (Main Street), the restaurant is one block past Watson Street on the left on the corner of Wellington Road. From the south on Highway 9 (Main Street) the restaurant is one block past the signal at Lincoln Street on the right on the corner of Wellington Road.

ESSENTIALS
Cuisine: Continental/German
Hours: 7 nights 5PM-9PM. Sun 10AM-2PM. JUN-SEP: Mon-Sat 11:30AM-2PM.
Meals and Prices: Lunch $6-$7. Dinner $16-$35. Sunday Brunch: adults $14, children $7.
Nonsmoking: All. Smoking only permitted in The Wine Cellar.
Take-out: Yes, upon availability.
Alcohol: Full Bar

Credit Cards: MC, Visa, Amx, Disc
Personal Check: No
Reservations: Highly recommended
Wheelchair Access: Yes, including restrooms
Dress: Dressy casual
Other: Coat room. Service charge of 15% may be added to parties of 5 or more. Service charge of 20% added for separate checks.

HISTORY, PERSONALITY AND CHARACTER

The Wellington Inn was built as recently as 1979, although when you walk in you'll swear it was built in 1879. The original restaurant was Weber's. In 1993, Hollie and Bill van der Hoeven purchased Weber's and opened The Wellington Inn on Thanksgiving of that year. They also gutted out the top floor adding luxury accommodations and performed a massive renovation of the entrance, lobby, waiting area and dining rooms to make the place look 100 years older than it really is. Hollie has been in the restaurant and hotel business since 1986 and manages the restaurant. Bill handles the bar in The Wine Cellar.

FOOD, SERVICE AND AMBIANCE

The Wellington Inn offers a variety of German and American dishes featuring veal, chicken, seafood, duck, pork, lamb and vegetarian. I decided on the pan-fried Rocky Mountain trout. A mini-loaf of soft, warm, fresh, homemade, honey wheat bread with poppy seeds was brought to my table. They also bake Bavarian dark bread in-house. For starters, I whet my appetite with creamed pickled herring, a tart and welcome alternative to soup or salad. The trout, seared and finished with capers and brown butter, was a firm, fresh, full filet. It was topped with a sprig of rosemary and served with a lemon wedge and sides of white rice, zucchini and very sweet carrots on a plate sprinkled with parsley and diced tomatoes. This is a very popular dish and one that I would certainly recommend.

Some of the soups, salads and starters to get you going on a wonderful evening of dining are baked brie with raspberry and Grand Marnier sauce, a bratwurst sampler platter, baked onion soup gratinée and traditional Caesar salad. The German entrées include weinerschnitzel, jagerschnitzel, sauerbraten and German beef stroganoff. There are other fine selections for you to choose from like chicken with sautéed lobster and fresh asparagus, pepper roasted duck, vegetable strudel in a golden pepper cream sauce, lobster thermadore, Colorado rack of lamb and beef Wellington Inn. Their veal Sargent dish, medallions sautéed with gulf shrimp and lobster tails, won First Place Entrée in the 1997 Taste of Breckenridge. The Wellington Inn prepares many fine homemade desserts to complete your dining experience: blueberry cobbler, apple strudel, various cheesecakes, chocolate fondue for two and bananas foster, a very popular dish that won Third Place for Best Dessert at the 1997 Taste of Breckenridge.

Their summertime lunch menu has some special items such as Wisconsin cheddar ale soup, portobello mushroom vegetarian grill and cheese tortellini Alfredo along with espresso, latte, cappuccino and about a dozen imported German beers. Salads, soups, omelets to order, desserts and a host of tempting dishes are highlighted on the Sunday brunch buffet. You can choose from home baked breads, salads, sausage gravy and biscuits, eggs benedict, cheese blintzes with blueberry and raspberry sauces, beef bourguignonne, chicken Alfredo, German sausages, waffles, chocolate fondue, pound cake, banana trifle, chocolate cake or mousse and fresh fruits.

My server was efficient and friendly. Classical music played quietly in the background. The atmosphere at The Wellington Inn is elegant, sophisticated and at times subdued, but not stuffy. The van der Hoevens must have gone to a lot of trouble to give the restaurant the look and feel of a 19th century Victorian hostelry. I entered the lobby through cherry wood doors with stained glass. To my right was a red brick column, a wood-burning fireplace and a waiting area with Victorian-style couches and chairs, a cherry wood cabinet and chairs and a walnut dresser and tables, all antiques. To my left were the two dining rooms adorned with blue and white, flower-pattern decorator plates and bowls, white-lace curtains and table covers, gold-framed mirrors on maroon, flower-pattern wallpaper, walnut finished walls and a fresh yellow columbine and lit white candle at each table. There are several Old World, small paintings in gold frames displaying lakes, sail boats, church steeples, open fields and marshes. Spotlighting the rear dining room is a large painting of a woman in a

BRECKENRIDGE

wedding gown titled "Portrait of Lady Agnew", 1928. "Escorting" Lady Agnew are several large paintings of flowers and one still life depicting bread, wine and a water pitcher.

The Wine Cellar downstairs houses their 200-bottle list from California, France and Germany in two wine cabinets, one set at 38 degrees for whites, the other at 58 degrees for reds. The Wellington Inn received the 1997 Award of Excellence from Wine Spectator Magazine. Besides the two wine cabinets, the Wine Cellar exhibits framed posters of the four seasons in Colorado; a warm, dark green leather sofa; rich, rust-red chairs; a wood burning stove; brass and green glass sconces and lamp shades; a Grgich Hills Cellar poster and sidewalk-level windows facing Main Street. You can sit at their small bar and order a glass of wine from their award-winning list or select one of their 35 single malt scotches. Visit The Wellington Inn, take a slow walk through the lobby, relax in The Wine Cellar, then delight in some fine Continental cuisine in a Victorian-looking setting.

SPECIAL ONE-TIME OFFER: Buy one entrée and receive a second entrée of equal or lesser value free OR receive 50% off one entrée. Not applicable for Special Holiday Menus. Please present to server at time of ordering.
_____ Owner/ Manager. _____Date.

Beef Wellington
(Serves 6)

6 8-ounce cuts of filet mignon
8 ounces duck liver pâté
1/2 cup fresh raspberries
1/2 teaspoon sugar
6 puff pastry sheets

Port Wine Sauce:
4 tablespoons unsalted butter
2 tablespoons port wine
2 tablespoons fresh lemon juice
1/2 cup red currant jelly or more to taste
2 tablespoons cornstarch

Béarnaise Sauce:
3 tablespoons white wine
1 tablespoon dried tarragon leaves
1 teaspoon lemon juice
1/2 cup butter
3 egg yolks
1 teaspoon fresh tarragon, chopped

1. In food processor, thoroughly mix pâté with raspberries and sugar. Set aside.
2. Sear meat to rare on all sides. Let cool slightly, then place tablespoon of pâté on top of fillets. Wrap in a 12-inch square of puff pastry, pinching together corners on bottom. Bake on middle rack at 350 degrees for 20 to 30 minutes. Check temperature with meat thermometer for desired temperature. Recommended medium-rare.
3. Port Wine Sauce: In small sauce pan, melt butter. Stir in remaining ingredients. Heat to boiling, stirring constantly.
4. Béarnaise Sauce: Combine the wine, tarragon, and lemon juice in a small sauce pan. Over high heat, reduce to 2 tablespoons, then strain. In another small sauce pan, melt the butter and heat to almost boiling. In a blender or food processor, process egg yolks until blended. With blender running, add the butter in a slow stream. With blender on slow, add reduced wine mixture. Process until blended, place in a serving bowl. Stir in the fresh tarragon. Yields 3/4 cup.
5. To serve, spoon port wine sauce on the plate, place beef on top, then drizzle with béarnaise sauce.

Wine Recommendation: Stag's Leap Wine Cellars, Cabernet Sauvignon Napa, California 1994

Recipe by: Hollie and Bill van der Hoeven

See top of page 51 for recipe photo.

CASTLE ROCK

Castle Rock was named by Dr. Edwin James, botanist on Major Stephen Long's expedition in 1820. He named the town after the large, castle-like rock formation nearby. Castle Rock is a community nestled among thousands of acres of rolling hills, scrub oak and ponderosa pine that used to be the hunting grounds for the Ute, Arapahoe and Cheyenne Indians. In the last quarter of the 19th century, Silas W. Madge quarried lava stone in the area that was used as building material.

In March of 1978, the county courthouse was destroyed by fire by a distraught lover who tried to free her imprisoned boyfriend. The new courthouse now stands in its place. Each year for the holiday season, a yule star is lit on top of the large rock marking the town. In the summer, Castle Rock is home to a PGA golf tournament — the International at Castlepines. Another major attraction is the factory outlet stores just north of town. Castle Rock is located in Douglas County, the fastest growing county in the nation in 1997.

The following two discoveries include an Italian trattoria in a 90-year old building that was a residence for over half a century and a Victorian house serving pasta, grill specialties and seafood.

Location of Town: 25 miles south of Denver on I-25.
Zip Code: 80104. Area Code 303. Population: 8,708. Elevation: 6,200'.

Augustine Grill

519 Wilcox Street, 814-3663
Directions: From the north on I-25, take Exit 182 and head east. The street will bend to the right (south) and become Wilcox Street. The restaurant is on the right a ½ block before the signal at 5th Street. From the south on I-25, take Exit 181 and head north on Wilcox Street. The restaurant is on the left ½ block after the signal at 5th Street.

ESSENTIALS

Cuisine: Pasta, Grill Specialties, Seafood
Hours: Tue-Sat 11am-3pm and 5:30pm-9pm. Sun 10:30am-3pm. Closed Mon.

Meals and Prices: Sun Brunch $6-$8. Lunch $6-$11. Dinner $7-$18.
Nonsmoking: Yes
Take-out: Yes
Alcohol: Full Bar

Credit Cards: MC, Visa, Amx, Disc
Personal Check: Yes
Reservations: Recommended, not required. Strongly recommended on weekends.

Wheelchair Access: Yes
Dress: Casual
Other: Available for bridal showers, rehearsal dinners, graduation parties and business meetings.

HISTORY, PERSONALITY AND CHARACTER

The Augustine Grill is in an old Victorian house built in 1904 and originally inhabited by the town lamplighter. A subsequent owner played an organ that could be heard in town during the evening. From 1965 until 1992, the house was The Golden Dobbin Restaurant. After The Golden Dobbin closed, the house became The French Bakery followed briefly by a German restaurant called The Winter Garden. The building laid vacant for about a year before the current owners, Mike and Anna Linney, opened the Augustine Grill in February 1997.

Mike has been in the restaurant business since 1972, Anna since 1975. They both worked in restaurants in Houston, New Orleans, San Francisco and Denver. Mike is also a food distributor for Sysco. Pam Morgan helps run the restaurant and tends bar. She also owns and operates the Carriage House gift shop behind the restaurant. Swiss immigrant Ruedi Elsener is the head chef. Since coming to the United States in 1991, he has cooked at the Sonnenalp in Vail and the Augusta in the Westin Hotel in Denver.

FOOD, SERVICE AND AMBIANCE

The seasonal soup, corn and potato chowder, sounded good, so I started dinner with that. I was not disappointed. It was thick and hot with ham and croutons. The classic Caesar salad which followed was a pleasant delight with fresh and crisp Romaine lettuce, shaved Parmesan cheese, herb and garlic croutons and a few anchovies, something I personally would like to see more restaurants do because they seem to go so well on a Caesar salad.

For my entrée, I chose the blackened yellow fin tuna with a corn and black bean relish, Mango salsa, a sprig of fresh oregano and grilled vegetables: zucchini, yellow squash, corn on the cob, red peppers and onions. It is a southwestern style dish full of spice and flavor.

Their dessert menu offers several delectable selections like raspberry almond crème brûlée, Castle Rock pie — Swiss chocolate with fresh whip cream and nuts — and fresh berries in a cookie cup with vanilla sauce. And yet, I went with the nightly special, strawberry shortcake prepared with fresh shortcakes baked that day, soft whipped cream and a fresh mint sprig. The

CASTLE ROCK

rim of the bowl was drizzled with raspberry and vanilla syrup making for a momentarily attractive and delicious dessert. Overall, I was impressed by the high quality of the ingredients used in my entire meal.

You can commence your dining experience at the Augustine Grill with popcorn shrimp or smoked chicken quesadilla for an appetizer or try a spinach salad or fresh fruit and grilled shrimp salad. Some of their mainstay entrées are southwestern chicken and shrimp fettuccine, grilled marinated flank steak and minted lamb loin chops. On Friday and Saturday nights in the summer, they offer an outdoor grill menu that includes Swiss veal bratwurst, Atlantic salmon, barbecue jumbo shrimp and a selection of steaks.

Spotlighting the lunch menu are Hawaiian tuna melt and portobello mushroom sandwiches, salads, pasta dishes like tomato basil fettuccine and garden primavera and a daily potpie special creation using meat, fish or vegetables. At their Sunday brunch, you can get a glass of champagne for a $1 to go with your omelet, Benedict, quiche, brioche French toast or burger. Whenever you go or whatever you order, you should be assured of quality, freshness and exceptional preparation.

Service was prompt, attentive and professional. They take good care of their people. Light jazz could be heard in the background. The dining areas downstairs are color coordinated very well with maroon walls and tablecloths, yellow and lime green curtains with maroon-color vases printed on them, several matching color pictures of fruits, flowers and tea pots in casual dining settings, hardwood floors, potted plants, flowers and a wreath. Upstairs are a yellow room referred to as the egg room and the garden room. Outdoors on the patio, live entertainers can be heard on Friday and Saturday nights singing and playing the violin, guitar and piano. This little white house in Castle Rock has a lot to offer.

See page 52 for restaurant photo.

Special One-Time Offer: Enjoy our cup ½ lunch entrée for $5.95. Includes ½ sandwich, field greens Augustine with peach vinaigrette and soup of your choice. Offer limited to four people. Please present to server at time of ordering. _____ Owner/Manager. _____ Date.

CASTLE ROCK

Roasted Red Pepper and Corn Chowder
(Serves 8 to 10)

Here's a great soup recipe to use up that extra corn on the cob from the barbecue. Before you turn off that grill, put your corn on and roast it to a golden brown. Also, while you're at it, put some whole red peppers on the grill until they turn black. Then peel the black skin off the peppers and shuck the corn off the cob. Now you are ready to make a soup that is sure to be a hit.

1 cup diced onion
1/2 cup diced celery
1/2 cup diced carrots
6 to 8 red bell peppers, roasted, peeled, and chopped

2 to 4 ears of corn, shucked and roasted
1/4 cup cream
Tri-colored tortilla chips

1. Sauté onions, celery, and carrots in a small amount of oil until soft.
2. Add chopped red peppers and corn and heat thoroughly.
3. In small batches, add vegetables to a mixer or food processor and puree.
4. Pour puree into pot and add cream* to soup. Stir until hot. Add salt and pepper to taste. Garnish with broken up tri-colored tortilla chips.

*1/4 cup chicken stock may be substituted for cream for a lighter version.

Wine Recommendation: Buena Vista Sauvignon Blanc

This recipe is a restaurant favorite.

CASTLE ROCK

Pino's Place
3 Wilcox Street, 688-8159
Directions: From the north on I-25, take Exit 182. Go left at the signal and over the bridge. The road will bend to the right taking you south on Wilcox street. Go straight at the signal at Fifth Street. The restaurant is five blocks past this signal on the right at the corner of South Street. From the south on I-25, take Exit 181, go north on Wilcox Street past Safeway on your right. The restaurant is on your left at the corner of South Street.

ESSENTIALS
Cuisine: Italian Trattoria
Hours: Mon-Fri 11AM-3PM. Mon-Thu 5PM-9PM. Fri-Sat 5PM-10PM. Sun 3PM-8PM.
Meals and Prices: Lunch/Dinner $7-$16.
Nonsmoking: Yes. Smoking permitted in bar area only.
Take-out: Yes
Alcohol: Full Bar
Credit Cards: All 5
Personal Check: Yes
Reservations: Not accepted, but call if your party is 6 or more.
Wheelchair Access: Yes
Dress: Mostly casual, some dressy.
Other: Private catering available in house, at your home or office.

HISTORY, PERSONALITY AND CHARACTER
    Pino's is in a building constructed in 1909 as a duplex. It was a residence until the early 1960s, then it became commercial property converting into a liquor store and boutique. In 1973, Pino and Pina Arini (Joseph and Josephine in English) moved to Castle Rock from Indiana to retire, purchased the building and opened a small liquor store with two apartments. In 1988, the Arinis sold the business but kept the property. In 1993, the liquor store closed. In April, 1994, Joseph and Josephine's son Tony, daughter Mary Ann, son-in-law Terry Reiff, and three grandchildren, Laura, Joe and Lauren, renovated the building and opened Pino's Place, an Italian trattoria.
    This is Tony and Mary Ann's first restaurant. Jeff Willoughby is the head chef and also part owner. He is graduate of the Colorado Institute of Art Culinary School.

FOOD, SERVICE AND AMBIANCE
    I spent a delightful spring afternoon here (or at least part of the afternoon), trying their zuppa del giorno, creamed carrot, and a portobello mushroom on crisp focaccia bread. The soup consisted of finely chopped carrot, a little onion, a sprinkle of parsley and a topping of grated Parmesan. It was both tasty and warm. The sandwich featured chive aïoli

and smoked Gouda with red peppers, Italian olives and lettuce on the side. Although a little messy, even with a serrated knife at hand (you wouldn't want to try this in your car while driving), I fancied the combination of flavors.

Their menu changes every few months. Many of the recipes are from the Arini family, some are from Chef Willoughby. For appetizers, they serve an antipasto plate. pan sautéed crab cakes, smoked salmon and fried calamari. The salads include an Oriental chicken, Caesar, spinach and a chef. The entrées offer a wide selection of meats, fishes, pastas, pizzas, calzones and vegetarian dishes. Meat lovers and vegetarians can both relish their spaghetti marinara, fettuccine Alfredo, linguini with basil pesto or lasagna, with or without the meats. Those who favor veal will like the veal scaloppine and osso bucco. Other delectable offerings include shrimp scampi, chicken saltimbocca or parmigiana, grilled pork chop with an apricot rosemary glaze, fish of the day prepared your way and the chef's selection of prime beef. For dessert, Pino's is recognized for their tiramisu which is made from scratch by Pina.

Service was quick, informal, courteous and friendly. Green shutters on the windows contrast with the red brick walls decked with pictures of chefs, ships, flowers and two girls playing on a sandy beach. In the front dining room there is a counter at the entrance, a bar to the rear and seating in-between at flower-pattern tablecloths. This is a two-room restaurant with a patio in front. This first and second generation family from Italy has given Castle Rock some authentic and delicious Italian cuisine.

Ossobuco Alla Fiorentina
(Serves 6)

4 ounces prosciutto
4 medium carrots, chopped
3 medium ribs celery, chopped
2 medium yellow onions
2 cups dry white wine
Salt and pepper
8 sprigs fresh thyme
2 bay leaves
6 veal shanks (2" to 2/12" thick)
About 1/2 cup flour

Olive oil
1 pound fresh Roma tomatoes
1 pound canned tomatoes, Italian imported
1 to 2 cups homemade chicken stock
3 to 4 peeled cloves of garlic
2 cups veal stock (beef broth may be used)

1. Cut prosciutto into fine pieces.
2. Rough chop carrots, celery, and onion.
3. Season veal with salt and pepper, lightly dredge in flour (all sides).
4. Place a large sauté pan with olive oil over medium heat. Sauté prosciutto for 3 minutes.
5. Add floured veal and brown for 2 minutes. Transfer veal and prosciutto into a large casserole dish and deglaze sauté pan with white wine.
6. Add all the remaining ingredients, make sure the veal is fully covered with liquid. Cover and simmer 3 hours at 350 degrees.

Wine Recommendation: Barolo Marcarini

Recipe by: Jeffrey S. Willoughby, chef

COPPER MOUNTAIN

Copper Mountain is often referred to as "the skier's mountain" and has been voted number one trail and slope design by Snow Country Magazine. This ski resort on the east side of Vail Pass offers ski lessons, snowboarding and cross-country skiing. In the summer, you can enjoy the Copper Creek Golf Club, one of the highest golf courses in the United States.

The restaurant listed here is a popular après ski, casual dining place at the base of the new high speed chair lift.

Location of Town: Central Colorado on I-70 between Frisco and Vail. Zip Code: 80443. Area Code: 970. Population: 150. Elevation: 9,700ft.

Double Diamond Restaurant

154 Wheeler Place (in the Foxpine Inn in the East Village at the base of the new high speed 6-seat chair lift). 968-2880

Directions: Take Exit 195 from I-70 and head south on Highway 91. Take the first right onto Copper Road. Go .2 miles and turn left onto Wheeler Place into the East Village. Parking is available in front of the Foxpine Inn. The Double Diamond is just past Breeze Ski Rentals to the left.

ESSENTIALS

Cuisine: Steaks, Ribs, Pasta, Seafood, Pizza
Hours: 7 days 11AM-9PM. Lunch until 5PM. Dinner from 5PM.
Meals and Prices: Lunch $5-$8. Dinner $9-$19. Pizza $11-$17.
Nonsmoking: Yes. Smoking permitted only at bar.
Take-out: Yes

Alcohol: Full Bar
Credit Cards: All 5
Personal Check: No
Reservations: No
Wheelchair Access: Yes
Dress: Ski attire, very casual
Other: Catering, in-house and out, evening delivery and box lunches available.

HISTORY, PERSONALITY AND CHARACTER

The Double Diamond was built in 1979 and originally used for conferences and banquets. Mogul Fields Restaurant was the first business to occupy the building from 1991 until 1993 when the Double Diamond opened. Wisconsin native David Luthi purchased the restaurant in July 1995. David has been in the restaurant business since 1980 managing, cooking

COPPER MOUTAIN

and bartending in Madison, Wisconsin, before coming to Colorado in 1982. Since 1982 he has handled banquets and managed at the Sonnenalp in Vail and at Farleys in Copper Mountain. Dave sets the menu and uses several cooks to handle different specialties.

FOOD, SERVICE AND AMBIANCE

The Double Diamond Restaurant specializes in homemade foods prepared daily like barbecue baby back ribs with an award-winning barbecue sauce, fresh Black Angus beef, fresh catches of the day, pasta and pizza. It was Friday, so I ordered the "all-you-can-eat" Alaskan Pollock fish fry with French fries and cole slaw. The fish was beer battered, firm, moist and excellent for dipping in tartar sauce. The steak fries were crisp and lightly seasoned. The cole slaw was creamy and a little sweet. Fish and chips lovers will savor these.

For a starter at lunch or dinner, try the smoked trout, crab dip with crackers, baby back ribs or Old Bay shrimp. Homemade soup is made fresh daily or you can order a classic Caesar salad topped with grilled shrimp or chicken. The lunch fare includes build-your-own sandwich beginning with a half-pound of ground beef or a grilled chicken breast, spicy red chili, linguini marinara, veggie burger and a cheesesteak or chicken hoagie. Highlighting the dinner entrées are prime rib, barbecued baby-back ribs, tenderloin filet, pasta primavera, spinach walnut fettuccini, chicken Marsala or shrimp scampi. If you choose the homemade, hand-tossed, made-to-order pizza, you can top it with pineapple, roasted garlic, fresh spinach, feta cheese or your other favorite ingredients. For your sweet tooth, the Double Diamond offers Snickers big blitz, Granny's apple pie and good olde fashioned vanilla ice cream with or without Hershey's chocolate syrup.

Service was fast, casual, accommodating and came with an English accent. They played low-keyed country and rock music. With its slope side location just 50 feet from the B-lift, this is a popular place with skiers at lunch or during après ski. If you arrive at one of these times expect a warm, good-time atmosphere.

The Double Diamond has a high slanted ceiling with pinewood log walls and windows facing the mountains. This is a great place for watching skiers outside or sports inside on their big screen television. A series of nature prints by Bev Doolittle is displayed throughout the restaurant exhibiting Indians, horses and wild animals: an Indian on horseback, a slumbering bear, bear footprints in the snow, a hare in the shadow of an eagle and an owl.

COPPER MOUNTAIN

Fern green-color heat ducts extend around the bar which is separated from the dining area by stained-glass artwork, several hanging philodendrons and a row of potted plants set on several rows of polished pinewood logs. The stained-glass artwork depicts an eagle soaring over snow-capped mountain peaks and evergreen trees with "Double Diamond" inscribed on the bottom. Completing this decorative theme are hanging plants over the windows and three large brown ornamented wreaths. Whether you are skiing or just visiting the area, stop in the Double Diamond for a relaxing break with a splendid outlook or join them on their sunny deck overlooking the Ten-Mile range!

<u>Special One-Time Offer</u>: Buy one entrée and receive a second entrée of equal or lesser value free (up to $18.95) OR receive 50% off one entrée (up to $9.50). Please present to server at time of ordering.
_____ Owner/ Manager. _____ Date.

Spinach Walnut Fettuccini
(Serves 4 to 6)

4 teaspoons garlic, finely diced
2 teaspoons shallots, finely diced
1 cup walnuts, chopped
1 cup mushrooms, sliced
1 ounce butter
4 ounces chicken stock
1 pound fresh spinach, chopped

1 cup white wine
1 cup heavy whipping cream
2 pounds cooked fettuccini
Salt and pepper to taste
4 tablespoons grated Parmesan cheese

1. Sauté garlic, shallots, walnuts, and mushrooms with butter. Add chicken stock, spinach, and white wine. Reduce by half.
2. Add heavy whipping cream. Reduce by half.
3. Add fettuccine and toss. Add salt and pepper (optional). Place in pasta bowls and top with Parmesan.

<u>Recipe by</u>: David Luthi

See bottom of page 51 for recipe photo.

CRESTED BUTTE

Crested Butte, the wildflower capital of Colorado, was founded by Howard F. Smith who bought the first mill here. The town was named for a nearby mountain whose top resembles the crest of a rooster's head. Ute Indians used the area around Crested Butte as summer hunting grounds. They were replaced by the gold and silver booms of the 1880s. In 1880, Crested Butte was incorporated and the following year, the town was connected to Gunnison, 28 miles to the south, by the Denver and Rio Grande narrow-gauge railroad. Also in 1880, coal was discovered in the area and it helped sustain the town until 1952 when the last mine was closed.

The economy struggled through the 1950s, but was revitalized with the birth of the ski resort on Mount Crested Butte just three miles to the north. In 1974, the entire town of Crested Butte was designated a National Historic District. One point of interest that you should catch while you are here is the world record elk rack displayed at the Conoco Station on the northwest corner of Elk Avenue and 4th Street.

Four very dissimilar restaurants are detailed here for your gastronomic pleasure: a small, unpretentious French and Continental restaurant; an American restaurant in a hotel on the National Register of Historic Places; a new restaurant just built in 1995 with a fresh, clean look advancing a cuisine described as global fusion; and a colorful pizzeria with a deck and gazebo.

Location of Town: Central Colorado on Highway 135 north of Gunnison
Zip Code: 81224. Area Code: 970. Population: 878. Elevation: 8,908ft.

Backcountry Gourmet
435 6th Street. 349-6733.
Directions: From the intersection of Highways 50 and 135 in Gunnison, go north 28 miles on Highway 135 to Crested Butte. Go two blocks past the first stop sign. The restaurant is on the left on the corner of 6th Street (Highway 135) and Sopris Avenue.

ESSENTIALS
Cuisine: Global Fusion
Hours: Mon-Fri 11AM-3PM. 7 days 5:30PM-9PM. Closed Mid-APR to Mid-MAY and early NOV to late NOV.
Meals and Prices: Lunch $6-$8. Dinner $18-$24.
Nonsmoking: All

CRESTED BUTTE

Take-out: Yes
Alcohol: Full Bar
Credit Cards: MC, Visa, Amx, Disc
Personal Check: Local with I.D.
Reservations: Highly recommended
Wheelchair Access: Yes
Dress: Crested Butte casual to dressed up

Other: Service charge of 18% added to parties of 6 or more. Split plate charge. Full Service catering available on and off premises with 48 hours notice. Restaurant may be rented. For more information contact their full page web-site at www.crestedbutte.com.

HISTORY, PERSONALITY AND CHARACTER

The original Backcountry Gourmet was in a log cabin on the same site as the current restaurant. Rose Konold, who conceived the name and her husband, Glenn Woelk, opened the restaurant in 1993. R. J. Harrington, Jr. and Doug Vaughan bought the Backcountry Gourmet in January 1995. The log cabin was moved and a new building was constructed in its place. The restaurant reopened on August 1, 1996.

R. J. grew up in the restaurant business working in his mother's restaurant in Pennsylvania serving frozen yogurt and sandwiches. He later attended Penn State University and obtained a degree in Hotel and Restaurant Management. In 1990, he moved to Crested Butte and helped open Giovanni's Restaurant in the Grand Butte Hotel (now the Marriott) in Mount Crested Butte. R. J. handles the front of the restaurant while Doug is the chef. Doug started in the restaurant business in 1983. He trained with chefs in Birmingham, Alabama; Prescott, Arizona, where he received traditional French training; and Boulder, Colorado. Doug came to Crested Butte in 1990 and worked at Jimmy's (now Lil's Land & Sea) and the Crested Butte Country Club. He eventually became executive chef at The Grand Butte on Mount Crested Butte.

FOOD, SERVICE AND AMBIANCE

Backcountry Gourmet provides an international selection of soups, salads, sandwiches, sushi, tapas and entrées. You will see words like West African, Asian, Grecian, Moroccan, Thai, Jamaican, Florentine, Indonesian, Southwestern and Italian on their menus. I tried two tapas for lunch. The sashimi rosettes were two servings of raw, fresh ahi tuna rolled like florets accompanied by slices of pickled ginger. They were served on a black lacquer plate drizzled with thinned wasabi and tamari sauce. It was fun picking up the sashimi and ginger with my chop sticks and swirling them in the wasabi and tamari. Equally tasty and entertaining were the Jamaican wontons: jerk-spiced chicken and cabbage dumplings in crisp deep-fried wontons with a flavorful sweet and sour (mostly sweet) bing cherry sauce for dipping. A red cabbage leaf and parsley sprig garnished the plate.

CRESTED BUTTE

Everything is made from scratch at Backcountry Gourmet. For starters, you might order Senegalese seafood stew, a salmon bisque with fresh dill and cream, a Grecian Caesar salad or Asian spinach with shitakes, leeks and water chestnuts. Highlighting the increasingly popular tapas, or "little meals" or appetizers, are imported and aged baked brie wrapped in pastry with apricots, a Moroccan pastry filled with curried chicken, a grilled veggie platter and a Florentine artichoke. Lunch sandwiches offer a southwestern chili tortilla filled with chicken, breaded eggplant in a Creole sauce, Italian meats, purple portobello grilled with spinach and cheesesteak.

Their worldly cuisine continues with the entrées featuring Indonesian prawns in a spicy basil-peanut sauce, a vegetarian delight with eggplant and polenta in two curries, apricot-pepper duck and char-grilled Atlantic salmon. Monday night is sushi night when you can choose your favorite raw fish with rice, like yellowfin tuna, barbecue freshwater eel, soft shell crab or fried shrimp. Monday is also the only night of the week that you will be able to dine on miso shiru soup, fresh vegetables in a blonde miso consommé, or gyoza, a steamed pork and vegetable dumpling. Save room for one of their homemade desserts like tiramisu, Grand Marnier (or Grandma's) chocolate tart, zebra pâté (sliced white and dark chocolate layered in a pâté tin served with raspberry coulis) or Doug's own recipe for homemade ice cream.

R. J. was my server. He was helpful, friendly and courteous. Lively jazz played in this restaurant with its 180° far-ranging view of seven peaks: Gothic Avery, Baldy, Whiterock, Mount Crested Butte, Cement Mountain and Round Mountain. The dining room is in the shape of an immense bay window with a row of nine windows. To the right of the entrance is a bar with a brass railing. Local photographer, Allen T. Brown, an Ansel Adams like photographer with adept use of shadow and light, beautified Backcountry Gourmet with his black and white photography depicting a wide range of subjects. His collection inclued Salton Sea and Brush, Alaskan Dory, Back-lit Aspen, Plywood, Screen Shadow, Ladder, Dew Drops, Jacket and Glasses, and 323 Whiterock.

Mary Brown's series "The Beauty is in You" further embellishes the setting with her black and white and color photography of provocative looking beautiful women. James Scott, who creates album covers, added a colorful portrait of a samurai golfer. Even one of the Backcountry Gourmet prep cooks lent an artistic hand with his airbrushed acrylic piece of a skier racing downhill in a blur titled "UFO". Take delight in the vista, relax in their comfortable atmosphere and let the Backcountry Gourmet's cuisine bring the world a little closer to you.

CRESTED BUTTE

SPECIAL ONE-TIME OFFER: Buy one entrée and receive a free glass of house wine (red or white) that you feel best accompanies your entrée selection. Valid for every member of your party. Please present to server at time of ordering. _____ Owner/Manager. _____ Date.

Thai Banderillas with Peanut Sauce

Your favorite assortment of vegetables
Beef, shrimp, or chicken

Clarified butter*

Peanut Sauce (makes 3 to 4 cups):
2 medium onions, diced
2 apples, peeled, cored, chopped
1/2 cup creamy peanut butter
1 tablespoon peanut or soy oil
1 tablespoon fresh ginger, minced
1/2 teaspoon cayenne
1 ripe banana

1. Sauce: Sauté onions and apples in clarified butter* until onions are translucent.
2. In a food processor, combine other ingredients and sautéed onion and apples. Puree until smooth, then refrigerate.
3. Skewer your vegetables and meats and char-grill until tender. Remove from grill and top with peanut sauce. Garnish with fresh orange and chives.

*Clarified butter (or ghee) is the clear yellow liquid created when butter is melted and the milky solids sink to the bottom of the pan.

Banderilla (Ban-dair-ree-yah) is the traditional name for the long decorated darts, or knives, used by the banderilleros (Ban-dair-ree-yairos) to provoke a bull to fight a matador. These darts are decorated with ribbons, feathers, and yarn. Each one is a personal statement of the matador and his cuadrilla, or troupe.

Our banderillas are so named because they mimic the tools of the banderilleros. Colorful vegetables and meats are skewered into a pattern that has become one of the culinary statements made at Backcountry Gourmet. Thai Banderillas refer to these skewers served with a spicy peanut sauce

Recipe by: R. J. Harrington, Jr. , owner and manager

CRESTED BUTTE

The Brick Oven Pizza

229 Elk Avenue. 349-5044.
Directions: From the intersection of Highways 50 and 135 in Gunnison, go north 28 miles on Highway 135 to Crested Butte. At the second stop sign, the four-way stop, turn left onto Elk Avenue. Go 3 blocks. The restaurant is on the right just past 3rd Avenue.

ESSENTIALS
Cuisine: Pizza, Pasta, Subs
Hours: 7 days 11AM-9PM. Closed Mid-APR to Mid-MAY.
Meals and Prices: Lunch/Dinner $6-$12 (more for pizza toppings)
Nonsmoking: All
Take-out: Yes
Alcohol: Full Bar
Credit Cards: MC, Visa, Disc, DC
Personal Check: Yes, with I.D.
Reservations: No
Wheelchair Access: Yes
Dress: Casual
Other: Free delivery 5PM-9PM.

HISTORY, PERSONALITY AND CHARACTER
　　The Brick Oven Pizza originated as three separate buildings built in the early 1880s. One of the buildings was the Bank of Crested Butte that opened in 1880 and failed in 1931. Meanwhile, the other two buildings were used as a drug store, post office and a mortuary. In 1931, the three buildings were combined under one roof. Lil and Phil Hyslop bought all three sections in 1958 and converted them into one, the Grubstake Building. Several different restaurants occupied the Grubstake Building beginning in the mid-1970s. First there was The Grubstake Restaurant. This was followed by Oscar's in the late 1980s. In 1991, The Bistro took over followed by McMahons in 1996. In November 1997, Eric Shaw, who started the original Brick Oven Pizza in December 1993, moved into the Grubstake.
　　Michelle Samuelson has been with The Brick Oven Pizza since it opened and manages the front. Eric deploys several cooks in the preparation of his menu.

FOOD, SERVICE AND AMBIANCE
　　Pizza being their specialty, I ordered one of their specialty pizzas, the Greek. It was a four-cheese white pie seasoned with olive oil instead of tomato sauce. All of their sauces are fresh and homemade. The four cheeses were feta, ricotta, Parmesan and mozzarella. My choice of toppings were shrimp and artichoke hearts. This thin crust pizza was baked just right, until the cheeses began to brown a little. I could taste the tart flavor of the artichoke hearts and the tender shrimps were the small variety rather than the baby salad shrimp that I usually see on pizzas. I liked the

texture of the pizza dough that they make from scratch and the quality of the ingredients. This was a tasty pie that I would recommend to all of you pizza lovers out there.

Brick Oven serves 12" and 16", thin and deep dish pizzas with your choice of 27 toppings including anchovies, bacon, basil, broccoli, chicken, garlic, red peppers, walnuts, spinach and sun-dried tomatoes. Traditional pies are made with tomato sauce and fresh grated mozzarella. The other specialty pizzas are the pesto made with basil sauce and the Texas bar-b-que prepared with Texas-style barbecue sauce. Pizza by the slice is also available and ready on hand. Spaghetti with garlic bread comes with marinara sauce, meatballs or sausage. The subs are on 8" white rolls and include steak or chicken and cheese, meatball or sausage marinara and a build your own vegetarian. The 24-item salad bar features six salad dressings highlighted by a sundried tomato basil, a honey French and an Oriental.

At Brick Oven, you place your order at the counter. They bring the food to your table from the kitchen or you take it from the counter. Signs request that you bus your table afterwards. Moderately heavy rock music played quietly in the restaurant. Red-framed windows on two sides face Elk Avenue and a deck and gazebo bordered by a white picket fence. The seating in the summertime expands about four-fold from 35 to 40 indoors to 150 with the deck. The gazebo comes equipped with full bar service.

The restaurant is decked in a festive mood with three posters of the Flausching Festival in Crested Butte from 1973 to 1975, two paragliding posters taken by the hang glider, and two bright and solid color character maps of the town emphasizing the Brick Oven building and truck. Enhancing this motif are posters of the Crested Butte Music Festival, Wildflower Festival, the Bols Alley Loop cross-country ski event and a spice poster. An excellent photo of a mountain peak and rainbow hangs on the back wall. The funniest item of decor had to be the sign "Warning: unattended children will be pickled and sold" over caricatures of three jars, each with the head of a pickled child. The Brick Oven Pizza is a fun place with good food.

SPECIAL ONE-TIME OFFER: Receive 15% off your order for all 12-inch or 16-inch pizzas, NOT valid for pizza slices or other menu items. Please present to server at time of ordering. _____ Owner/Manager. _____ Date.

CRESTED BUTTE

Greek Pizza
(Makes one 16-inch pizza)

1 18-ounce pizza dough/crust (Feel free to use your own pizza crust or pre-made, store bought crust. Just make sure there is enough for 16" pizza.)
1 ounce seasoned olive oil
1/2 cup ricotta cheese
1/2 cup shredded mozzarella cheese
1/4 cup feta cheese, crumbled
1/4 cup fresh grated Parmesan cheese
1/2 cup artichoke hearts
1/4 cup shrimp
1 tablespoon fresh, chopped garlic

Feel free to use more or less of these ingredients to meet your desired taste.

1. Spread olive oil evenly over entire crust, up to the edges.
2. Evenly spread ricotta layer over olive oil. Next add crumbled feta, Parmesan and mozzarella.
3. Add artichoke hearts and shrimp.
4. Add your garlic last. It will cook off better in the oven giving a better taste. Sprinkle evenly over entire pizza.
5. Bake 10 to 15 minutes in a preheated 450-degree oven. Keep close watch so as not to burn. Crust should be golden brown and cheese on top should start to brown.

<u>Beverage Recommendation</u>: Your favorite beer or Chardonnay

<u>Recipe by</u>: Eric Shaw, owner

The Forest Queen

129 Elk Avenue. 349-5336. 800-937-1788.
Directions: From the intersection of Highways 50 and 135 in Gunnison, go north 28 miles on Highway 135 to Crested Butte. At the second stop sign, the four-way stop, turn left onto Elk Avenue. Go 4 blocks. The restaurant is on the right just past 2nd Street.

ESSENTIALS
Cuisine: American
Hours: 7 days 7:30AM-10PM. Closed early MAY to early JUN and early OCT to early NOV.
Meals and Prices: Breakfast $3-$8. Lunch/Dinner $3-$17
Nonsmoking: Yes
Take-out: Yes
Alcohol: Full Bar
Credit Cards: MC, Visa, Amx, Disc
Personal Check: Local only
Reservations: Accepted
Wheelchair Access: Yes
Dress: Casual
Other: Service charge of 15% added to parties of 8 or more. Catering services available. Seven rooms for rent.

HISTORY, PERSONALITY AND CHARACTER

The Forest Queen was built in 1881 as a bar, boarding house and brothel. In the 1930s, it became Perko's Service Store, a general store. Today, it is a hotel and restaurant on the National Register of Historic Places with seven newly renovated rooms reflecting the spirit of the West.

Doug Cooper has owned The Forest Queen since October 1996 and has owned Sgt. Preston's Restaurant and Bar in Lafayette, Indiana, since November 1980. He has been in the restaurant business since the early 1970s. Manager Rob Horesovsky started at The Forest Queen in October 1996 and began in the restaurant business in 1988. He previously worked at restaurants in Boulder, Colorado, and Orlando, Florida.

FOOD, SERVICE AND AMBIANCE

The Forest Queen is a good lunch stop for a hot cup of soup and a hot or deli sandwich, which is just what I did. The homemade soup of the day was a very thick provincial vegetable with potatoes, broccoli and tomatoes. My selection from the deli was bacon, avocado and tomato on a French roll with mayonnaise, Grey Poupon, lettuce and pickle. This was a great combination with plentiful portions yet still easy to handle.

The Forest Queen offers make-your-own deli sandwiches with a host of ingredients like chicken salad, corned beef, ham, roast beef and turkey. You have your choice of breads, from whole grain and sour dough to sesame roll and rye, as well as toppings. The list of hot sandwiches also

CRESTED BUTTE

presents a variety that includes buffalo or garden burger, grilled Cajun chicken, breaded pork tenderloin and breaded cod. If you are in the mood for Mexican food, The Forest Queen can provide that also with beef or chicken tacos and black bean or ground beef burritos.

For starters, you can choose among Buffalo wings, stuffed mushrooms, a nacho platter, jalapeño poppers and a cheese and vegetable plate. For a light meal, try one of The Forest Queen's many salads such as crabmeat, chicken taco, chicken Caesar or fruit with one of their dressings like poppy seed or honey mustard. They also serve zesty Italian, French and raspberry vinaigrette fat-free and lo-cal dressings. For an entrée, elect a steak, pork loin, teriyaki or smothered chicken, swordfish, stuffed shrimp or the fish of the day. A selection of beers, house wines, liquors and non-alcoholic beverages are on hand to accompany your meal. To complete it, try one of their pies or cheesecakes.

The breakfast fare features buckwheat or buttermilk pancakes or waffles, French toast and create-your-own omelets. Spotlighting the house specialties are eggs benedict, baggins made with eggs and green chili sauce, huevos rancheros, a breakfast burrito plate and steak and eggs.

Service was amicable and accommodating while contemporary rock tunes played throughout the dining area. The Forest Queen is a one-room restaurant with an original oak wood bar, a mirror along the back bar and several period pieces. Headlining the habiliments were a big, old, round, antique clock over the front window; a Forest Queen Hotel and Restaurant, Inc. iron black safe on wheels; an old toboggan with iron runners hanging from the ceiling and antiquated rolls of butcher block paper.

A painting of the Forest Queen and Kochivar's Restaurant next door, antlers, the 1939 sales tax license for Perko's Service Store and old town photos of horse-drawn carriages and downtown Crested Butte embellish the walls. Extending this theme are mining photos of Big Mine and Peanut Mine. Philodendrons and brass lamps on brass chains hang from the ceiling. The windows on the right look down upon rushing Coal Creek. In the summertime, there is creek side patio dining at tables under umbrellas. At The Forest Queen, you will receive a worthy meal at reasonable rates and a bit of nostalgia to swallow as well.

SPECIAL ONE-TIME OFFER: Receive 10% off your TOTAL FOOD bill for the lunch and dinner menu. NOT valid for the breakfast menu. Please present to server at time of ordering. _____ Owner/Manager._____ Date.

Provincial Vegetable Soup
(Makes 3 to 4 Quarts)

2 small zucchinis, sliced
4 medium carrots, sliced
1/2 head of cauliflower, chopped in large pieces
8 ribs of celery, chopped
2 medium potatoes, skin on, diced large
1/2 head of broccoli, chopped in large pieces
1 28-ounce can crushed tomatoes
1 46-ounce can V8 juice
1/2 teaspoon crushed garlic
3 tablespoons olive oil
1/4 cup fresh basil
Salt and pepper

1. Slice zucchini, carrots, celery to 1/4 inch slices. Dice potatoes to 1/2 inch. Break up cauliflower and broccoli.
2. Cook vegetables in V8 juice. Bring to a boil and continue to cook at low heat.
3. Add tomatoes, olive oil, garlic, and basil. Cook 20 to 30 minutes. Add salt and pepper to taste.

Soupçon

127A Elk Avenue. 349-5448.
Directions: From the intersection of Highways 50 and 135 in Gunnison, go north 28 miles on Highway 135 to Crested Butte. At the second stop sign, the four-way stop, turn left onto Elk Avenue. Go four blocks. Turn right onto 2nd Street. Go ½ block. The restaurant is down the alley to the left.

ESSENTIALS
Cuisine: French/Continental
Hours: 7 days 6PM-10PM
Meals and Prices: $19-$35
Nonsmoking: All
Take-out: No
Wheelchair Access: Yes
Dress: Casual
Alcohol: Full Bar
Credit Cards: MC, Visa, Amx
Personal Check: Preferred and accepted with I.D.
Reservations: Highly recommended
Other: Available for small receptions and private groups.

HISTORY, PERSONALITY AND CHARACTER
     Soupçon was originally half its present size when it was built by the Kochevar family in 1916. It was first used as a residence for the coal miners. In the 1930s, Carolyn (Kochevar) Tezak lived here. When the Kochevars

installed running water in the log cabin in 1962, Lynn and Kolbe Schrichte began The Fondue Place. It operated until 1965. Bea Norris reopened the building in 1967 with The Swiss Fondue House. She was replaced in 1971 by A Pot of Stew and Sanchos, a Mexican restaurant. David Laskey followed in 1972 with the opening of the Bacchanale. When he moved his restaurant to Elk Avenue the building was briefly occupied by Chez Danielle.

Candy Smith, chef and owner, opened Soupçon in 1975. She was succeeded by Jeff Keys and Craig Ling. In 1982, current owners Mac and Maura Bailey bought the restaurant. Mac, the creative mind in the kitchen, adheres to using only the freshest ingredients available and staying actively involved with the cooking process. Maura establishes and maintains the relaxed atmosphere in the front of the house through her warm personality. They also own The Slogar in Crested Butte. Head Chef Paul Tillger started at Soupçon in 1995. He is a graduate of the Culinary Institute of America in Hyde Park, New York, and has been in the restaurant business since the mid-1980s. Paul previously cooked at the Crested Butte Mountain Resort, in Hawaii and at Square One in San Francisco.

FOOD, SERVICE AND AMBIANCE

Mac believes that involvement with the food is what makes Soupçon so special. Over the years, he has developed many unique dishes on his changing menu. All meals are made to order. The soups and sauces are all homemade and they bake their own breads. For starters, I selected the Brie soup, a creamy chicken velouté, or stock-based white sauce, with French Brie cheese, onions and celery liquefied together. This delicious cream soup was enhanced with a sweet apple-pecan turnover. A small Caesar salad followed with red pepper and crunchy croutons.

For the entrée, I chose the Colorado rack of lamb, roasted with a rosemary infused zinfandel reduction. These were two high-quality, delicate, tender ribs that were fresh, flavorsome and moist. The sauce, prepared with the lamb's juice and zinfandel wine reduced or thickened over heat, was wonderful. This dish was so good I wish I had ordered the four rib rack.

Going along with the lamb were potatoes au gratin with just the right amount of cheese to improve the taste but keep it light, sweet asparagus strips and spaghetti squash topped with sesame sauce, and a small loaf of French bread with a whole-grain roll. Mac's mission to use fresh ingredients, start from scratch and make good food was accomplished as far as I was concerned.

There are several other appetizers on the menu that sound delectable like French red pepper soup with lump crabmeat, house made duck pâté, Jack Daniel's marinated and cherry wood smoked quail salad, and long-time favorite oysters aïoli. Elk, beef, duck and fresh fish are the mainstays on the menu. Some variations that you may see are elk tenderloin with dried blueberries, roast duck with ginger brandy peach sauce, beef tenderloin with Madeira green peppercorn sauce, and fresh salmon with raspberry Grand Marnier sauce. A pasta dish like gnocchetti with pesto and shrimp is another possibility. Soupçon is also prepared to serve vegetarian meals on request. If you give them a little advance notice, they can be more creative with your selection. Choose a wine from Maura's list of some 100 vintages to accompany your meal. To complete the dining experience, take delight in one of Soupçon's homemade desserts such as cappuccino cheesecake, fresh berry cobbler with homemade buttermilk ice cream, mango sorbet, white chocolate Neapolitan or chocolate truffle torte.

    Service was quick, friendly, attentive and with a good attitude. I enjoyed listening to the classical guitar music. Soupçon is a small two-room, log cabin restaurant with red-painted wood door and window frames. Candlelight dining is on tables with flower-pattern covers. Posters of the Crested Butte Wildflower Festival, the Wildflower Capital of Colorado and the Antique Botanical Cascade adorn the pastel blue and white wallpaper. Paintings of the town of Crested Butte, white water falls, columbines, and rivers and trees in winter complement the setting. Large oak wood log walls and vegas, a stained-glass window and white lace curtains augment this rustic ambiance. Visit Soupçon and I think you will agree that their slogan is true: "A small unpretentious French restaurant, big on gourmet cuisine."

Hazelnut Ice Cream Cake
with Chocolate Rum Sauce
(Makes one 11"x17" Cake)

Hazelnut Ice Cream Cake:
6 ounces hazelnuts
6 ounces almonds
1 1/4 cups granulated sugar
1/4 cup flour
10 to 12 egg whites
Pinch of salt

Chocolate Rum Sauce:
4 ounces unsweetened chocolate
1 ounce unsalted butter
1 cup heavy cream
1 cup granulated sugar
1 teaspoon vanilla extract
1/4 cup Myers dark rum

CRESTED BUTTE

1. Line bottom of 11"x17" jelly roll pan with parchment (baking) paper and butter the sides of the pan.
2. Roast and skin hazelnuts. Grind hazelnuts and almonds with 1/4 cup sugar in processor.
3. Using oversized bowl, mix together ground nuts, remaining sugar, and flour.
4. Beat egg whites with a pinch of salt until stiff, not dry. Quickly fold egg whites into mixture, in three additions, being careful not to over mix.
5. Bake in a 325-degree oven, approximately 45 minutes, or until cake pulls away from sides of pan.
6. Cool cake and remove from pan; cut into 3 equal pieces and assemble with high quality vanilla ice cream. Freeze until firm.
7. <u>Chocolate Rum Sauce</u>: Melt chocolate and butter in double boiler. Mix in cream and sugar and cook over low heat until sugar is dissolved.
8. Remove from heat and stir in vanilla extract and rum.
9. Refrigerate and re-heat gently for use.
10. Slice cake and serve with warm sauce.

<u>Recipe by</u>: Mac Bailey, owner and chef

DURANGO

Durango is derived from the Basque word Urango meaning "watering town or place": "ur" meaning "water" and "ango" meaning "town". Durango was the name of a town in the Basque Province of northern Spain. The "D" was later added by the Spanish. Former Territorial Governor A. C. Hunt named the town after returning from Durango, Mexico. Durango was the watering station for the stage coach line and wagon trains.

Durango reflects three cultures — Native American, Anglo and Hispanic — and is a center for ranching, farming and recreational activities. Once a predominant coal mining community and commercial center, Durango today is known for its Victorian architecture and the Durango and Silverton narrow gauge railroad.

Variety is the order of the day at the four restaurants shown below. I have a Mediterranean café in a turn-of-the-century home, a Swiss restaurant and bakery with Mexican and American influences, a New York style Italian restaurant using family recipes and a modern American grill with a seasonally changing menu.

Location of Town: Southwest Colorado where Highways 160 and 550 intersect.
Zip Code: 81301. Area Code: 970. Population: 14,300. Elevation: 6,523ft.

Cyprus Café

725 East 2nd Avenue. 385-6884.
Directions: From the intersection of Highways 160 and 550, go north on Highway 550 to the first signal and turn right onto College Drive (6th Street). Go three blocks and turn left onto 2nd Avenue. The restaurant is 1½ blocks down on the left.

ESSENTIALS
Cuisine: Mediterranean
Hours: JUN-SEP: 7 days 11:30AM-3PM and 5PM-10PM. OCT-MAY: Mon-Fri 11:30AM-2:30PM, Mon-Sat 5PM-9PM. Closed Sun.
Meals and Prices: Lunch $6-$7. Dinner $7-$15.
Nonsmoking: All
Take-out: Yes
Alcohol: Full Bar
Credit Cards: MC, Visa, Amx
Personal Check: Yes, with I.D.
Reservations: Not accepted

DURANGO

Wheelchair Access: Yes, including the restrooms
Dress: Casual
Other: Service charge of 17% added to parties of six or more. Catering available.

HISTORY, PERSONALITY AND CHARACTER

The Cyprus Café is in a turn-of-the-century home that did not convert to a business until Lola's Restaurant opened here in 1994. The building is old enough to garnish a few ghost stories involving an old miner. In October 1996, Alison Dance and Kelly Rogers opened the Cyprus Café. Alison created the menu and is the executive chef. She has been in the restaurant business since the early 1970s starting at the Red Rooster in Pine Junction, Colorado before moving on to Denver and San Francisco. In 1980, Alison bought her first restaurant, a pizzeria/art gallery. Between 1984 and 1996, she worked at Asimako Poulos, a Greek restaurant in San Francisco. Kelly, who worked in restaurants to put himself through college, tends bar at the Cyprus Café.

Joelle Riddle is the dining room manager and hails from a family that has owned restaurants in the Durango area. Sous chef Lisa Carr graduated from the California Culinary Academy in 1989 and cooked in San Francisco before coming to Colorado in 1993. She was a pastry chef at the Tamarron Resort north of Durango before coming to the Cyprus Café. Kitchen manager Vera Hansen has worked and catered in Durango her entire life.

FOOD, SERVICE AND AMBIANCE

The Cyprus Café uses fresh, locally grown ingredients in preparing their wholesome, health-conscious foods. After having an appetizer and an entrée for lunch, I felt like I had finished a nourishing meal, full but not bloated. This was a lot of food, but its light nature did not weigh me down. The bruschetta consisted of diced tomato, capers, onion and olive oil on toasted French bread with lemon wedges and lettuce. Very fresh tasting and plentiful with six toast slices stacked high, yet not heavy. The entrée was a tilapia filet, a fresh water fish grown in the San Luis Valley of Colorado, on a baguette topped with onion slices and lemon wedge. Sliced Roma tomatoes, hummus, tzatziki, lettuce, kalamata olive, pepperoncini and homemade mayonnaise with raspberry dill were served on the side. They also prepare a homemade mayonnaise with lemon dill and one with chili pepper basil. The tilapia was light, flaky, slightly breaded and sprinkled with parsley. The baguette was warm and toasty, crisp on the outside, fluffy on the inside.

Their Mediterranean menu offers several Greek and Lebanese dishes. For appetizers, start with warm chèvre (goat) cheese and roasted red peppers in grapeleaves, spanakopita, baba ganoush (eggplant) or the soup of the day, like Mediterranean clam chowder with a tomato base. If you prefer, you can select a warm spinach, Greek, Kota (chicken) or house salad. Highlighting the lunch entrées are falafel (fried chickpea patties) souvlaki, gyro, gardenburger and sandwiches like spicy pork sausage, eggplant and grilled vegetable. For dinner, choose from such foreign delights as salmon with goat cheese and grapeleaves, penne pasta with tomatoes and spinach, Tunisian prawns or Imam Biyaldi, stuffed half eggplant with basmati rice.

Service was friendly and courteous. Snappy vocal jazz played in the background. This is a charming, century-old Victorian house with a small patio in front and a garden patio on the side featuring a river rock wall and trellis. The building's exterior is very colorful with purple and yellow trim, red and green windowsills, a green roof and yellow walls. In the summertime, people sit at big tables under green umbrellas and listen to live jazz, gypsy jazz or a flute player three to five nights a week. A bar in the back placed in front of the rock wall provides the libations while cherry and pear trees, wild flowers and herbs contribute to the atmosphere. They have an ideal location for viewing the Fourth of July fireworks.

Andrew Rush, Alison's artist uncle from Arizona, contributed many of the artworks found inside including two etchings of bathers and a bar and grill, both signed "To Alison". Garlands of dried fruit and spice hang in front of the windows and on the fireplace mantel. Enhancing the diverse ambiance are sketches of people on "no smoking" signs over the dining room entrance, a ram's head over the entrance to the kitchen, a wine rack and an abstract ink and watercolor of a bird in clouds over the fireplace mantel. Seating is on wrought-iron framed chairs with wood seats. Revel in some salubrious ethnic cuisine in a cozy setting at the Cyprus Café.

See page 150 for restaurant photo.

DURANGO

Salmon sto Fourno
(Serves 6)

12 grape leaves
6 salmon filets, 6 to 8 ounces each
8 ounces olive saltza*
6 ounces goat cheese
1 lemon sliced into rounds
6 parchment papers, 18"x18"

*Olive Saltza:
1 cup assorted olives, pitted and chopped
1 tablespoon capers, chopped
3 shallots, peeled and finely chopped
1 medium red onion, peeled and finely chopped
Juice from one lemon
1/4 cup of extra virgin olive oil
3 tablespoons quality red wine vinegar, not balsamic

1. Place two grape leaves on working surface overlapping each other.
2. Place a salmon filet in the center of the grape leaves with one ounce of the olive saltza, one ounce of goat cheese, and one lemon round.
3. Wrap the grape leaves around the entire portion. Place the portion on a parchment paper square on the lower third of the paper.
4. Fold the outside edges of the parchment paper over the salmon. Fold the lower edge in and roll into a package.
5. Repeat the process with the remaining salmon filets.
6. Bake in a hot oven (425 degrees) for 20 minutes or until paper browns and puffs up. Unwrap and serve immediately.
7. Olive Saltza: Place all of these ingredients in a medium mixing bowl and toss.

Wine Recommendations: Penfolds Chardonnay, Australia or Preston Cuvée de Fumé, Dry Creek Valley 1995

Recipe by: Alison Dance, owner and executive chef

See page 149 for recipe photo.

Le Rendezvous

750 Main Avenue. 385-5685.
Directions: From the intersection of Highways 160 and 550, go north on Highway 550 to the first signal and turn right onto College Drive (6th Street). Go two blocks and turn left onto Main Avenue. The restaurant is 1½ blocks down on the right.

ESSENTIALS

Cuisine: Swiss, American, Mexican
Hours: Tue-Sun 7AM-3PM. Closed Mon. Closed end of OCT to beginning of NOV.
Meals and Prices: Breakfast/Lunch $5-$7.
Nonsmoking: All
Take-out: Yes
Alcohol: Beer and wine
Credit Cards: MC, Visa, Disc
Personal Check: Local only

Reservations: No
Wheelchair Access: Yes
Dress: Casual
Other: Children's Menu. No separate checks. Service charge of 15% added for parties of 6 or more. Box lunches to go. Available for small banquets. Special order cakes for weddings and anniversaries available with delivery.

HISTORY, PERSONALITY AND CHARACTER

Le Rendezvous is in a building that dates back to 1883. It had been the New York Bakery for many years before Swiss native and Swiss-trained Pierre André opened Le Rendezvous in 1992. Pierre has been in the restaurant business since 1977. He came to the United States in 1981 and cooked in Santa Fe, New Mexico, for 10 years. Jeromy Nicholas, who cooked at Henry's in the Strater Hotel for 3½ years, assists Pierre in the kitchen with the pastries and preparation. Sheri Eicenzo has been managing the restaurant since 1994. Prior to that, she worked in restaurants in northern California beginning in 1971.

FOOD, SERVICE AND AMBIANCE

Le Rendezvous is a Swiss bakery and restaurant offering fresh baked goods and healthy and nutritious meals, daily. Linda and I had Sunday breakfast at Le Rendezvous. I ordered one of their stuffed buttery croissants; the tasty Florentine cooked golden brown and filled with creamed spinach, Swiss cheese and scramble eggs. Mixed fruits were served on the side. Linda had the fruity and wholesome blue corn blueberry pancakes made

DURANGO

with fresh blueberries (when in season) with blueberry compote on top. Other breakfast specialties include espresso drinks, three egg omelets, huevos rancheros, meat or veggie burritos, French toast, green chili potatoes, and banana walnut pancakes.

Highlighting the lunch menu are sandwiches using their freshly baked baguettes and country or whole wheat breads, croissants, French onion soup, salads, quiches, pizzas and desserts. Among the possible choices are albacore tuna, honey ham with Swiss cheese, grilled eggplant, stir fry teriyaki chicken, quiche Milanaise with ham and Swiss cheese, smoked chicken salad with blue cheese and pecans (their most popular salad), a Greek pizza with eggplant and sundried tomatoes, and homemade pastries and pies.

Service was quick and efficient taking our order and serving our food. This is a cherubic place with hand paintings of fish, mushrooms and a village scene on the pink stucco walls. The stucco is in patches allowing some of the red brick underneath to show through. There are posters depicting the various varieties of mushrooms and Tabasco sauces and a comical poster of a rabbit eating watermelon. Handmade crafts including handcrafted jar lids enhance the quaint ambiance. The restaurant hosts both a full bar with bottles of beer on the back shelf and a bakery with cookies, muffins, croissants, cinnamon rolls and pies. They have been baking at the place now called Le Rendezvous for over a century. Stop in for some fresh, out-of-the-oven-bakedgoods or a healthy meal.

See top of page 151 for restaurant photo.

Special One-Time Offer: Buy one entrée and receive a second entrée of equal or lesser value free (up to $7.00) OR receive 50% off one entrée (up to $4.00). Please present to server at time of ordering.

_____ Owner/ Manager. _____ Date.

Vol Au Vent
(Serves 4 to 5)

10 ounces mushrooms
1 1/2 pounds chicken breast
4 ounces butter
4 ounces all purpose flour

1 1/2 cup water
8 ounces of chicken stock or 1 cube bouillon to make 8 ounces of chicken stock
1 quart heavy cream

1. Cut mushrooms in quarters. Sauté them in butter until all water is reduced. Set aside.
2. Boil chicken breast in water until cooked, approximately 10 to 15 minutes. Cool and rinse with cold water, then cut in 1/4" cubes. Set aside.
3. Make a roux. Melt butter and add flour. Mix together. Set aside.
4. Begin sauce with boiling chicken stock. Add your roux to it.
5. Continue to boil and stir vigorously making sure not to burn bottom of pan.
6. Add 1 quart of heavy cream slowly, keep stirring until mixture boils, then turn off burner. Sauce should be thick and creamy
7. Add mushrooms and chicken. Salt and pepper to taste.
8. Serve in pastry shell or bread.

<u>Wine Recommendation</u>: Any white wine
<u>Recipe by</u>: Pierre André

Mama's Boy

3690 Main Avenue. 247-0060.
Directions: From the intersection of Highways 160 and 550, go north on Highway 550 about ½ mile to the intersection of Main Avenue just past 14th Street. Bear left onto Main Avenue and proceed north. The restaurant is on the right where the highway bends to the right between 36th and 37th Streets across from Pizza Hut.

<u>ESSENTIALS</u>
Cuisine: Italian
Hours: 7 days 4PM-10PM.
Meals and Prices: Dinner $8-$15
Nonsmoking: Yes, smoking only in the bar and lounge.
Take-out: Yes
Alcohol: Full Bar
Credit Cards: MC, Visa, Disc
Personal Check: Local only with I.D.
Reservations: Not accepted
Wheelchair Access: Yes
Dress: Casual
Other: Available for meetings and parties of up to 50 people.

<u>HISTORY, PERSONALITY AND CHARACTER</u>
Mama's Boy is in a building originally used as a Creamland Dairy circa 1940s. The building has a varied and colorful history having been used as an auto garage, a Ski Barn ski rental place, a Mexican restaurant and Smokey Robins Barbecue. Mama's Boy opened here in 1993. The original Mama's Boy began in Hermosa, 11 miles north of Durango, in 1988 and is still there.

DURANGO

Current owner James Salzillo grew up in a tight Italian family in the Bronx in the 1950s and 1960s. He began his culinary career as a line cook in Warwick, New York in 1968. During the 1970s, he worked at The Assay Office and The Hobbit Hole in Durango. Patti Kuttler, his current manager, owned the latter. In the 1980s, James would work winters as a cook at Purgatory Ski Resort when he wasn't skiing. Patti started at the Mama's Boy in Hermosa in 1988 before coming over to the Durango Mama's Boy in 1994. Christopher Dodge and Bryan Gasior are the kitchen co-managers. Christopher has been cooking since the late 1980s and has been at Mama's Boy since 1994. Bryan came to the restaurant in 1997 and has been in the restaurant business since the mid-1980s.

FOOD, SERVICE AND AMBIANCE

Most of the dishes at Mama's Boy are family recipes that originated with James' grandmother or mother. I delighted in the wonderful pasta della casa: ziti noodles topped with a mouth-watering array of sautéed mushrooms, prosciutto, green peas and red onions with a delicious layer of marinara sauce and herbed ricotta in-between. This was a hearty bowl full and well seasoned with basil and oregano. Mmwahh! A mini loaf of homemade bread was served on the side. I also visited the Mama Mia's in Hermosa, a small one-room pizza shop, and sampled their appetizing hand tossed, hand rolled, baked-to-order New York style pizza. You can't go wrong with the pizza or the pasta.

There are daily fish specials like grilled mahi mahi with green chili cream sauce, a children's menu and a list of Italian and domestic wines. Save room for one of their homemade desserts, if you can, like peach, pumpkin or blueberry pie; white chocolate raspberry or chocolate walnut cheese cake; a no-flour chocolate raspberry torte; tiramisu; cannoli or spumoni.

Service was pleasant, hospitable and with a smile. Light jazz and new age music played in the background. This is a surprisingly elegant place considering the inconspicuous exterior. Spanish arch entrances lead to two candle-lit dining rooms with white-laced curtains, plants in baskets and ceiling fans. The artwork is a blend of Colorado valleys and Italian villas; a mixture of grape vines painted on one arch by Vicki Roberts, a painting of the Trimble Hot Springs Pool by Ed Kreuse and art works portraying Italy's small towns by Paul Falwell. Posters of various cheeses and wines of Tuscany combine with a painting of a speedboat on a lake. An Italian-made cappuccino machine is set in one of the arch openings between the lounge and dining room, strictly for looks. Behind the granite bar are three arches with mirrors along the back wall. The more time I spent here, the more it felt like I was back in Italy. The food, the atmosphere and the friendly people will make you feel like you are in Italy too.

<u>Special One-Time Offer</u>: Buy one entrée and receive a second entrée of equal or lesser value free (up to $15.00) OR receive 50% off one entrée (up to $7.50). Please present to server at time of ordering.
_____ Owner/ Manager. _____ Date.

Pasta della Casa
(Serves 3 to 4)

2 tablespoons olive oil
3 cloves fresh garlic, minced
2 to 3 ounces dry red wine
6 ounces sweet peas, cooked
12 ounces medium mushrooms, quartered
1 medium red onion, julienne
1 tablespoon dry basil
1 tablespoon dry oregano
1 tablespoon dry parsley

Salt and black pepper to taste
1 pound desired pasta (like penne, fusilli, ziti or any other form of pasta that will allow plenty of sauce to cling to it)
12 ounces ricotta cheese
2 cups marinara sauce (spaghetti sauce)
Fresh grated Parmesan cheese

Optional: Add 6 to 8 ounces of prosciutto or Italian salami

1. Put pasta into 7 to 8 quarts of boiling water.
2. In the meantime, heat marinara and ricotta separately either in pans or in a microwave oven.
3. Place a large sauté pan on moderately high heat and add olive oil. Sauté garlic until translucent being careful not to brown. Add wine and then onions, mushrooms, and peas.
4. Sprinkle in dry herbs and salt and pepper to taste. Sauté vegetables until tender, tossing occasionally.
5. When pasta is al dente, drain and place into bowls.
6. Ladle marinara on pasta, then follow with ricotta cheese and sautéed vegetables.
7. Sprinkle with fresh Parmesan and MANGIA!

<u>Wine Recommendations</u>: Cakebread, Cabernet Sauvignon, or Gabbiano Chianti Classico

<u>Recipe by</u>: James Salzillo, owner
See bottom of page 151 for recipe photo.

DURANGO

Seasons Grill

764 Main Avenue. 382-9790. Fax 382-0452.
Directions: From the intersection of Highways 160 and 550, go north on Highway 550 to the first signal and turn right onto College Drive (6th Street). Go two blocks and turn left onto Main Avenue. The restaurant is 1½ blocks down on the right.

ESSENTIALS
Cuisine: Modern American
Hours: Sun-Thu 5PM-10PM, Fri-Sat 5PM-11PM.
Meals and Prices: Dinner $13-$17.
Nonsmoking: All
Take-out: No
Alcohol: Full Bar
Credit Cards: MC, Visa, Amx, Disc

Personal Check: No
Reservations: No
Wheelchair Access: Yes
Dress: Casual, business suits, a "little of everything".
Other: Service charge of 15% may be added to parties of 8 or more.

HISTORY, PERSONALITY AND CHARACTER

Seasons occupies a building originally constructed as a sundry shop in the mid-1890s. During the 1960s and 1970s, a place called Hafeys sold newspapers, magazines and cigars on this spot. In the 1980s, a restaurant called Marco Polo moved into the location for a short while. Right before Seasons opened on Christmas Eve 1994, an art gallery existed here.

Current owner of Seasons Roger Roessler has been in the restaurant business for 30 years and owns Old Tymer's Café in Durango, Seasons in Albuquerque, Ogelvie's in Taos and the Swiss Hotel in Sonoma, California. General Manager Jim Nichols has been working in restaurants since 1980 having previously managed at Dos Juans, now Gazpachos and the Palace Grill, both in Durango. He has been with Seasons since August 1994 and worked on the initial setup and hiring for the new restaurant. Jason Daub and Amy Nordby are co-chefs. Jason has two associate degrees, one from the Florida Culinary Institute and one from the Colorado Institute of Art. He has been cooking since 1988. Amy worked as a sous chef at Geronimo's in Santa Fe and other New Mexico restaurants before coming to Seasons in 1995.

FOOD, SERVICE AND AMBIANCE

Seasons' menu, quite appropriately, changes with the seasons, four times a year. I ordered off their fall menu selecting the chopped romaine (the lettuce of choice for Caesar salads) salad with grated Parmesan, garlic croutons and anchovy-garlic dressing. The lettuce, croutons and Parmesan slivers were all very crisp and I loved the dressing. It was just the right amount, too. One slice of white and one slice of wheat bread were served for dipping. A bottle of olive oil is set on the table.

My entrée was the grilled Australian lamb sirloin in a balsamic mint jus with a goat cheese-caramelized onion crostada and a side of refreshing greens. The lamb was seven slices of heavenly, medium-rare lean meat with a little fat and seared on the edges. The red, meaty-flavored au jus sauce added a wonderful flavor to the delicious meat. The crostada was a savory slice of cheese-onion pie. The greens, firm and fresh, included radicchio, frisée, arugula, baby spinach leaves and field greens. This was a delectable, not overfilling, meal.

For an appetizer, deep-fried calamari with a grilled tomato salsa and lemon aïoli is offered year-around. In winter or spring, you might order crisp fried onion strings with chipotle ketchup; while in the fall, you could choose pan seared crab cakes or the house cured Atlantic salmon. Imaginative salads are available like the Nicoise with house cured tuna or the romaine heart with pears and toasted walnuts in Maytag blue cheese dressing. Depending on the season, you may find linguine carbonara, grilled salmon fusilli, braised duck pappardelle or farfalle on their list of pan roasted-sautéed entrées. The house specialty rotisserie-grill items include spit-roasted chicken, double cut pork rib chop and Black Angus garlic and black pepper ribeye. A fine selection of after dinner drinks from espressos to ports, grappas and cognacs can accompany your tiramisu, chocolate crème brûlée or berry brioche bread pudding dessert.

Servers are what I like to call "upscale casual" with white shirt, tie and jeans. They are also efficient, friendly and professional. This is a long, rectangular dining room with a bar to the left of the entrance and an open kitchen to the right in the rear. Ceiling fans hang from the high ceiling and blown-up micro shots of flowers, a rose, a white Lilly and a yellow mum, decorate the yellow textured plaster walls. The red brick walls are adorned with a large mural of eight horses in full gallop and photos taken by local artist, David B. Wilkins, depicting a grotto in the Grand Canyon. A patio behind the restaurant hosts eleven tables in a setting of aspen trees around a wood-burning, adobe-style fireplace. Seasons has been a popular, frequently well-talked about restaurant since its opening. The attention that it has mustered is well deserved.

DURANGO

Grilled Australian Lamb Sirloin with Goat Cheese, Caramelized Onion Crostada, and Balsamic Mint Jus
(Serves 4)

Lamb and Marinade:
Zest of 1 lemon
6 garlic cloves, minced
1 tablespoon fresh thyme leaves, chopped
1/4 cup pure olive oil
2 teaspoon coarsely ground black pepper
4 6-ounce lamb sirloins (lamb chumps)

1. Mix together the first 5 ingredients. Coat the lamb pieces in the mixture and marinate at least 8 hours or overnight.

Goat Cheese-Caramelized Onion Crostada:
For the pastry:
1 cup all purpose flour
1/2 teaspoon salt
1/2 teaspoon sugar
4 ounces chilled, unsalted butter, cut into 1/4 inch dice
1/4 cup ice water, plus droplets more, if needed

1. Place flour, salt, and sugar in the bowl of a food processor and pulse 2 to 3 times to combine. Add the diced butter and pulse 5 to 6 times.
2. All at once, add the ice water and pulse 3 to 4 times. The dough will look crumbly and lump, but will hold together when pressed between fingers.
3. Quickly turn the dough out onto a work surface, form a rough ball, wrap with plastic wrap, and refrigerate at least 1 hour.

For the filling:
6 ounces mild goat cheese, such as Montrachet
6 ounces ricotta impastata cheese
1 peeled russet potato, boiled soft, and mashed with 1/4 cup heavy cream and 1 tablespoon butter
1 egg
1/2 teaspoon each chopped fresh thyme, rosemary, and Italian parsley
1 large onion, julienne, and cooked in 2 tablespoons butter until dark golden brown
Salt and pepper to taste

1. Place the first five ingredients in a large bowl (or in a bowl of an electric mixer) and combine well.
2. Add 1/2 of the caramelized onion, reserving the other half to top the crostada. Add salt and pepper. Refrigerate for about an hour.

Making the crostada:
1. Heat the oven to 400 degrees.
2. Grease a cookie sheet, or line it with bakers' parchment paper.
3. Unwrap the pastry and place it on a floured work surface. Roll the pastry out into an approximate circle of about 12 inches in diameter and transfer it onto the prepare cookie sheet.
4. Place all of the filling in the middle of the pastry, flattening it somewhat, but leaving a 2-inch margin of dough around the perimeter.
5. Begin folding and pleating the edges of the crostada up around the filling to create a free-form crust, leaving the filling exposed in the center.
6. Place the remaining caramelized onion on top of the visible filling, and bake for about 25 minutes or until golden brown.

Balsamic-Mint Jus:
1/4 cup balsamic vinegar
1 1/2 cups beef or veal stock
2 tablespoons chopped fresh mint
Salt and pepper to taste
1 tablespoon butter

1. In a small sauce pan, combine the first 3 ingredients and cook over high heat until the mixture is reduced by half. Taste and add salt and pepper. Whisk in the tablespoon of butter until completely incorporated.

For presentation: Grill the lamb sirloins to desired temperature. Slice each sirloin against the grain into five pieces. Serve with a wedge of the warm crostada. Ladle about 2 ounces of the jus over the meat. Garnish the plate with a handful of mixed baby greens and serve.

Wine Recommendation: Ravenswood Sonoma Zinfandel

Recipe by: Amy Nordby, chef

See top of page 152 for recipe photo.

EL JEBEL

El Jebel, meaning "The Rock" in Arabic, is unincorporated. It is a community, rather than a town. The area around El Jebel was predominantly developed by Floyd Crawford, a land owner, rancher, and trailer park owner.

This American provincial restaurant operated by a couple with Aspen experience, was a splendid find.

Location of Town: Central Colorado on Highway 82 between Glenwood Springs and Aspen
Zip Code: 81628. Area Code: 970. Population: 1,000. Elevation: 6,480ft.

Blue Creek Grill

68 El Jebel Road. 963-3946.
Directions: Take Exit 114 from I-70 and go north to the signal. Turn right onto Highways 6 and 24 and go to the next signal. Turn right onto Highway 82, go over I-70 and continue on this road for 11.7 miles to the intersection with Highway 133. Continue straight on Highway 82 for 8 miles to the second signal and turn left onto El Jebel Road. The restaurant is one block down on the right.

ESSENTIALS
Cuisine: American Provincial
Hours: Tue-Sun 5PM to close (usually between 9PM and 10PM). Closed Mon.
Meals and Prices: Dinner $11-$19
Nonsmoking: All
Take-out: Yes
Alcohol: Full Bar
Credit Cards: MC, Visa

Personal Check: Local only
Reservations: Recommended
Wheelchair Access: Yes
Dress: Casual
Other: Service charge of 18% added to parties of 6 or more. Catering, banquets, receptions and weddings available for parties of 25 to 300.

HISTORY, PERSONALITY AND CHARACTER

Chris Sapp and his wife, Carolyn Fisher, opened The Blue Creek Grill on April 5, 1994, in a building constructed in the 1960s. A banjo shop and, in the early 1990s, Szechuan Chinese Restaurant previously occupied the premises. Chris has been in the restaurant business since 1978 and was sous chef at Gordon's in the late 1980s and at Syzygy in the early 1990s, both restaurants in Aspen. Carolyn, who has been working in restaurants since 1975, worked previously at Gordon's, the Little Nell Hotel in Aspen and the Swiss Hotel in Boston. She also owns and operates her catering company, Fabulous Food. Chris and Carolyn are also the head chefs at the Blue Creek Grill.

FOOD, SERVICE AND AMBIANCE

Chefs Carolyn and Chris serve an eclectic array of fanciful salads, tempting appetizers and intricate entrées from pasta and seafood to steak, lamb, pork and chicken. All of the sauces, soups and desserts at the Blue Creek Grill are homemade. For starters, I selected the scallion pancakes topped with big mounds of smoked salmon, sour cream and capers in a chive vinaigrette and crème fraîche. The three pancakes were soft, chewy, tasty and just the right size for eating with your hands. A side salad of field greens, baby spinach, arugula, mâché, red oak, radicchio and frisée accompanied these savory tidbits. My server also brought warm wheat bread with a sprig of oregano to the table. My main course was the popular cornmeal crusted mountain trout from Idaho with roasted pecan butter, mashed potatoes topped with chives and vegetables. The open trout filet was nicely browned. The cornmeal crust added crunch to the moist, fresh trout and the pecan butter augmented the flavor in a very complementary way.

You can begin your meal at the Blue Creek Grill with duck and kielbasa sausage gumbo; a tossed house, Caesar, field greens or spinach salad; grilled shrimp or a spicy steak quesadilla. Choices of entrées include fettuccini with roasted and grilled vegetables, herb roasted chicken, grilled double cut pork chop, dry-aged New York strip and Colorado lamb chops. Chris and Carolyn also prepare several seafood specialties like mussels provençal, grilled mahi mahi, sea scallops and sautéed shrimp. For a delectable dessert, choose one of their homemade creations such as chocolate bread pudding with warm caramel and fudge on a bed of crème anglaise with whipped cream topping, crème brûlée, strawberry shortcake biscuit style or a warm apple tart.

Service was efficient and accommodating. Chef Chris allowed me to substitute mashed potatoes for the new potatoes on the menu. Blues rock music played very softly throughout the restaurant. The decor for the Blue Creek Grill begins at the entrance where the door handle was in the shape of a large fork. The warm, peach and orange-color walls of this two room restaurant are painted with blue, gold, black and white pictographs

EL JEBEL

by Carolyn's sister, Suzanne Kfoury. The Blue Creek Grill was an exquisite discovery in this little town, one that you would expect to find in a place like Aspen.

Roasted Strawberry and Cherry Meringue Pie
(Make one 9-inch pie)

Pie Crust:
2 1/4 cups sifted all purpose flour
3/4 teaspoon salt
3/4 cup vegetable shortening

Meringue:
6 egg whites
3/4 cup sugar
1/4 teaspoon salt

Filling:
1 pint washed, halved strawberries
2 cups pitted dark sweet cherries
Juice of one lemon
1 cup sugar
1/2 cup water
3 tablespoons cornstarch

1. Preheat oven to 400 degrees.
2. Crust: Combine flour and salt in a large bowl. Remove 1/3 of the mixture to small bowl and add 1/2 cup cold water to make a paste. In a large bowl, cut shortening into flour until it resembles course meal. Add paste to large bowl and mix with a fork until it forms a ball. Divide dough into 2 pieces, reserve one piece for later use. Roll dough on lightly floured surface until 1/8 inch thick. Place dough into 9-inch pie plate, cover with foil, and weight with dried beans or rice. Bake shell 20 minutes. Cool. Lower oven to 350 degrees.
3. Filling: Toss strawberries and 1/2 cup sugar in a shallow baking dish, roast in 350 degree oven 20-25 minutes until soft and bubbly. Cool. In a medium sauce pan, combine cherries, 1/2 cup sugar, lemon juice, and 1/4 cup of water. Bring to a boil, add cornstarch mixed with 1/4 cup water. Bring to another boil, let cool.
4. Meringue: In a bowl, over simmering water, whisk egg whites, sugar, and salt, until sugar dissolves and whites are warm to the touch. Transfer to mixing bowl and whip until stiff, glossy peaks form.
5. To Assemble: Fill cooled pie with cool filling. Cover the top of the pie thoroughly with meringue all the way to the edges. Bake at 350 degrees until golden brown, 20 to 25 minutes.

Wine Recommendations: A port or Gewürztraminer

Recipe by: Carolyn Fisher, owner and chef

EVERGREEN

First called The Post, after Amos F. Post, son-in-law of Thomas Bergen who settled nearby Bergen Park, the name was changed to Evergreen by D. P. Wilmot in honor of the dense forests of evergreen trees in the area. Ute Indians used to camp along nearby Soda Creek. Evergreen has had a varied history of trappers, traders, gold miners, ranchers and lumberjacks.

My two Evergreen samplings feature a steak and seafood house by the lake and golf course and a newly remodeled international restaurant in town.

Location of Town: West of Denver
Zip Code: 80439. Area Code: 303. Population: 4,500. Elevation: 7,040ft.

The Columbine
28186 Highway 74. 670-3651.
Directions: From I-70 heading west take Exit 252, heading east take Exit 251 (The El Rancho/Evergreen Exit). Follow Highway 74 south for 8 miles into Evergreen. The restaurant will be on your right, set in from the street, just past Highway 73.

ESSENTIALS
Cuisine: International
Hours: Tue-Sat 11AM-2PM and 5:30PM-9:30PM. Sun 10:30AM-2PM and 5:30PM-9PM. Closed Mon.
Meals and Prices: Lunch $5-$7. Sun Brunch $4-$9. Dinner $9-$17.
Nonsmoking: All. Smoking only at the bar.
Take-out: Yes
Alcohol: Full Bar
Credit Cards: MC, Visa, Amx

Personal Check: Yes, with I.D.
Reservations: Not necessary except for Holidays. Accepted for parties of 6 or more.
Wheelchair Access: Yes
Dress: Casual
Other: Available for banquets, business lunches and private parties. Catering in house or on site. A 17% service charge may be added to parties of 6 or more.

HISTORY, PERSONALITY AND CHARACTER
The building occupied by The Columbine was once a Food King, Evergreen's sole grocery store. It was also a Safeway store. In 1988-89, the building was renovated from a grocery store and made into a space for a restaurant. In the early 1990s, Lizbeth's Restaurant became the first

EVERGREEN

restaurant to occupy the premises. In 1995, Peter Ertl moved The Columbine from its location of 3 years on Highway 73 to its current location. Peter is also the head chef. He began cooking at Marlino's in Evergreen and has since earned fans not only from America but around the world. He is backed by sous chef Adrian Lundgreen and general manager Susan McIntosh, who started at The Columbine in February 1998. She has managed restaurants since 1978. Susan grew up in Colorado Springs where she owned a restaurant and lounge and managed several night clubs. She also owned a restaurant and lounge in Cheyenne, Wyoming.

FOOD, SERVICE AND AMBIANCE

Linda and I started dinner with an appetizer of calamari: about a half dozen breaded strips served with a spicy cocktail sauce. The calamari had a firm texture, yet were light, very tender and had a delicate taste. From here, we ventured to their southwest-style cream of celery soup prepared with onions and cayenne pepper to give it some zing. Then it was a salad with Gorgonzola-dill dressing. Our taste buds were all a tingle and we had not even gotten to the main courses! My entrée was a large, succulent rack of veal prepared medium-rare with roasted red peppers, onions and herbs. It was served with rice, julienne carrots and snow peas. Linda ordered the shrimp Sicilian: five plump, superb shrimps well seasoned with capers to give it tang on a bed of linguini with a mild tomato sauce. This dish is now available on their "make your own pasta" menu that lets you choose from five pastas and three sauces. Ask for some extra homemade bread for the sauce. We were both very pleased with our selections.

Their dinner menu demonstrates creative style and international cuisine combined with unique specials. Some of the varied dishes are Spanish paella, Cajun jambalaya, Jamaican jerk chicken, homemade pizza and Pacific Rim vegetarian stir-fry. Depending on your mood, appetite or lifestyle, you can choose from three nightly special categories. "Down home" specials present good inexpensive home cooking and family-style dinners. "Spa cuisine" specials will acquaint you with healthy low-fat ingredients and preparations that do not sacrifice taste. "Decadent" specials are available if you want to throw caution to the wind and satisfy your heart's desire for rich foods. Their menu does change periodically, but they will prepare a former menu item on request. Lunch offerings include egg dishes for a late breakfast, homemade soups, salads, sandwiches and pasta. The mimosa Sunday brunch features Belgian waffles, Swiss pancakes and a variety of egg entrées as well as pasta, sandwiches, soups and a catch of the day.

Our servers were hard working and our dinner did take a little longer because it was Valentine's Day. Since our visit, the servers have changed their look and are now wearing black Dockers jeans and brightly colored T-shirts. Peter remodeled the entire restaurant in July 1997. The stucco walls in the dining room are sponge painted in a combination of light beige, California poppy and burnt amber. The formerly green tables are covered with copper flake paint. The old green cushion bench seats with yellow specks complement this new look very well. The restaurant appears bright, cheerful and inviting.

Beautifying the bright yellow, beige and amber walls are sconces, dried flowers, leaves and cones, and the artworks of Joe O'Connor displaying mountain scenes with old, abandoned homes, creeks and waterfalls. A wine rack with a basket of dried flowers is set between two columns adjacent to the bar. There is a fireplace along the far right wall and a series of glass doors leads to patio dining directly above Bear Creek where you can watch ducks float by. The Columbine is a restaurant for any season with creative fine dining and just a dash of elegance.

SPECIAL ONE-TIME OFFER: Buy one entrée and receive a second entrée of equal or lesser value free up to $15.00 OR receive 50% off one entrée up to $7.50. _____Owner/Manager. _____ Date.

Jamaican Jerk Chicken
(Serves 4)

3 tablespoons Scotch bonnet, habanero, or jalapeño chilis, seeded and minced
6 cloves garlic, minced
2 tablespoons brown sugar
1 teaspoon cinnamon
3 teaspoons allspice
1 teaspoon ground clove

1/2 cup canola oil
3 tablespoons lime juice
2 green onions, minced
2 tablespoons fresh ginger, chopped
Salt and pepper to taste
4 large chicken breasts

EVERGREEN

1. Puree all ingredients, except chicken, in a food processor.
2. Rub chicken breasts all over with puree. If chicken breasts have skin on, peel back skin and rub some puree underneath. Cover and refrigerate at least 2 hours or overnight.
3. Grill over coals or on gas grill until cooked through. Turn frequently to keep from burning.
4. Serve with rice and sautéed vegetable medley. Garnish with fresh fruit such as pineapple, mango, guava, kiwi, etc.

Wine Recommendations: Chardonnay, Sauvignon Blanc, or White Zinfandel

Recipe by: Peter Ertl, owner and chef

Keys on the Green
29614 Upper Bear Creek Road. 674-4095.
Directions: From I-70 heading west take Exit 252, heading east take Exit 251 (The El Rancho/Evergreen Exit). Follow Highway 74 south for 8 miles into Evergreen. The highway comes down a hill and narrows to one lane as it approaches Evergreen Lake. You will come to a fork where the main road bends to the left. Go straight, leaving Highway 74. Go .1 miles to a stop sign and turn right. The restaurant is ½ mile down on the left.

ESSENTIALS
Cuisine: Steaks, Seafood, Prime Rib
Hours: Mon-Sat 11AM-10PM. Sun 9AM-9PM. Summer (when golf course is open) APR/MAY-OCT/NOV: Also open Mon-Sat 7AM-11AM.
Meals and Prices: Breakfast/Brunch $4-$8. Lunch $4-$7. Dinner $10-$21.
Nonsmoking: Yes. No cigar or pipe smoking.
Take-out: Yes
Alcohol: Full Bar
Credit Cards: All 5
Personal Check: Yes, if out-of-town, I.D. required
Reservations: Only accepted for parties of 6 or more
Wheelchair Access: Yes
Dress: Nice casual
Other: Banquet facilities available. Service charge of 15% added to parties of 6 or more. No separate checks. Extra plate charge $3.

EVERGREEN

HISTORY, PERSONALITY AND CHARACTER

Keys on the Green was originally a golf clubhouse built in 1925. It was refurbished and converted into a restaurant in 1979. Current owner and manager David Rodriguez from Montana purchased the restaurant in 1982. Troy Nelson is the kitchen manager and has been with the restaurant since 1996. He has a degree in culinary arts from Elgin Community College in Chicago and has been cooking since 1988.

FOOD, SERVICE AND AMBIANCE

I was in the mood for steak and could not resist the owner's own house special, steak David. It was preceded by spinach orzo soup, a spice mild soup served temperature hot consisting of spinach, tomato, chicken broth, soft orzo, a tiny rice-shaped pasta, celery and onion. Perfect for a snowy December evening. The thick-cut tenderloin was nicely charbroiled and medium rare (just the way I ordered it), topped with "melt in your mouth" crab meat and fresh, long asparagus spears. Three of my favorite foods! This was an excellent steak dish. It came with béarnaise sauce, a side of plain but flavorsome squash, two long white bread rolls and a red carnation on a leaf of radicchio lettuce for garnish.

Several appetizers will get your dinner started at Keys on the Green: everything from chicken wings and sautéed mushrooms to steak bits in teriyaki sauce and a colossal deep-fried onion. Prime rib "while it lasts" is another house special. If you decide on steak, they have top sirloin, New York pepper steak and filet mignon. If you are undecided on, get an 8-ounce sirloin with shrimp, lobster or crab. Fresh trout and chicken entrées like chicken Oscar and fried chicken complete the dinner menu. A blend of Cajun spice may be added to any meat or fish entree for $1. For dessert, try some Montana huckleberry pie, triple chocolate fudge cake, Snickers cheesecake, turtle pie, homemade carrot cake or homemade pineapple upside down cake.

Some of the highlights from the summer breakfast/Sunday brunch menu are New York strip steak and eggs smothered with green chili, smoked pork chops and eggs, eggs Benedict, giant burritos and taco or chef's salad. Lite lunches like a stuffed tomato or avocado, a spinach salad or veggie sandwich are available for the mid-day meal along with burgers, sandwiches, green or red chili and house specialties such as chicken fried steak and a hot turkey plate. There is a children's menu with every meal.

My servers were very prompt, efficient and "on the ball". They were extremely quick on refills and clearing plates. Country music could be heard throughout these Arcadian chambers. Several large paintings of Indians in winter wilderness scenes adorn the log wood walls. My favorite is

EVERGREEN

a fox with two Indians on horseback camouflaged by aspen trees and snow. The centerpiece of this rustic restaurant, however, is the four-sided rock fireplace. Tucked away behind Evergreen Lake in the midst of pine trees and Bear Creek, Keys on the Green is a preferred mountain retreat possessing a natural setting combined with warm ambiance and service.

See page 153 for restaurant photo.

Montana Huckleberry Pie
(Makes one 9-inch pie)

4 cups huckleberries
1 1/4 to 1 1/12 cups of sugar (to taste)
1/3 cup flour
Pinch of salt
1 tablespoon lemon juice

1 tablespoon butter
1/2 teaspoon cinnamon
1/2 teaspoon nutmeg
Pastry for 9-inch double crust pie

1. Mix together sugar, flour, salt, cinnamon, and nutmeg. Toss huckleberries in flour mixture. Add lemon juice. Set aside while preparing pastry.
2. Spoon huckleberries into pie crust, dot with butter, and cover with top crust.
3. Slit top to let steam escape. Bake 40 to 50 minutes at 425 degrees.

Recipe adapted by: Troy Nelson, kitchen manager

FAIRPLAY

Once known as South Park City and Tarryall City, Fairplay was founded by gold seekers who were upset to discover that the best placers at nearby Tarryall were taken. Finding other rich deposits, they established their own camp calling it "Fair Play" and nicknamed their rival camp "Graball".

The following restaurant serves country-style American food in an historic hotel dating back to 1873.

Location of Town: Central Colorado where Highways 285 and 9 intersect. Zip Code: 80440. Area Code: 719. Population: 387. Elevation: 9,920ft.

The Historic Fairplay Hotel Restaurant

500 Main Street (Highway 9), PO Box 1987, 836-2565. 888-924-2200.
Directions: From the intersection of Highways 285 and 9 in Fairplay, go north on Highway 9 for 1/2 mile. The hotel and restaurant are on the right at the southeast corner of Main Street and 5th Street. From the north on Highway 9 (coming from Breckenridge), the restaurant is on the left just past the park with the Park County Library.

ESSENTIALS
Cuisine: Country-Style American
Hours: Memorial Day through SEP: 7AM-9PM (10PM Fri/Sat). OCT to Memorial Day: 7 days 7AM-3PM (Breakfast to 11AM, Lunch 11AM-3PM) and 5PM-9PM.
Meals and Prices: Breakfast $4-$8, Lunch $5-$8, Dinner $7-$14.
Nonsmoking: All. Smoking only permitted in bar.
Take-out: Yes
Alcohol: Full Bar

Credit Cards: MC, Visa
Personal Check: Yes, with I.D.
Reservations: Recommended for parties of 10 or more or on holidays
Wheelchair Access: Yes, but 3 steep steps at the entrance
Dress: Casual
Other: No separate checks. Service charge of 15% added for parties of 6 or more. Banquet facilities. Rooms available year-around for about $50/night.

HISTORY, PERSONALITY AND CHARACTER
The Fairplay Hotel and Restaurant was originally established in 1873 and known as the Valiton Hotel, after Louis and Marie Valiton. It survived a fire in 1873 and went through several name changes — McLain Hotel, Bergh

FAIRPLAY

House, Vestel House and Windsor Hotel — until 1921 when another fire destroyed the original building. Construction on a new building began in the same year and it opened on June 9, 1922, with a dining room, kitchen wing and sun porch.

A magnificent mahogany bar built by Brunswick (the pool table company) of Chicago was transported on wagon carts, before the railroads arrived, to Rachel's Place, a saloon in Alma, Colorado, right after its construction in 1883. In the 1920s, it was moved to the Fairplay Hotel. In 1934, the sun porch was converted into the Silverheels Lounge. As with many 19th century hotels in Colorado, this one is also purportedly haunted. The reported specter is a woman seen walking down the hallways talking to herself.

Olga Chambers from Washington State has owned the Fairplay Hotel and Restaurant since 1987 when she had the kitchen renovated. Scott Atchison is the manager of the hotel, restaurant and bar. He is an Ohio State University graduate in hotel and restaurant management, came to Colorado in 1990 and worked for restaurants and lodging in Vail, Keystone, Breckenridge and Arapahoe Basin before coming to the Fairplay Hotel in 1995. Liz Glendenning is their certified head chef who worked at the Hilton in Breckenridge before starting at the Fairplay Hotel Restaurant in 1995.

The Historic Fairplay Hotel has 21 recently renovated rooms with period antiques, iron beds, new bathrooms and modern plumbing and heating.

FOOD, SERVICE AND AMBIANCE

Meals at the Fairplay Hotel Restaurant are a home-cooked affair with everything made from scratch. I have taken pleasure in both breakfast and lunch at the Fairplay Hotel Restaurant. Their chicken fried steak has crispy breading and creamy white gravy. The eggs done over easy are just right. The pancakes are thin, light and airy. Their homemade mashed potatoes with thick, brown gravy is a likable change of pace. Just good country food prepared by good country folks.

The breakfast menu also features homemade biscuits with homemade sausage gravy, several omelet selections, breakfast burritos, huevos rancheros, French toast and breakfast sandwiches. Highlighting the country-style lunch menu are Liz's award winning green chili at the 1997 and 1998 Fairplay Chili Cookoff (her red chili placed 3rd in 1998), deli sandwiches, blackened chicken with the Fairplay's own special Cajun seasoning, beef burgers and garden burgers. Lunch specialties included pot roast that is slow roasted for 24 hours, homemade beef stew and fried chicken.

Tablecloths and candlelight enhance the ambiance for dinner which showcases prime rib, ribeye, broiled salmon, chicken with a homemade pesto sauce, buffalo burgers, seafood fettuccini, pasta primavera and the lunch specialties. There is a children's menu and you can complete your meal with a warm piece of fresh baked apple, blueberry, pecan pie á la mode or brownie sundae made with homemade brownies.

A table of 8 and another one of 7 came in right before I arrived for lunch so I had a bit of a wait. My server commented, "We believe in old fashion service". I guess things moved slower back in those days. I wasn't in a hurry so I didn't mind. (Service was much faster on my second visit for breakfast.) Besides, there's a lot to absorb and look at in a place that's over 100 years old. To the right of the restaurant's entrance is a tapestry depicting peaches. The shelf along the back wall is decked with a kerosene lamp, glass colored bottles, an old washboard, a toy donkey, a sack of potatoes and a tin of lard. Most of the fixtures and the structure, the mahogany wood beams and posts and the oak wood floors are original dating back to 1922.

A radio playing rock oldies could be faintly heard in the background. Artwork describing the Californian coastline, a log wood fence with aspen trees and mountains, and a trade meeting between Indians and white men on the plains embellished the dining room decked with white curtains and frosted and stenciled chandeliers and sconces. The opening for the rock fireplace is filled with red bricks. Wine bottles and kerosene lamps are set on the mantel while overhead is a large mirror. To the right of the fireplace is a platform used for bands after 9PM.

I passed over uneven, creaky floorboards as I entered the Silverheels Lounge with its restored oak wood floors and discovered that the fireplace is double-sided with a bullhead and horns over the mantle. The saloon is adorned with red cloth curtains, a picture of the hotel circa 1930, three heads of deer with antlers and old, wagon wheel chandeliers with gas light switches. To the right of the lounge is a meeting room used for special parties. My placemat described the Fairplay Hotel as "homey, historic and hospitable" and the restaurant definitely possessed all three. The Historic Fairplay Hotel Restaurant is a place filled with many family artifacts and a wealth of country flavor.

FAIRPLAY

SPECIAL ONE-TIME OFFER: Buy one entrée and receive a second entrée of equal or lesser value free up to $10.00 OR receive 50% off one entrée up to $5.00. _____Owner/Manager. _____ Date.

Green Chile
(Serves 8)

1 pound pork, diced
1 medium onion, chopped
1 medium green pepper, chopped
1 tablespoon jalapeños, diced
1 1/3 cups canned diced tomatoes in juice
1 1/4 cups canned chopped green chilies
1 quart pork or chicken stock
1 tablespoon ground cumin or to taste
1 1/2 tablespoons New Mexico ground chili or chili powder to taste

1. Sauté diced pork in small amount of oil.
2. Add onion, green pepper, and jalapeño. Sauté 5 minutes or until vegetables begin to soften.
3. Add the remainder of the ingredients. Bring to a low boil.
4. Reduce heat and simmer for 1 to 2 hours.
5. Thicken with desired amount of roux.

Wine Recommendation: Trapiche Malbec from Mendoza, Argentina

This award-winning recipe at the 1997 and 1998 Fairplay Chili Cookoff is by Liz Glendenning, head chef.

See bottom of page 152 for recipe photo.

FRISCO

Swedish immigrant Henry A. Recen built Frisco's first log cabin in 1871. In 1875, Indian scout Henry Learned named the townsite "Frisco City" after the short form of San Francisco. In its early days, Frisco was known for its dance halls and saloons. Today it is the center of Summit County with easy access to several surrounding ski areas.

The contemporary bistro shown here serves a diverse menu in a former tire garage.

Location of Town: Central Colorado on I-70 between Dillon and Vail
Zip Code: 80443. Area Code: 970. Population: 1,601. Elevation: 9,050ft.

Uptown Bistro
304 Main Street. 668-4728.
Directions: Take Exit 201 from I-70. Go east on Main Street for one mile. The restaurant is on the right just past Third Avenue.

ESSENTIALS
Cuisine: Contemporary
Hours: Mon-Sat 11AM-4:30PM. Sun Brunch 9AM-3PM. Appetizers and pizza 3PM-5PM. 7 nights 5PM-10PM.
Meals and Prices: Brunch $4-$8. Lunch $6-$8. Dinner $12-$27. Pizza $6-$9.
Nonsmoking: Smoking only in bar.
Take-out: Yes
Alcohol: Full Bar
Credit Cards: MC, Visa, Amx, Disc
Personal Check: Local only with I.D.
Reservations: Suggested
Wheelchair Access: Yes
Dress: Casual to dressed up
Other: Available for wedding receptions, birthday parties and other special events for up to 30 people. Locals discount 10%.

HISTORY, PERSONALITY AND CHARACTER

The Uptown Bistro opened in December 1996 in what was formerly the Frisco Tire Garage. New owners Wayne and Cindy Spaulding did a remarkable remodeling job converting the former auto garage into a restaurant. They also own the Blue River Bistro in Breckenridge and have been in the restaurant business together since 1979.

Floor Manager Diane Cook is from Cape Cod, has been in restaurants since the late 1970s and previously managed The Wellington Inn and Blue Spruce Restaurants in Breckenridge. Chef Donovan Cornish taught culinary school in New England, has been cooking since 1979,

FRISCO

worked previously at Beano's Cabin in Beaver Creek and formerly owned Café Paradiso in Denver. Diane and Donovan have been with the Uptown Bistro since its inception. Jen Slivatz does the baking for both of the Spauldings' restaurants. The Uptown Bistro was the winner of both the Judge's Choice and People's Choice Grand Award at the 1997 Taste the Summit.

FOOD, SERVICE AND AMBIANCE

Uptown Bistro presents a fundamental environment serving an inventive menu that changes seasonally four times a year. This is fine dining in a casual environment. For a first course, I tried a cup of grilled vegetable puree, the soup du jour. It was a very hot and flavorsome mix of squash, onion and peppers that went well with the homemade thick focaccia and sour dough breads. Their breads, made fresh daily, were served with olive oil seasoned with herbs, red pepper and black peppercorns.

For my main course, I could not resist the mixed grill of ostrich and venison tenderloin. Both had game flavor and, although I found the venison to be more tender and sweeter than the beef-tasting ostrich, I liked them both. They were a good combination with mashed potatoes, braised garlic sauce with whole garlic cloves, crisp grilled asparagus and green beans and a toasty waffle with the distinctively sharp and savory flavor of rosemary. Wild game lovers will like this dish.

Uptown Bistro serves several select first courses: grilled marinated quail with lingonberry sauce, roasted beet and fried squash ravioli salad, smoked crab enchilada, tuna tartare and seared lamb cakes to name a few. For a main course, you have your choice of pork tenderloin stuffed with herb goat cheese, grilled Colorado lamb chops, wood oven baked penne pasta with gulf prawns, grilled duck breast and jambalaya crab cake, or grilled tofu and Asian vegetable stir fry, all prepared in special ways. They also use that wood oven to make fired pizza including a Greek style, one with wild mushrooms and grilled chicken, and a pizza topped with prosciutto and fresh pineapple. A wine list of about 90 different bottles is at your disposal to go with your meal or afterwards with one of their homemade desserts like chocolate Tuaca mousse cake, amaretto cheesecake, key lime pie, cappuccino flan or fruit crisp.

Their lunch and Sunday brunch menus also have some tempting selections. In addition to the appetizers and pizzas offered on their dinner menu, lunch favorites include a calzone, corn-fried shrimp and oyster po-boy sandwich, Thai chicken salad and chili marinated salmon tacos. Some special items highlight the Sunday brunch like prosciutto, the Uptown benedict on herb scones, apple-smoked bacon, a wood oven baked frittata, snow crab hash, seafood crêpes, granola pancakes, pizza and brunch cocktails.

My server was full of smiles, friendly and very helpful. Light jazz played in the background. Uptown Bistro is a long, rectangular restaurant with rock columns, hanging plants and high windows to the left where the bay door entrances used to be for the auto garage. To the right of the entrance is a bar and lounge. Further down is a counter with high chairs facing the open kitchen where you can watch the chefs at work. There is a painting of a pestiman flower between the bar and kitchen and another painting of black-eyed Susans in the separate dining area in the rear. Uptown Bistro serves an exquisite menu in a relaxed atmosphere.

<u>SPECIAL ONE-TIME OFFER</u>: Purchase two entrées and receive one complimentary appetizer. Please present to server at time of ordering. _____ Owner/Manager. _____ Date.

Grilled Colorado Lamb Chops with Garlic and Raspberry Sauces
(Serves 6)

18 lamb chops

<u>Veal Stock:</u>
5 veal or beef bones (raw)
1/2 cup tomato paste
Pinch of thyme
1 large carrot, chopped

2 onions, quartered with skin on
3 ribs of celery
Cold water

1. Place raw bones in a roasting pan and smear tomato paste on bones. Place in a 450-degree oven, uncovered.
2. Roast bones until dark brown and nicely caramelized. This provides color and flavor to your stock.
3. In a stock pot large enough to fit bones into, place the cut vegetables and thyme leaf in the bottom of the pot and add the roasted bones. Fill the pot with cold water just covering the bones.
4. Put on the stove and bring to a slow simmer. Cook for at least 8 hours or overnight. Refill with water if necessary.
5. When done, strain, keeping only the liquid (discard bones and vegetables). Refrigerate.

FRISCO

6. <u>For demi-glace</u>: Take stock, put in a stock pot large enough to hold liquid. Place on stove and simmer until the stock is reduced by half. This concentrates the color and flavor by evaporating the water out of the stock.

<u>Garlic Sauce</u>:

1 medium carrots, diced	2 tablespoons pure olive oil
3 medium celery ribs, diced	3 cups red wine
1 onion, diced	2 bay leaves, whole
Thyme to taste	1 quart demi-glace
8 garlic cloves, whole, peeled	15 garlic cloves, whole, peeled
1 tablespoon whole peppercorns	Salt and pepper to taste

1. Sweat carrots, celery, onion, garlic, peppercorns, and thyme in olive oil in a hot pot until they begin to caramelize. Let them get brown, but do not burn them.
2. Add the wine and bay leaves and reduce this until it reaches the tops of the vegetables.
3. Add the demi-glace and garlic cloves and simmer this for another half hour. Season with salt and pepper.

<u>Raspberry Sauce</u>:

1/2 cup sugar	1 pint raspberries
1/2 lemon	1/4 cup demi-glace
1/2 cup water	

1. Combine sugar and water in heavy bottomed pot and squeeze in juice from half of a lemon, no seeds. Bring to a boil. Remove from heat.
2. Pour hot sugar syrup over raspberries. Add demi-glace then puree. Strain through a fine sieve.

Season lamb chops with a little olive oil, salt, and black pepper. Place on a hot grill, turning a 1/4 turn (for nice marks and even cooking) until they reach the desired doneness.

<u>Presentation</u>: Place mash potato in the center of a plate. Rest 3 lamb chops against the potato, stick green beans in mashers. Place raspberry sauce around the whole place and pour garlic sauce over the top of chops and potato.

<u>Wine Recommendation</u>: David Bruce Pinot Noir

<u>Recipe by</u>: Donovan Cornish, chef
See top of page 154 for recipe photo.

GLENWOOD SPRINGS

Glenwood Springs, home of the world's largest hot springs pool, was originally called Defiance for the defiant attitude of the miners towards the Indians who controlled the hot springs. The name was changed to Glenwood Hot Springs in 1883 after Glenwood, Iowa, and the mineral springs in the area. It was later shortened to Glenwood Springs. The Ute Indians were the first people to use the mineral hot springs. Later visitors included Doc Holiday, Kit Carson, Buffalo Bill Cody, President Theodore Roosevelt and Tom Mix, the actor. Doc Holiday is buried in a cemetery in Glenwood Springs.

For your dining delight, I have chosen a café and bakery serving homemade and healthy food in a 19th century building and two Mexican restaurants. One serving Sonoran-style Mexican food in a continuously upgraded building. The other uses recipes from Trinidad, Colorado, and has been serving dishes since 1975.

Location of Town: West of Denver on I-70 between Vail and Grand Junction
Zip Code: 81601. Area Code: 970. Population: 6,561. Elevation: 5,763ft.

Daily Bread
729 Grand Avenue. 945-6253.
Directions: Take Exit 116 from I-70. Go to the signal north of I-70 and turn right onto 6th Street (Highways 6 and 24). Go to the next signal, turn right and go over the bridge. The restaurant is on the right corner at the first signal past the bridge.

ESSENTIALS
Cuisine: Cafe/Bakery
Hours: Mon-Fri 7AM-2PM, Sat 8AM-2PM, breakfast until 11AM, lunch from 11AM. Sun 8AM-12PM, breakfast only.
Meals and Prices: Breakfast $3-$7. Lunch $4--$7.
Nonsmoking: Yes
Take-out: Yes
Alcohol: No

Credit Cards: MC, Visa, Disc
Personal Check: Yes
Reservations: Not Accepted
Wheelchair Access: Yes, including restroom
Dress: Casual
Other: Children's menu. Senior, over 60, 10% discount. Low-fat, fat-free menu available.

GLENWOOD SPRINGS

HISTORY, PERSONALITY AND CHARACTER

The Daily Bread Cafe and Bakery is in a building dating back over 100 years. It was previously a mortgage company, then a pet store followed by a taco place before John Leibundgut (meaning "Good Love" in German) and Terry Brass opened the Daily Bread in 1982. Terry formerly owned her own catering business, Bread and Roses, in Denver from 1978 to 1982. John is a former musician.

FOOD, SERVICE AND AMBIANCE

Daily Bread is a very popular place with both the locals and frequent visitors to Glenwood Springs. Located at the foot of the bridge over I-70, it is a busy place outside with lots of traffic passing by. Some of that traffic finds its way into Daily Bread and for good reason. They serve fresh baked goods and dishes with a smile in a comfortable, down-home atmosphere.

Being a lover of Greek food — I was in Greece in 1994 — I ordered the Greek omelet: a big concoction of fluffy eggs with fresh leaf spinach, chopped tomatoes, black olives and chunks of melted feta cheese seasoned with tangy lemon and spicy oregano. Linda opted for their scrambled eggs special with salmon and red onion. The salmon was also fresh and flavorful. You could really taste the salmon. Both meals came with potatoes that still had the skins on and toast. We were both delighted and highly recommend these breakfast entrées.

Homemade and healthy are the key ingredients to their cuisine. They bake their own muffins, bagels, fruit croissants, cookies and cakes. For breakfast, you'll see fresh ground coffee, several homemade toasts, French toast made with either their own sourdough bread or fresh baked cinnamon rolls, a vegetarian Benedict that substitutes Canadian bacon with spinach, artichoke hearts, tomatoes and scallions, and a host of other American and Mexican plates. A number of fruit juices, espresso, cappuccino and flavored lattes are available. The lunch selections feature their favorite deli sandwiches, like the tuna grill, the chicken club and Rueben on their homemade breads. Also offered are a bunch of burgers, a slew of salads with homemade dressings, a quiche of the day, homemade soup and desserts. Showcasing the low-fat, fat-free menu are the following fat-free items: whole wheat bread, granola, cream cheese, gazpacho soup, toast, mayonnaise, croutons and salad dressings.

Service is friendly, very attentive and first rate. Our coffee mugs were always filled and our server returned twice to ask how our meals were. As you enter the restaurant, there is a red brick wall to the left with framed posters displaying fresh bagels, apples with a slice of green pepper, and one of France. Also exhibited are oil and watercolor paintings by local artists revealing Gore Creek in Vail and the New Zealand countryside alongside flowers and nature scenes. Completing the decor are white-laced curtains, wood booths with flower-pattern tablecloths under glass and a wood trellis separating the baked goods counter from the kitchen. Daily Bread is a worthwhile stop on a busy street for health-conscious diners, good food lovers, vegetarians and carnivores.

Cream Cheese Peanut Butter Pie
(Makes one 10-inch pie)

Crust:
1 cup graham cracker crumbs
1/2 cup pecans, finely chopped
6 tablespoons unsalted butter, melted
2 tablespoons sugar
1/4 teaspoon cinnamon

Filling:
1 1/4 cups creamy peanut butter
8 ounces cream cheese, room temperature
1 cup powdered sugar
1/4 stick unsalted butter, melted
1 1/4 cups chilled whipping cream
1 tablespoon vanilla

Glaze:
1/2 cup whipping cream
4 ounces semi-sweet chocolate

1. Crust: Mix all ingredients and press firmly into bottom and up sides of a 10-inch pie pan that has been sprayed or buttered. Freeze while preparing filling.
2. Filling: In Kitchen Aid, beat peanut butter, cream cheese, 1/2 cup sugar, and melted butter. Using hand mixer, beat whipping cream with remaining 1/2 cup sugar and vanilla. Stir into peanut butter mixture and spoon into prepared crust. Refrigerate until firm.
3. Glaze: Bring cream to a boil. Reduce heat and add chocolate. Stir until completely blended and smooth. Cool glaze until it reaches spreading consistency.
4. Spread over pie leaving a 1 1/2-inch border all around so you can see the peanut butter filling. Decorate with whole peanuts.

Recipe by: Terry Brass, owner and cook

See bottom of page 154 for recipe photo.

GLENWOOD SPRINGS

Dos Hombres

51783 Highways 6 and 24. 928-0490.
Directions: Take Exit 116 from I-70 and go north to the first signal. Turn right onto Highways 6 and 24 and go .6 miles. The restaurant is on the left.

ESSENTIALS
Cuisine: Sonoran-Style Mexican
Hours: 7 days 11AM-10PM
Meals and Prices: Lunch/Dinner $5-$11.
Nonsmoking: Yes
Take-out: Yes
Alcohol: Full Bar
Credit Cards: All 5
Personal Check: Yes, with I.D.
Reservations: Not necessary
Wheelchair Access: Yes
Dress: Casual
Other: Available for banquets, receptions, weddings and other special events. Ample parking for large RVs, buses and trailers.

HISTORY, PERSONALITY AND CHARACTER

Dos Hombres is in a freestanding building built in 1982 for K-Bob's Steakhouse. K-Bob's closed in 1987 and the building laid vacant until 1992. Dos Hombres opened for business in June of that year after an extensive remodel inside and out. The remodel was a combined effort of the building's owner George Demos and one of the co-founders of Dos Hombres Restaurants in Colorado, Del "Spike" Howard. In 1995, a patio was added on the south side of the building. The current co-owner, operator John Webber, continues to upgrade and renew the restaurant on a regular basis.

Dos Hombres was founded in 1977 by Gloria, Scott and Spike Howard in Grand Junction, Colorado. The Howards started in the restaurant business in 1974. Just out of college, Scott and Spike were eager to get into any kind of business. Williams Deli was for sale at the time and the Howards were able to work out a lease-purchase arrangement with Danny Williams. Williams Deli in Grand Junction had some Mexican entrées and from there the Howards expanded on the Mexican items. In 1977, the family was able to take over a location less than a mile from the Deli and open Dos Hombres in April. Spike also owns the Dos Hombres in Clifton, just east of Grand Junction. Scott owns the restaurant in Grand Junction and two in Colorado Springs. Gloria has since retired and advises her sons.

John has been in the restaurant business since 1988. He opened Eye-talian restaurant and catering in Chicago before coming back to Colorado in 1994 to purchase the Quizno's Subs franchises on the western slope with partner Spike. In January 1995, he traded part of his investment in

GLENWOOD SPRINGS

the franchises to be a partner with Spike in the Glenwood Springs' Dos Hombres Restaurant. John is constantly making improvements to the restaurant, whether it be a new sign out front, a new-look exterior, a fresh coat of paint inside or an addition to their expansive collection of southwest art. He also takes a hands-on approach to the business to keep on top of things. You might find him cooking, tending bar or waiting tables. He does it all. Most of the recipes on the menu are the creation of Ann Stout, the kitchen manager in the Clifton restaurant.

FOOD, SERVICE AND AMBIANCE

Dos Hombres uses the Sonoran style of cooking from Sonora, Mexico, and prepares their food fresh daily. Chips are fried every morning in 100% peanut oil. Guacamole is made fresh daily. Sopapillas are made with 100% vegetable shortening. Only real sour cream and dairy products are used. Margaritas are prepared in a soft-serve ice cream machine for consistency and quality.

Wanting to try a little of everything, I ordered a combination of chicken enchilada, chili relleno and tamale with three different sauces. The chili relleno stuffed with Monterey Jack cheese and a soft bread coating came with the hot Dos Hombres green chili sauce with a green chili and tomato base and diced pork. The enchilada filled with plain shredded chicken and a soft flour tortilla was served with the mild green chili derived from a green chili, tomato and chicken broth base. The tamale with the soft, granular corn tortilla had the mild red chili with stripped beef. The trio made for a delicious variety. Homemade chips with their own tomato-based salsa with green peppers and onions were served before the meal.

Dos Hombres offers an extensive menu of appetizers, salads, combinations, fajitas, enchiladas, wraps, chili, daily specials and your Mexican favorites. Highlighting the lighter fare are Texas toothpicks, fresh cut onions and jalapeños dipped in light batter and deep fried; chili con queso spicy cheese dip; char-broiled chicken quesadillas; taquitos, chicken or beef rolled tightly in a corn tortilla; and Cancun salad with grilled chicken breast and pineapple. Featured on the list of favorites are a vegetarian special, a flauta (flour tortilla filled with rice and stripped beef or chicken), a Navajo taco, a fajita chimichanga, blue corn enchiladas, Kelly's special (beef or chicken fajitas rolled into enchiladas), burrito con chorizo and Old Mexico-style tacos fried crisp. They also make a variety of green and red chilies, hot and mild, and a white chili from Great Northern white beans and chicken breast. There are several delectable-sounding desserts with a Mexican twist, like fry bread with honey, Mexican chocolate mousse with a hint of cinnamon, strawberry sopapilla, flan Mexican custard, apple or

GLENWOOD SPRINGS

cherry empanada and a Margarita pie. If your mood is north of the border, try the key lime pie or chocolate brownie sundae.

Service was quick, courteous and efficient. Contemporary music played quietly in the background. Dos Hombres is a large restaurant that can handle a high volume of people with quick turnover. The Santa Fe-style textured walls are embellished with elaborate southwest/Native American/Mexican decor, most of it derived from Santa Fe, New Mexico. Spotlighting this theme are Mexican rugs, a map of Mexico, photos of old Mexican women, paintings of American Indians including some abstract ones, artificial cacti and chili ristras. Further enhancements include handmade sconces, cushioned booths in southwest pattern and colors, Budweiser Beer labels, Coca-Cola labels, a Clifford Peck poster and a painting titled "10 Little Rabbits" with 10 rabbits snuggled into 10 Mexican blankets. The bar and lounge up front presents Denver Broncos play-action photos and two televisions. The rock enclosed patio in front of the lounge has tables, umbrellas and a grand view of Red Mountain across I-70. Come to Dos Hombres for variety and variations on Mexican cuisine served in a festive atmosphere.

SPECIAL ONE-TIME OFFER: Buy one entrée at the regular price and receive 50% off a second entrée of equal or lesser value. Please present to server at time of ordering. _____ Owner/Manager. _____ Date.

White Bean Chili
(Makes 9 one-cup servings)

2 tablespoons oil
1 medium onion, chopped
2 cloves minced garlic
1 pound boneless, skinless chicken breast, cubed small
3 14 1/2-ounce cans chicken broth
2 15-ounce cans Northern white beans, drained

8 ounces green chilies, chopped
1 teaspoon oregano
1/2 teaspoon cumin
1/4 teaspoon dried cilantro
1/8 teaspoon ground habanero chili (optional, this is very hot)
Season salt and pepper to taste

1. Heat oil in frying pan or large sauce pan over medium heat until hot. Add onions, garlic, and chicken.
2. Cook until chicken is done and then stir in remaining ingredients. Bring to a boil and simmer for 15 minutes, stirring often.

3. Pour into bowls and garnish with cubes or shredded Jack cheese and onions.

Recipe by: John Webber, owner and chef

See top of page 155 for recipe photo.

Los Desperados

0055 Mel Ray Road. 945-6878.
Directions: Take Exit 116 from I-70 and go north. At the first signal, continue straight for ½ block. The restaurant is on the left.

ESSENTIALS
Cuisine: Mexican
Hours: Mon 5PM-10PM. Tue-Sat 11:30AM-10PM. Sun 11AM-9:30PM.
Meals and Prices: Lunch $5-$9. Dinner $6-$12.
Nonsmoking: All. Smoking only permitted at the bar or on the patios.
Take-out: Yes
Alcohol: Full Bar

Credit Cards: All 5
Personal Check: In state with I.D.
Reservations: Recommended
Wheelchair Access: Yes, including restrooms
Dress: Very casual
Other: Children's menu. Service charge of 15% added to parties of 8 or more. Banquet facilities available.

HISTORY, PERSONALITY AND CHARACTER

Jim and Annibet Griffin opened Los Desperados in 1975. Manager Rudy Lallier has been with the restaurant from the beginning. Cook Tim Marren started at Los Desperados in March 1998. He has extensive southwestern cooking experience and spent 15 years cooking with the Marriott Hotel Corporation. All the recipes used at Los Desperados are from Trinidad, Colorado.

FOOD, SERVICE AND AMBIANCE

I remember Los Desperados as a favorite dinner stop in the 1980s after a canoe trip on the Colorado or Gunnison Rivers on the western slope of Colorado. A more recent visit revealed that this popular Mexican restaurant has lost none of the food quality that I so fondly recall. I ordered the macho burrito, a large flour tortilla loaded with refried beans, seasoned ground beef and green chili. This very tasty, soft tortilla that you can cut with a fork was topped with a delicious homemade green chili, melted

GLENWOOD SPRINGS

cheddar, lettuce, tomato and a mild red cherry pepper. I found this dish to be very flavorful, yet fairly mild. Accompanying the meal were homemade chips and homemade salsa with green pepper and some jalapeño fire.

For lunch or dinner appetizers, Los Desperados offers chicken wings, nachos or quesadilla olé, guacamole or bean dip and Mexican potato skins. For late risers wanting an egg dish, Los Desperados serves a poblano omelet with creamy cheese and homemade poblano sauce, Yucatan eggs and three variations of huevos: rancheros, machacas and a la Mexicana. Headlining the lunch entrées are homemade chili rellenos, homemade pork tamales, tacos made with soft corn tortillas, enchilada plates, chalupas, fajitas, chimichangas and tostados. Also available are sandwiches and salads such as a Southwest sandwich with green chili strips and avocado, fajita sandwich, chicken melt, taco salad and stuffed avocado. For dinner, you can choose from combination plates, enchilada dinners, taco dinners, chimichangas, ensaladas, gringo dinners and seafood dinners. Their specialties include tamales, chalupa, arroz con pollo prepared with rice and green chili, relleno royale and taquitos. Most menu items can be ordered vegetarian style. For a sweet ending to your meal, deep-fried bananas with strawberry brandy sauce, apple chimi, fried ice cream and chocolatier's delight cake are featured.

Service was quick and helpful. Spanish music played throughout this Southwest-style restaurant regaled with two life-size figures of desperados, art work, and several papier mâché toucans and parrots perched on swings overhead. A pair of 55-gallon fish tanks and the desperados sitting over the stairwell were evident when I entered the restaurant. Original murals decorate some of the walls. The carpet with its Southwest diamond pattern in turquoise, maroon, pink and yellow complemented the natural setting and rugged, western look. A seasonal outdoor patio is at your disposal in pleasant weather. Hole up at Los Desperados for a while when you are in Glenwood Springs and you will be treated to some fine Mexican flavors.

See page 156 for restaurant photo.

SPECIAL ONE-TIME OFFER: Receive 20% off your total lunch or dinner bill for six or fewer people. Please present to server at time of ordering. _____ Owner/Manager. _____ Date.

GLENWOOD SPRINGS

Yucatecan Soft Shell Tacos
(Serves 4 to 6)

2 to 3 pounds pork roast
6 poblano chilis
1 large onion
1 teaspoon salt
1 tablespoon red chili pepper
    powder

12 flour tortillas

Tomatillo Sauce:
6 tomatillos (look like green tomatoes)
3 chili habaneros (also called Scotch bonnets, very spicy)
6 cloves garlic
1 onion

1. In a large pot, cover roast with water and boil until the meat can be shredded, approximately 2 hours. Add water as needed.
2. Remove meat, save stock.
3. Cut poblanos and onions into 1/8 inch strips. Put about 1/2 cup of the stock back into the pot and bring to a boil.
4. Add poblanos, onion, salt, and chili powder.
5. When onion becomes transparent, add the shredded pork and stir.
6. Cover, reduce heat, and simmer for 10 minutes.
7. Serve folded in warm flour tortillas with tomatillo sauce.
8. Sauce: While meat is cooking, remove outer skin of tomatillos. Place in boiling water for 2 to 3 minutes or until they begin to change color. Remove and place in blender. Add onion, habaneros, and garlic. Blend well. Let stand to cool. This sauce will thicken as it cools. Add salt to taste.
9. Hint: Lay the flour tortillas on top of the pork mixture to heat before serving. This dish goes well with black beans. A little sour cream cuts the "fire" if the chilis are too hot for your personal taste.

Wine Recommendation: Concha y Toro, a Chilean Merlot

Recipe by: Jim Griffin, owner
See bottom of page 155 for recipe photo.

*Salmon sto Fourno from the Cyprus Café in Durango.
Photo by Laurie Dickson.*

*The Cyprus Café in Durango.
Photo by Laurie Dickson.*

Le Rendezvous in Durango.
Photo by Pierre Andre.

Pasta della Casa from Mama's Boy in Durango.
Photo by James Salzillo.

Grilled Australian Lamb Sirloin with Goat Cheese, Caramelized Onion Crostada and Balsamic Mint Jus from Seasons Grill in Durango.
Photo by Jim Nichols.

Green Chili from The Historic Fairplay Hotel Restaurant.
Photo by David J. Gruber.

Southwestern Fettuccine from The Table Mountain Inn in Golden.

The Table Mountain Inn in Golden.

**Double Peppered Flank Steak from the
Back Street Steakhouse in Grand Lake.
Photo by Carey Barnes.**

**Fish Tacos from Su Casa in Keystone.
Photo by David J. Gruber.**

Shrimp Enchiladas with Jalapeño Cream Sauce from E. G.'s Garden Grill in Grand Lake.

E. G.'s Garden Grill in Grand Lake.

*Coconut Cream Pie from the Country Peddler in Granite.
Photo by Vi Matteson.*

*The Country Peddler in Granite.
Photo by Vi Matteson.*

*Oven Fried Chicken from J. C.'s Deli and Bakery in Limon.
Photo by Julie Coontz.*

*J. C.'s Deli and Bakery in Limon.
Photo by Julie Coontz.*

*Pulpos Guisdos from The Loop in Manitou Springs.
Photo by Mathew Gray.*

*The Loop in Manitou Springs.
Photo by Mathew Gray.*

The Historic Stagecoach Inn in Manitou Springs.

Refried Beans from Chili Willy's in Minturn.
Photo by Al Brown.

The Crystal River Way Station in Marble.

GOLDEN

Second capital of the Colorado Territory from 1862 to 1867 (Colorado City was the first), Golden was originally called Golden City and named after pioneer Thomas L. Golden. He, along with fellow settlers James Saunders and George W. Jackson, established a temporary camp near the mouth of Clear Creek Canyon in 1858. The building used for the Colorado Territorial Capital is still located on the corner of Washington Avenue and 12th Street. Once a railroad center associated with the metal production industries, today Golden is a tourist town and the county seat of Jefferson County. It is also home to the Coors Brewery, established in 1872 by Adolph Coors Sr., the Colorado School of Mines founded in 1874 and Hakushika Sake USA brewery which opened in 1992.

The restaurant described below is strong on southwestern flavor, both in decor and cuisine.

Location of Town: West of Denver
Zip Code: 80401. Area Code: 303. Population: 13,116. Elevation: 5,674ft.

Table Mountain Inn

1310 Washington Avenue. 277-9898. 800-762-9898. Fax 271-0298.
Directions: From Denver, take 6th Avenue (Highway 6) west past C-470 and Colfax Avenue (Highway 40). Turn right at the signal at 19th Street in Golden. Drive 6 blocks and turn left onto Washington Avenue. The restaurant is 6 blocks down on the left on the corner of 13th Street and Washington Avenue. From north Denver, take I-70 to Exit 265 and go west on Highway 58 to the Washington Avenue Exit. Go south (left) on Washington Avenue for 5 blocks. The restaurant is on the right. From Boulder, go south on Highway 93 into Golden and turn left onto Highway 58. Exit Washington Avenue and go south (right) for 5 blocks. The restaurant is on the right.

ESSENTIALS
Cuisine: Southwestern
Hours: 7 days 6:30AM-10:30AM, 11AM-3PM and 5PM-10PM. Mesa favorites 3PM-5PM. Sun Brunch 6:30AM-2PM.
Meals and Prices: Brunch/Breakfast $6-$10. Lunch $7-$9. Dinner $14-$20.
Nonsmoking: Yes
Take-out: Yes
Alcohol: Full Bar
Credit Cards: All 5
Personal Check: Yes

GOLDEN

Reservations: Accepted, not required
Wheelchair Access: Yes
Dress: Casual

Other: Banquet facilities and catering available for meetings and private parties.

HISTORY, PERSONALITY AND CHARACTER

The Table Mountain Inn originally opened in 1925 as the Hotel Berrimoor. Named after its founder John Berrimoor, it has the historic distinction of being the longest operating hotel in Golden. Distinctive Moorish architecture and brick mined and made in Golden was used in the $60,000 building. The hotel failed briefly during the Great Depression but reopened in the 1930s as the Cody Hotel, named after Colonel William F. "Buffalo Bill" Cody who is buried on Lookout Mountain above Golden. The Cody Hotel changed owners and names in the 1940s and took an art deco style in 1946.

In 1948, Lu Holland purchased the Inn, renamed it the Holland House and operated it successfully for nearly 35 years until he retired. During most of the 1980s, the hotel fell into disrepair and eventually closed altogether. In the early 1990s, two successful restaurateurs, Bart Bortles and Frank Day, invested $3 million for a complete renovation and overhaul of the hostelry, restoring it to its original splendor and southwestern décor.

Frank has been in the restaurant business since 1969, owns the historic Hotel Boulderado and founded the Rock Bottom Breweries, the Walnut Brewery and Jose Muldoon's in Boulder and Colorado Springs. Bart, who has been in the restaurant business since 1970, founded Woody's Wood-Fired Pizza that has six locations on the Front Range. He travels to Santa Fe, New Mexico, to pick up new food ideas and buy chilies in bulk. Bart also uses a local tortilla maker. General manager J. Allen Adams brings a quarter of a century of experience in the restaurant and hospitality business and has been with the Table Mountain Inn since 1995. Executive Chef Jeff McCleary began his culinary career in 1985 and received his training under John Bouchette in Atlanta and Chicago before joining the Table Mountain Inn in 1993.

FOOD, SERVICE AND AMBIANCE

I have dined here for both lunch and dinner with Linda and members of her family so I have had the opportunity to try several of their menu items. They use blue, red and yellow corn tortillas for their Table Mountain nachos with all of the usual toppings. The salsa made with cilantro and leeks was one on the best that I have found. They also serve a great burger here. The range burger was charbroiled, tender, very lean beef with pepper Jack cheese. Scrumptious! The Sierra club, spotlighted with avocado and herbed cream cheese and served on homemade Navajo flat bread, was a vegetarian delight. These are just the lunch samplings that I have tested.

On our dinner visit, we were treated to red and green jalapeño corn muffins with our meal. For an appetizer, we shared an order of their grilled wild mushrooms. It consisted of portobellos, shitakes and chanterelles, grilled in balsamic and soy, served with corn, black beans, sliced tomato and red onion, on top of roasted garlic smashed potatoes. Mouthwatering! The roast chicken tortilla soup was a southwestern pleasure featuring roast chicken, peppers, zucchini, carrots, celery, yellow squash and pimentos in a tortilla broth with strips of green, red and yellow corn tortilla laid on top. The red chili vinaigrette on the mixed greens salad with jicama and carrot was sweet and tangy. They also offer tequila-lime vinaigrette.

They have fresh fish and wild game specials every night. Ahi tuna on Spanish rice with pineapple pesto was the special this particular evening. The tuna was tender and moist, presenting a mesquite-grilled flavor. Reduced soy/balsamic vinaigrette was drizzled on the plate for an eye appealing and appetizing presentation. Crispy crab fritters filled with crab, rice and black beans provided the perfect side dish along with string beans. For dessert, we delved into a chocolate cherry tamale, a very unique presentation of warm chocolate and sundried cherries in a cinnamon-laced graham cracker masa with grilled corn ice cream, served in a corn husk with a mint leaf. Simply delicious! Other dessert options are caramel flan, Aztec mousse made with Kahlúa and coffee and apple berry crisp.

Brunch is a taste treat as well. You can wake up to fresh squeezed orange juice or, if you desire something stronger, order the Mesa Mary with pickled jalapeño and pepperoncini. Then choose one of their delectable entrées like cinnamon French-style Texas toast, Santa Fe benedict with chipotle hollandaise or the Table Mountain frittata with chorizo sausage and fresh pico de gallo. Lunch headliners include coyote salad with mesquite grilled chicken or salmon, pizza and club sandwiches made with Navajo flatbread and southwest specialties like chili rellenos con queso.

Start your dinner off right with a chicken quesadilla or the queso fundido, a baked crock of three cheeses with cilantro and chilies. Highlighting the list of evening entrées are Rocky Mountain buffalo rubbed with ground chipotle chilies and salmon or cumin pork loin slow smoked over cherry wood. The Table Mountain Inn submits a special "Wine on Wednesday" or the "WOW" as they refer to it. Lists of wines, margaritas, your tequilas, frozen specialties using liquor, specialty coffees, small batch

GOLDEN

bourbons and fine single malt scotch whiskies are on hand to complement dining experience

This is a very popular place for lunch or dinner but any wait that you may incur is well worth it. The Table Mountain Inn is a true southwest-style restaurant with its resurfaced stucco exterior, cedar wood vegas and white adobe walls embellished with strings of red chilies. Further enhancing this ambiance are frosted windows with scenes of Indians and horses standing on a mesa and the banderas used for napkins in colorful patterns of turquoise, yellow and red with prints of Indian pottery and arrowheads.

The bar and lounge to the far right was an addition used as a coffee shop when the building was the Holland House. Today it is adorned with Indian horse baskets, paintings of Indian pottery and a picture of a buffalo in a snowfield. Around to the left of the inn's entrance is the Lakota Room used for buffets, bars and fireside dinner. Adjacent to this room are the three banquet rooms: the Arapahoe Room, the Kokopeli Room, named after the Navajo tribe and the Del Rio Room. This restaurant can truly please the culinary senses. If you have been looking for some excitement for your palate, bring it here. The Table Mountain Inn is a testament to the flavor, atmosphere and spirit of the great area we live in!

See bottom of page 157 for restaurant photo.

Southwestern Fettuccine
(Serves 4)

Red Pepper Coulis:
1 3-pound can roasted red peppers
1 cup barbecue sauce
1 teaspoon chipotle chile
2 teaspoons cumin
2 teaspoons garlic salt
1 teaspoon white pepper
1 pint half and half

1 1/2 pound fettuccine

3 ounces chile oil
4 teaspoons minced garlic
3 6-ounce chicken breasts, boneless, skinless, diced
10 to 12 shiitake mushrooms, julienne
1 red onion, julienne
2 red bell peppers, julienne
2 yellow bell peppers, julienne
20 large shrimps (21 to 25 per pound), peeled, deveined, tails optional
4 teaspoons chipotle chile powder, ground
3 teaspoons seasoned salt
4 ounces toasted piñon (pine nuts)
3 tablespoons parsley and cilantro, chopped

1. <u>Red Pepper Coulis</u>: Drain and puree canned red peppers. In a large sauce pan, combine puree with remaining coulis ingredients, adding cream as necessary for consistency and desired heat. Bring to a simmer, stirring constantly. Add seasoning for heat (spice) as you like. If it is too hot, add more cream.
2. Pour 6 ounces of Zaca Mesa Pinot Noir into a glass for the cook to enjoy while no one is looking.
3. Cook the fettuccine to al dente. You'll need 6 ounces cooked per serving.
4. Heat sauté pan to the smoking point, then add chile infused oil and minced garlic, allowing the garlic to toast. Add diced chicken breast, brown well on all sides.
5. Add mushrooms, onion and peppers. Add shrimp.
6. Season with chipotle powder and seasoned salt.
7. Add your roast red pepper coulis. You'll be able to tell by looking, about 32 ounces is what you'll need.
8. Add cooked pasta. Toss thoroughly and serve in a large hot bowl, top with piñon and garnish with cilantro and parsley around the rim. This should make four big servings. Enjoy!

<u>Table Mountain Inn Hints</u>: Chipotle -- a smoked and dried jalapeño is used here in its powdered or ground form; not in adobo. Seasoned salt at our restaurant is black and white pepper, onion salt, garlic salt, and cayenne. We make traditional barbecue sauce and then add cilantro and orange juice. Chile oil is found readily in many stores or to make your own simply bring olive oil and dried chiles to a slow boil; quickly remove from heat, and let sit for at least an hour. The longer it sits, the more like chile your oil will taste.

<u>Wine Recommendation</u>: Zaca Mesa Pinot Noir (of course) or Gold Margaritas
<u>Recipe by</u>: Jeff McClary, Executive Chef.
See top of page 157 for recipe photo.

GRAND LAKE

Grand Lake was a mining settlement founded by the Grand Lake Town and Improvement Company, a group of Kentuckians. The town is located at the headwaters of the Colorado River and on Grand lake, the largest natural body of water in Colorado. Grand Lake is the western gateway to Rocky Mountain National Park. In the winter, the town is considered the Snowmobile Capital of Colorado.

Presented for your delectation is a classic American restaurant in a lodge off the main highway and an eclectic selection with a southwest flair in one of Grand Lake's three original buildings.

Location of Town: North-central Colorado at the west end of Rocky Mountain National Park
Zip Code: 80447. Area Code: 970. Population: 259. Elevation: 8,380ft.

Back Street Steakhouse

604 Marina Drive (in the Daven Haven Lodge). 627-8144.
Directions: From Highway 40 in Granby, go north on Highway 34 for 14.5 miles and take the right turn-off for Grand Lake. Go .2 miles and turn right on Center. Go ¼ mile and turn left on Marina Drive. Go another ¼ mile. The restaurant is on the right in the Daven Haven Lodge on the corner of Cairns Avenue.

ESSENTIALS

Cuisine: Classic American
Hours: Mid-MAY to Labor Day and Mid-DEC to Early-JAN: 7 days 5PM-9PM (10PM Sat). Labor Day thru OCT: Tue-Sat 5PM-9PM (10PM Sat). Closed Sun-Mon. Early JAN thru MAR: Wed-Sat 5PM-9PM (10PM Sat). Closed Sun-Tue. Closed APR to Mid-MAY and NOV to Mid-DEC.
Meals and Prices: Dinner $10-$28
Nonsmoking: All. Smoking only permitted at bar and on patio.
Take-out: Yes
Alcohol: Full Bar
Credit Cards: MC, Visa, Disc

Personal Check: Yes, with 2 I.D.'s
Reservations: Recommended for weekends and holidays. Suggested otherwise.
Wheelchair Access: Yes
Dress: Casual comfortable
Other: Children's menu. Service charge of 17% added to parties of 5 or more. Extra plate charge $3. Senior citizens special split entrée on Wed, 5PM-6PM. Full service catering on and off premises for groups up to 200. Available for special parties and receptions.

GRAND LAKE

HISTORY, PERSONALITY AND CHARACTER

The Daven Haven Lodge was originally opened in the 1930s by Les and Cornelia Piper and her mother, Mrs. Davis. At that time, the main road into Grand Lake was the street in front of the main lodge. The lodge originally consisted of a gas station and several small tourist cabins. Today, the tourist cabins are used as employee cabins. The Pipers and Mrs. Davis owned and operated the lodge until 1968 when they sold it to Tom and Betty Sowell. Over the years, the Daven Haven has been a popular destination family summer resort. Many people keep coming back to relive childhood memories, their wedding or honeymoon.

Carey and Greg Barnes have owned the Daven Haven Lodge and Restaurant since 1990. In 1993, they changed the name of the restaurant to the Back Street Steakhouse in honor of their rather obscure location. Carey began working in restaurants in Chicago in 1971 and has been in the lodging business with Greg since 1980. Head chef Kevin Mack started cooking in restaurants in 1976 and has been at the Back Street Steakhouse since 1994. He previously worked at the Brown Palace, the Marquis and Moulan Rouge Restaurants in the Fairmont Hotel and the restaurant in the Scanticon Hotel, all in Denver. He has worked with two of Denver's most respected and talented executive chefs, Christian Schmidt and Peter St. John. Bon Appetit featured the Back Street Steakhouse in their November 1997 issue.

FOOD, SERVICE AND AMBIANCE

The Back Street Steakhouse serves well-prepared, high-quality meats and seafood. Linda and I tried them both. She ordered the fresh-tasting and savory crab stuffed trout with meunièr sauce and spicy roasted pecans. Linda also enjoyed the New England clam chowder with very tender clams, celery, red pepper and mushrooms. I went with the dry-aged 12-ounce char-broiled New York Strip au poivre. This lean meat dish with very little fat had a flavorsome black coating, was topped with scallions and dice tomatoes and was spicy and delicious. A spinach salad with a sweet vinaigrette dressing, mushrooms and bacon bits preceded the entrée. Mixed sautéed vegetables accompanied the steak.

Chef Kevin changes the menu from winter to summer. Some of the appetizers and light entrées that you may see are smoked oyster canapés, crab and cream cheese stuffed artichoke hearts, baked Brie or beef Thai sticks with a spicy peanut dipping sauce. You can also start out with a teriyaki chicken salad, chicken Caesar salad or French onion soup. The Back Street is noted for aged and slow roasted prime rib served with a hearty au jus and USDA choice steaks. Jack Daniel's pork chops is their

GRAND LAKE

house signature item. They also have a variety of house specialties like filet medallions with crab and roasted pepper hollandaise, lemon-nut sea bass, jumbo prawns scampi, pasta puttanesca and barbecued chicken and baby-back ribs. For dessert, the Back Street offers homemade pies, cheesecakes and Kevin's special ice cream.

Our server was very friendly and courteous on a busy Saturday night. The Wurlitzer juke box in the corner where we sat was playing some soothing instrumental pieces. The dining room possesses rustic charm with nature scenes and family antiques and artworks. A series of Tom Dooley oil paintings adorns the walls presenting the Colorado Mountains, eagles in flight, horses fenced in, and old houses and barns made of wood and rock. H. W. Hansen depicts a cowboy and Indian on horseback in the desert west. A Frederick Remington painting shows a wagon train crossing a river while under attack from Indians.

The rock fireplace in the center of the dining room is decked with lots of greenery and a wooden duck. Wreaths hang on the walls and garlands draped the ceiling beams. Enhancing the surroundings are mini-photos of a foxhunt, embroidery by Carey's grandmother and several of the collectable "Daddy Long-legs" dolls placed throughout the dining room. Augmenting the environment further are a red water pump, Aunt Gert's clock with a sailboat scene and an old Alcazar stove dated 1913. The Back Street Steakhouse is a true "off the beaten path" restaurant that is well worth finding for its superb food and Arcadian allure.

SPECIAL ONE-TIME OFFER: Buy one entrée at the regular price and receive a complimentary beverage of your choice. Valid for every member of your party. Please present to server at time or ordering. _____ Owner/Manager. _____ Date.

Double Peppered Flank Steak
(Serves 4 to 6)

2 pounds flank steak

1/2 cup cracked black pepper
1/4 cup thyme, chopped

Sauce:
1/4 cup shallots, sliced
2 tablespoons whole butter
1 cup crimini mushrooms, sliced
2 Rome apples, peeled, cored, and sliced
1/4 cup brandy
1 cup demi-glace (brown sauce)
1/2 cup heavy whipping cream

Marinade:
5 ounces red pepper paste
2 tablespoons Worcestershire
1 1/2 teaspoons chopped garlic
1 tablespoon garlic chili sauce
1 tablespoon granulated onion

1. In a bowl, mix together ingredients for marinade and coat flank steak completely.
2. Mix together pepper and thyme and pack mixture on both sides of meat. Cover and marinate at room temperature for 3 to 4 hours or refrigerate overnight.
3. In a hot skillet, sear steak until crispy on both sides. Don't overcook. Place on a baking sheet and cook to internal temperature of 130 degrees.
4. Sauce: Grill apple slices until lightly tender. Set aside slices from one apple for garnish. Dice remaining apple. In a sauté pan, brown shallots in butter. Add mushrooms and diced apples. Sauté 2 minutes. Flame with brandy. Now add demi-glace and whipping cream, reduce by 1/3.
5. If you do not wish to make demi-glace from scratch, you may use Knorrs packaged sauce which you can find in your local grocery store in the soup or sauce sections.
6. To Serve: Slice 4 to 6 ounces of meat across the grain and fan onto the plate. Ladle 3 to 5 ounces of sauce over meat and garnish with a grilled apple slice. Serve with desired vegetable and starch.

Wine Recommendations: George Du Boeuf, Beaujolais Villages, 1995 or Chateau Souverain Cabernet Sauvignon, 1996

Recipe by: Kevin Mack, head chef
See top of page 158 for recipe photo.

GRAND LAKE

E. G.'s Garden Grill

1000 Grand Avenue. 627-8404.
Directions: From Highway 40 in Granby, go north on Highway 34 for 14.5 miles and take the right turn-off for Grand Lake (bearing left will lead you into Rocky Mountain National Park). Go about 1 mile into town on Grand Avenue to the stop sign at Garfield Street. The restaurant is on the right on the southeast corner of Grand Avenue and Garfield Street.

ESSENTIALS

Cuisine: Eclectic with a Southwest Flair
Hours: JUN-SEP: 7 days 11AM-10PM. OCT-MAY: Thu-Tue 12PM-9PM. Closed Wed.
Meals and Prices: Lunch $7-$11 Dinner $12-$24.
Nonsmoking: All. Smoking only permitted at the bar.
Take-out: Yes
Alcohol: Full Bar
Credit Cards: MC, Visa, Amx, Disc

Personal Check: Yes, with I.D.
Reservations: Accepted
Wheelchair Access: Yes
Dress: Casual
Other: Children's menu. Service charge of 15% may be added to parties of 5 or more. One check per table. Split entrée plates $4 extra. On or off premise catering. Available for private parties, receptions and banquets.

HISTORY, PERSONALITY AND CHARACTER

E. G.'s Garden Grill is in one of three original buildings in Grand Lake built in 1910. It began as a hotel providing lodging for summer tourism. From the early 1970s to 1992, it was Squeaky Bob's Restaurant. In 1992, Judy Lorens and her two sons, E. G. and Stanton, opened E. G.'s Garden Grill. E. G. has been in the restaurant business since 1978. He graduated from the New England Culinary Institute in 1989, served an internship in San Diego and worked previously at Caroline's Cuisine in Grand Lake and the Grand Lake Lodge. E. G. is the kitchen manager. Stanton began working in restaurants in the mid-1980s as a waiter at the Grand Lake Lodge. He is your host and server. Judy prepares the desserts. E. G.'s. was chosen "Best Out-of-Towner" restaurant by Greg Moody in the October/November issue of "5280", Denver's Mile-High Magazine.

FOOD, SERVICE AND AMBIANCE

E. G.'s presents "a potpourri of creative cuisine" with made from scratch stocks, soups and sauces. I stopped here for lunch and ordered one of their specialty sandwiches, E. G.'s club sub. It came with turkey, black pepper bacon, avocado and cilantro mayonnaise on a pleasing, lightly toasted French roll. This was a tasty, flavorful mixture of fresh ingredients. For dessert, I treated myself to a piece of Judy's homemade key lime pie with a creamy, sweet, tart and delicious filling on a light graham cracker crust. It was topped with whipped cream and a twisted lime slice and presented on a plate drizzled with chocolate. Mmmm!

Other specialty sandwiches on the menu were the shrimp po boy with Havarti cheese and the mustard catfish. From the grill, E. G. offers a Colorado sirloin burger, New York steak sandwich and Barb's baby-back ribs with E. G.'s homemade barbecue sauce. Pizza is another option with 12" pies in either the traditional style with tomato sauce or the special gourmet variety with olive oil, garlic and fresh herbs.

For an appetizer at lunch or dinner, you might try the fried calamari, Baja fish taco or the basket of onion rings. The dinner only small plates include buffalo flautas with homemade green chili, sautéed wild mushrooms and filo wrapped Brie cheese. Homemade soup of the day, homemade green chili, grilled chicken salad and Green salad are available for your enjoyment. Highlighting the dinner entrées are shrimp enchiladas, grilled pork tenderloin with mango habanero sauce, one-half roasted duck, stuffed chicken breast and linguini with sundried tomato pesto and asparagus spears. For a sweet ending to your meal, you should select one of their cheesecakes or homemade desserts like mud pie, banana cream pie or a Mexican chocolate sundae.

Stanton was a most gracious host and server greeting locals by their first name and out-of-towners like myself with equal aplomb. Classic tunes and light jazz filled the air. E. G.'s is a one-room divided restaurant with a fireplace and rock hearth at one end and a piano in the corner. Local artist Lola Clark has embellished the dining room with her watercolors representing Grand Lake, Rocky Mountain grandeur, an Indian pueblo, a downhill skier and Jimmy the Jester. Adorning the corner walls where the piano was located are two engaging art works. One is a picture of seven waiters in black coats, black ties and white skirts carrying wine bottles and glasses on trays. The other is a large color caricature map of the "Polo Lounge" by Lee Roy Nieman with numerous Hollywood great personalities like Gregory Peck, Johnny Carson, Dean Martin, Frank Sinatra, Cary Grant and Humphrey Bogart. Stained-glass artworks depicting a deer in the mountains and a fruit basket beautify the right wall.

In the spring of 1998, a new wood floor was installed in the dining room. By the summer of 1999, E. G.'s will also be a bed and breakfast. At the entrance to E. G.'s is Barb's Bar and Beer Garden serving lunch and dinner during the summer months. Visit E. G.'s and you will be treated to fabulous food served by friendly people in an old-fashioned atmosphere.

GRAND LAKE

See bottom of page 159 for restaurant photo.

Shrimp Enchiladas with Jalapeño Cream Sauce
(Serves 5)

Enchilada Filling:
- 1/2 red bell pepper, cut into thin strips
- 1/2 green bell pepper, cut into thin strips
- 1/2 red onion, cut into thin strips
- 1/8 cup olive oil
- 1 tablespoon minced garlic
- 2 pounds raw shrimp, peeled and deveined
- 1 teaspoon ground coriander
- 1 teaspoon chili powder
- 1/2 teaspoon onion powder
- 1/2 teaspoon garlic powder
- 1/2 teaspoon ground cumin
- Salt and pepper to taste

Cream Sauce:
- 1 quart heavy cream
- 1/4 cup diced, pickled jalapeños
- 3 tablespoons juice from pickled jalapeños
- Salt and pepper to taste
- Cornstarch

15 5-inch corn tortillas (3 per person)
2 1/2 cups cooked black beans

Garnish:
- Cheddar cheese
- Fresh tomatoes, sliced
- Zucchini, sliced, grilled
- Fresh cilantro, chopped

1. Filling: Sauté the peppers and onion in olive oil and garlic until tender. Add shrimp and all herbs to onion and pepper mix. Continue to sauté about 5 minutes until shrimps are cooked through. Cool before wrapping in corn tortillas.
2. Sauce: Bring all ingredients to a boil. Thicken with cornstarch to a sauce consistency.
3. Roll enchiladas and place 3 per person on an oven-proof plate. Place 1/2 cup cooked black beans on plate with enchiladas. Ladle cream sauce on top and place in a 400-degree oven for 20 minutes.
4. Garnish with white cheddar cheese, sliced fresh tomatoes, and grilled zucchini and fresh chopped cilantro.

Wine Recommendations: Bouchaine Russian River Gewürztraminer or Dry Creek Fume Blanc

Recipe by: E. G. Stanton, owner and chef

See top of page 159 for recipe photo.

GRANITE

Named after the barren, rocky granite deposits in the area, Granite was originally a gold-mining camp. It was once the seat of Lake County and the temporary seat of Chaffee County.

Submitted for your approval is a country restaurant serving home-cooked meals in a former housing unit for railroad workers.

Location of Town: Central Colorado on Highway 24 between Leadville and Buena Vista.
Zip Code: 81228. Area Code: 719. Population: 25. Elevation: 8,928ft.

Country Peddler

43169 Highway 24. 486-1679.
Directions: From the signal at Main Street in Buena Vista, go 17 miles north to the town of Granite. The restaurant is in a yellow building on the left (west) side just north of the Texaco Station. From the north on Highway 24, go 2½ miles south of Highway 82. The restaurant is on the right.

ESSENTIALS
Cuisine: Country-Home
Hours: End of APR-End of SEP: Mon-Sat 7:30AM-9PM. Sun 8AM-8PM. Breakfast until 11:30AM, Lunch from 11:30AM, Dinner from 4PM. Closed End of SEP-End of APR.
Meals and Prices: Breakfast/Lunch $3-$6. Dinner $5-$13.
Nonsmoking: No
Take-out: Yes
Alcohol: No
Credit Cards: MC, Visa
Personal Check: Yes, with I.D.
Reservations: Accepted
Wheelchair Access: Yes
Dress: Casual
Other: Available for meetings, receptions and catering.

HISTORY, PERSONALITY AND CHARACTER
The building occupied by the Country Peddler was originally an old railroad section house for railroad employees. In 1989, it was damaged by fire and repaired by Vi and Frank Matteson who turned the rental into a small deli. When the old railroad house was built is unknown, but during the Matteson's renovation, they discovered pieces of an old newspaper with articles about Rutherford B. Hayes, President of the United States from 1887 to 1881.

GRANITE

When their deli customers began asking for breakfast, Vi started a low-key operation with no menus. Vi would just ask what they wanted, then "go into the kitchen and whip it up". From this inconspicuous beginning, the Country Peddler has grown into a complete restaurant offering three meals daily. Vi and Frank have also owned the Granite Store next door since 1984. Vi manages the restaurant and cooks breakfast and lunch while Frank handles the store. Bill Shirlaw has been their night chef since 1991. He has also worked in Alaska and at the Mount Princeton Hot Springs Resort about 25 miles to the south.

FOOD, SERVICE AND AMBIANCE

I stopped at this quaint, small one-room restaurant for dinner and ordered the steak and shrimp combination. The soup and 25-item salad bar goes with all dinners and is highlighted by krab salad, potato salad, creamed pea with cheese salad, cole slaw and hard-boiled eggs. The soup du jour was temperature hot, but mild, beef vegetable with cabbage and onion. Four large breaded and fried shrimp came with the entrée. They were very crisp on the outside and moist on the inside. The four-ounce filet was wrapped in bacon and tender, despite being well done. The accompanying vegetable was crisp cauliflower topped with melted Monterey Jack and cheddar cheeses. Add some real mashed potatoes with brown gravy and I had one full platter of food! Expect good, down-home cooking and generous portions when you dine here.

Breakfast offers the usual eggs, omelets, pancakes, French toast, breakfast burrito, biscuits and gravy and chicken fried steak. For lunch, try a hamburger, soup, salad, hot sandwich like a Philly, Reuben, or teriyaki chicken or a cold corned beef sandwich. Their dinners specialize in hamburgers and steaks such as filet mignon and ground sirloin, ham, grilled halibut, chicken fried chicken or steak, country fried chicken, orange roughy and spaghetti. The soups are homemade by Vi as are the dessert pies.

Service was casual in this attractive and clean restaurant with a "home-spun friendly atmosphere". Weavings by Vi's daughter and paintings by William Stephan Coleman adorn the white wallpaper with a blue and red pattern. Matching this are white plastic table covers, white wooden chairs and white-laced curtains. The artworks depict apple trees, farm houses, rivers, trees and windmills. Complementing the white are blue-painted walls with blue wallpaper bordering the ceiling. The weavings also have a lot of blue and white in them. The Greeks would love this place! You will appreciate the simple, unpretentious country flavor found in their food, service and ambiance.

See bottom of page 160 for restaurant photo.

Special One-Time Offer: Buy one entrée and receive a second entrée of equal or lesser value free (up to $12.00) OR receive 50% off one entrée (up to $6.00). Please present to server at time of ordering.
_____ Owner/ Manager. _____ Date.

Coconut Cream Pie
(Makes one 9- or 10-inch pie)

2 eggs	1 teaspoon vanilla
3/4 cup sugar	1 tablespoon butter
3 heaping tablespoons flour	1/2 cup shredded coconut
7 large marshmallows	9" or 10" pie crust
Pinch of salt	8 ounces whipping cream
1 1/2 cups milk	Toasted coconut

1. Separate eggs. Beat egg whites until stiff. Set aside.
2. Combine egg yolks, sugar, flour, marshmallows, salt, and milk. Cook over medium heat until full boil, stirring constantly.
3. Remove from heat, add vanilla, butter, and coconut.
4. Pour into cooked pie shell. Cool then cover with whipped cream and toasted coconut.

This recipe was given to me by my mother-in-law who got it from her mother. The original recipe did not have coconut in the filling, only on top of the whipping cream. We took the recipe and adjusted amounts and ingredients until we came up with this foolproof recipe that has become one of our customers' favorite pies.

Recipe by: Vi Matteson, owner and chef

See top of page 160 for recipe photo.

KEYSTONE

Keystone's history is both rich and mysterious. As early as 1810, mountain trappers discovered gold and silver in the creeks and rivers but managed to keep it a secret until 1859 to protect their peaceful beaver ponds. John C. Fremont, guided by Kit Carson, led the first government survey and mapping expedition through Summit County in 1843. The first reported silver strike in Colorado was in 1863 near Saints John, 10 miles up the Montezuma Canyon from Keystone Village. The famous Comstock Lode was uncovered there in 1865.

My selection of dining establishments includes a restaurant and cantina serving California Mexican food in a fun atmosphere and a contemporary American tavern that is a restaurant and a mini-brewery.

Location of Town: Central Colorado on Highway 6 between I-70 and Loveland Pass.
Zip Code: 80435. Area Code: 970. Population: 325. Elevation: 9,547ft.

Great Northern Tavern

0091 River Run Road, Suite C6. 262-2202.
Directions: Take Exit 205 from I-70 and continue in a southeasterly direction on Highway 6 for 7.7 miles. Turn right onto Keystone Road (not marked), just past the sign stating "Skier Parking Use Gondola Road". This is the turnoff for people skiing at Keystone. Go 100 feet and turn left onto Gondola Road. Go .1 mile and park in the parking area on the right. Walk towards the south into River Run Village. Great Northern Tavern is the first restaurant on the right. It is behind a stone sculpture of an Indian with an eagle-wing headdress.

ESSENTIALS
Cuisine: Contemporary American
Hours: NOV to Mid-APR: 7 days 11am-10pm. Mid-APR to early MAY: 7 days 5pm-10pm. Memorial Day Weekend thru SEP: Tue-Sun 5pm-10pm. Closed Mon. Closed early MAY to Memorial Day Weekend and OCT.
Meals and Prices: Lunch $7-$13. Dinner $13-$26.
Nonsmoking: All. Smoking only permitted in bar area.
Take-out: Yes
Alcohol: Full Bar
Credit Cards: All 5
Personal Check: Yes, with I.D.
Reservations: Recommended in ski season and summer.
Wheelchair Access: Yes
Dress: Ski cloths and casual

Other: Service charge of 18% added to parties of 8 or more.

Available for banquets, weddings and large parties.

HISTORY, PERSONALITY AND CHARACTER

Bill Ferguson, Buck Warfield and Donna Crown opened the Great Northern Tavern on March 1, 1997, in a new building. Bill has owned the Avenue Grill in Denver since the late 1980s and opened the Great Northern Tavern in the Denver Technological Center in the spring of 1998. Buck is in charge of operations at both Great Northern Taverns and helped launch the Rock Bottom Breweries in Denver and across the country.

General manager Bob Fowles came to the Great Northern Tavern in December 1997 after working at Keystone Resort for 3½ years. He has been in the restaurant business since 1991, owned his restaurant in Bend, Oregon, and is a certified sommelier. Executive chef Tim Anderson is classically trained, has been in the restaurant business for over 30 years and developed the menus for the Great Northern Tavern. He has worked as an executive chef in Denver, Dallas and Minneapolis. Chef Larry Johnson has been with the restaurant since its inception and began cooking in 1994 at Keystone Resort.

FOOD, SERVICE AND AMBIANCE

My entrée at the Great Northern Tavern (GNT) was three delicious Colorado lamb chops rubbed with olive oil, garlic and rosemary that rubbed me just the right way. They were savory, juicy and flavorful. The chops came with roasted red peppers, corn on the cob, zucchini and red potatoes. I loved the taste of the roasted vegetables. They were excellent! Some sprinkles of rosemary on top of the dish provided some fine seasoning for this marvelous meal. A house salad with a sweet and tasty herb vinaigrette consisting of oregano and other herbs preceded the entrée. The salad was not tossed but rather comprised mixed greens topped with carrot swirls with sliced tomatoes on one side and chopped mushrooms on the other.

You can start your dinner at GNT with rock shrimp cakes; GNT onion soup, a true vegetarian soup made with porter beer, or a wild mushroom strudel. The tempting salads include pork tenderloin, smoked chicken and Caesar. For a lighter meal, try the chipotle-garlic rubbed burger topped with poblano-wild mushroom butter. Spotlighting GNT's "things from the grill" are London broil; the all-American, honey-glazed, Porterhouse pork chop; Atlantic salmon with a celery-herb sauce and a daily grilled shrimp special.

KEYSTONE

Specialties "from the stove top and elsewhere" are Rocky Mountain farfalle with buffalo sausage and smoked chicken, Great Northern venison stew, lamb and goat cheese meatloaf and roasted herb chicken. To complete your dining experience select from GNT's brownie terrine, chocolate crème brûlée, New York cheesecake and root beer float. Except for the grilled items, the same menu in smaller portions is served for lunch with the addition of a bacon burger, a burger with house made barbecue cole slaw, a grilled chicken sandwich and a Santa Fe chicken sandwich.

Some summer alternatives to the menu are spinach and grapefruit salad, mahi mahi with rock shrimp stuffing, Castillian shrimp and chicken fettuccine, Atlantic salmon with lemon zest cous cous and roasted chicken substituted for smoked chicken. Besides GNT's own brewed ales, stouts and wheat beer, they have an excellent and extensive wine list plus a prime selection of single malt scotches, blended scotches, cognacs, armagnacs, small batch bourbons, tequilas and ports.

Service was amiable and helpful. Light jazz and 1950s classics played quietly through the restaurant. Glass-covered, framed posters of national parks of the west featuring Glacier, Grand Canyon, Yosemite, Zion and Yellowstone beautify the walls. A captivating Honduran mahogany chandelier with a black lacquer finish and gold frosted glass hangs in the middle of the dining room. Additional lighting overhead is provided by what could best be described as "railroad track lighting". At the end of the dining room is a mammoth rock fireplace. The windows on the right faced the deck in front and the village square. The windows on the left facing the mini-brewery are stenciled in gold with the names of GNT's beers: Great Northern, Dakota, Cascadian, Western Star and Empire Builder. All of their beers are named after the Great Northern Railroad trains and their routes.

The Great Northern Tavern boasts two decks. The one in front uses a gas fireplace for après ski. To get to the one in back, you walk through the bar area and past a magnificent curved bar. This deck has a red brick floor, wrought-iron patio furniture and is used just in the summer. The Great Northern Tavern provides high-quality fare served by warm, sociable people in a relaxed, comfortable atmosphere with a touch of class.

SPECIAL ONE-TIME OFFER: Receive 10% off your entire bill excluding happy hour drink specials. Please present to server at time of ordering. _____ Owner/Manager. _____ Date.

Colorado Lamb Chops
(Serves 4)

4 ounces olive oil	12 lamb chops, cut and trimmed
2 to 3 sprigs fresh rosemary, stripped of stem, roughly chopped	1 tablespoon kosher salt
	1 teaspoon ground black pepper
2 teaspoon minced garlic	1 tablespoons ground dry rosemary

1. In a bowl, mix together olive oil, rosemary, and garlic. Add lamb chops, completely coating. Let marinate to 1 1/2 to 2 hours.
2. In separate bowl, mix salt, pepper, and dry rosemary.
3. Remove chops from marinade. Let excess oil drain.
4. Season chops on both sides with dry rosemary mixture. Place on hot grill. Cook to desired temperature. Serve with roasted red potatoes and vegetables.

<u>Wine Recommendation</u>: Ferrari Carano, Merlot, Sonoma Valley

<u>Recipe by</u>: Tim Anderson, executive chef

Su Casa

22869 U.S. Highway 6. 262-9185.
Directions: Take Exit 205 from I-70 and continue in a southeasterly direction on Highway 6 for 7 miles. Go one mile past the Keystone Resort on the right. The restaurant will be on the left on the northeast corner of Rasor Road and Highway 6 in the Mountain View Plaza.

<u>ESSENTIALS</u>
Cuisine: California Mexican
Hours: 7 days 11:30AM-2PM and 5PM-10PM.
Meals and Prices: Lunch $5-$9. Dinner $6-$14.
Nonsmoking: All. Smoking only permitted in the cantina.
Take-out: Yes
Alcohol: Full Bar
Credit Cards: MC, Visa, Amx
Personal Check: Local only with I.D.
Reservations: Recommended
Wheelchair Access: Yes
Dress: Casual
Other: Full service catering available in your home or at one of three restaurants in Summit County. Private dining room for special parties, banquets and receptions. Service charge of 15% added to parties of six or more.

KEYSTONE

HISTORY, PERSONALITY AND CHARACTER

Su Casa Mexican Restaurant and Cantina is the newest member of the Storm Enterprises family of Summit County Restaurants. It was formerly the Gulch Tavern in the 1980s, the New England Raw (oyster) Bar from 1988 until 1990 and the Bandito Cantina from 1990 until the spring of 1997. Then the building was extensively remodeled and redecorated to create a festive atmosphere in their large cantina and a cozy home feeling in their upstairs dining room. In November 1997, Dick Carleton and Jane Storm opened Su Casa, a sister of the Mi Casa Restaurant that they own and operate in Breckenridge. They also own and operate Hearthstone Casual Dining in Breckenridge.

General manager Pam Sletten has been in the restaurant business since 1987. She was the general manager at the Kickapoo Tavern in Keystone and worked previously at the Hearthstone and Prospector restaurants in Breckenridge. Both Pam and assistant manager Chris Johnson are dedicated to consistency of quality, offering a value-based experience.

Chef de cuisine Lisa Kahute has been cooking since 1982 and has an Associates Degree in Culinary Arts from the New England Culinary Institute in Vermont. She worked for Four Seasons Resorts in the West Indies, the Caribbean and Hawaii before coming to Summit County. Lisa cooked for six years at the Sunshine Café in Silverthorne and the Kickapoo Tavern in Keystone before coming over to Su Casa when they opened. She and corporate chef Bruce Carlton are constantly refining and changing the menu to offer a variety of new and up-to-date cuisine. They have both traveled to Mexico for special training. Though only in business since November 1997, the staff at Su Casa is eager to show you "the new kids on the block" can meet and exceed your expectations.

FOOD, SERVICE AND AMBIANCE

Su Casa provides many of the same authentic, unique Mexican dishes that you will find at its sister restaurant, Mi Casa, in Breckenridge. Two different homemade salsas and homemade chips are brought to your table. One salsa is mild with tomato, green pepper, onion and cilantro; the other is much spicier with serrano peppers.

The wonderful flavors of Mexican food came out in all the items that I feasted on for dinner. For starters, there was their homemade corn chowder with potatoes, tomatoes, green peppers, celery and green chili in a thick and creamy vegetable stock, sprinkled with red pepper and seasoned with Tabasco for a "touch of fire". It definitely hit the spot on a cold winter night. The main course was one of their house specialties, poblano relleno: fresh, fire-roasted poblano chilies with the seeds removed, filled with rock shrimp, cream cheese and achiote, a chili paste made from very hot peppers roasted. The stuffed chilies were encrusted in blue corn meal and served with rich roja, a beef based enchilada sauce. This dish had just the right mix of taste and seasoning. It came with black beans sprinkled with Parmesan cheese, a southwest medley of vegetables and two warm flour tortillas. For added touch and savor, the chilies and black beans were drizzled with strings of sour cream.

You can begin your Mexican meal with chili con queso (a Mexican cheese fondue), jalapeños stuffed with cheese, nachos supreme or Mexican pizza. Other house specialties include rock shrimp simmered or sautéed in one their distinctive sauces, hand-cut pork chops in a red chili and mango sauce and spice rubbed sea bass. For a lighter fare, you can order the tostado grande or chipotle Caesar salads. Their fine Mexican selection features veggie or chicken breast quesadillas, seafood enchiladas, taco burritos and combinations. Filet mignon, hamburgers and sea bass in light lemon butter are available for American food lovers. They offer some great Margaritas, I tried a couple of them, and specialty coffees and liquors to enhance your dining. For a finish, try their deep-fried ice cream, sopapillas or flan.

Service was very courteous and attentive throughout the evening. Su Casa is a two-story restaurant with a balcony dining room overlooking a cantina on the lower level. The cantina looks out onto to the Keystone ski slopes where you can watch skiers day or night. The dining room faces a wall of red bricks, tan rocks and false blue windows with shutters to provide the illusion that you are witnessing a street party below while you dine. Wagon wheel chandeliers and fans hang from the turquoise ceiling over the cantina. The dining room has a bamboo ceiling with in-set lights.

In direct opposition to the more subdued tones found in Mi Casa, Su Casa has a playful look with lots of solid, bright colors on the walls – pinks, greens, yellows and reds; and posts painted in splashy stripes of green, white, red and orange. Papier-mâché and plastic cutout skulls from Mexico and a giant three-foot high Boyson pocket watch made of metal add to the frantic environment. This wildly colorful décor is found in the bright solids of the red doors with blue door frames and the blue windows with green windowsills. The ambiance runs from the ridiculous to the righteous; from a toy monkey wearing a sombrero and Mexican blanket to the many Mexican religious artifacts of crosses and the Virgin Mary. Just past the host's stand, there is a "Day of the Dead" display with skeleton dolls playing music. An after life party is a popular conviction in Mexico where it is believed the real party starts after you die. In the summertime, you can dine on the glass-enclosed, open-top patio with wet bar, tables and

KEYSTONE

umbrellas. If you are looking for a fun time mixed with genuine dishes from Mexico, Su Casa is the place to be.

Fish Tacos
(Serves 4)

Batter:
32 ounce beer*
1 tablespoon salt
1 1/2 teaspoons black pepper
1 tablespoon granulated garlic
1 1/2 tablespoons baking powder
3 1/2 cups flour

*We use American-style lager for our batter. Any type of beer will work, so feel free to experiment with different flavors.

Tacos:
8 3-ounce cod fillets
1 cup flour
Vegetable oil
8 6-inch flour tortillas
1/2 cup cilantro, minced
2 cups shredded red cabbage

Sauce:
1 cup plain yogurt
1/2 cup sugar
2 limes for juice
1/2 cup cilantro, minced

1. Sauce: Combine all ingredients in a plastic or glass container. Mix until all sugar dissolves. Refrigerate until ready for use.
2. Batter: In a large bowl, combine beer, salt, garlic, pepper, and baking powder. Using a whisk, gradually whisk in flour, stirring constantly to prevent lumping. For a thicker bread batter, whisk in more flour. For a lighter, crispier batter, use a little less.
3. Tacos: Dredge each cod fillet in flour and shake off excess. Dip each floured fillet in batter, letting excess drip off then deep fry in vegetable oil at 360 degrees for 5 to 7 minutes or until golden brown and cooked through. Remove from oil and drain on paper towel.
4. Warm tortillas in a 250 degree oven for 3 to 4 minutes.
5. Top each tortilla with 1 tablespoon of sauce, 1 tablespoon minced cilantro, 1/4 cup cabbage, and 1 fried cod fillet. Fold and serve.

Beverage Recommendation: Cerveza or your favorite beer

See bottom of page 158 for recipe photo.

LA JUNTA

La Junta was originally named Otero after Miguel Otero who established the town in 1875 when the Santa Fe railroad was built through the area. The name was changed to La Junta, which means "the junction" in Spanish, and refers to the joining of the Santa Fe Railway and the Kansas Pacific Railroad. Two places of interest are the Koshare Indian Museum and Bent's Old Fort.

The following American regional restaurant with European countryside style offers a touch of class in a turn-of-the-century building.

Location of Town: Southeast Colorado on Highway 50.
Zip Code: 81050. Area Code: 719. Population: 7,637. Elevation: 4,066ft.

Café Grand'mere

408 West 3rd Street. 384-2711.
Directions: From Highway 50 (known as 1st Street in La Junta) turn south onto Lincoln Avenue (one block east of Maple Avenue and one block west of Carson Avenue). Go two blocks and turn left onto 3rd Street. The restaurant is ½ block down on the right.

ESSENTIALS

Cuisine: American Regional with European Countryside Style
Hours: Mon-Fri 11AM-2PM. Thu-Sat 5:30PM-9PM or by appointment.
Meals and Prices: Lunch $7-$9. Dinner (5-course) $22.
Nonsmoking: All. Smoking only permitted on patio.
Take-out: Yes
Alcohol: Beer, wine and limited mixed drinks.

Credit Cards: MC, Visa
Personal Check: Yes, with I.D.
Reservations: Preferred
Wheelchair Access: Yes
Dress: Casual
Other: Full service catering, on and off premises. Café available for special parties up to 30 people.

HISTORY, PERSONALITY AND CHARACTER

Café Grand'mere (Grandmother's Café in French) is in a turn-of-the-century building originally used as a carriage house for horses. The building was used for a barbershop in the 1950s and 1960s. Then, it was converted

LA JUNTA

into an apartment building before Rosita's Mexican Restaurant took over from 1980 to 1994. The property laid vacant for a year before Ron Charlton opened Café Grand'mere on September 14, 1995.

Ron started cooking in Southern California in 1981. He graduated from the Culinary Institute of Art in Hyde Park, New York, in 1988 and worked as an apprentice in Grand Rapids, Michigan. After spending two summers in Alaska, he moved to La Junta and turned to catering for 3½ years before opening Café Grand'mere, his first restaurant. Ron, who has been featured in Country Inns Magazine, is assisted in the kitchen by Jerome King. Jerome is from nearby Swink and did an apprenticeship with the American Culinary Federation.

FOOD, SERVICE AND AMBIANCE

When I arrived at Café Grand'mere, I was greeted on the street-side patio by the very affable Ron Charlton. He presented an enticing description of their five-course dinner that led me into his restaurant for a delightful evening of fine food and good conversation. The first course was a salad of fresh greens with onion, carrot, mushroom and tomato in a homemade raspberry vinaigrette. This was followed by deliciously piping hot autumn squash puree sautéed in onion and garlic with parsley and yellow droplets of squash. A fresh cantaloupe sorbet was a cool and refreshing interlude to dinner. The main course was an artful presentation of salmon in the shape of two onion rings in beurre blanc on top of saffron rice. White wine, basil and rice wine vinegar seasoned the savory salmon. It was delicate and broke easily with a fork. Buttered zucchini sautéed in onion for great flavor, cucumbers in a dill cream sauce and homemade bread rolls accompanied the salmon. This delectable meal was satisfying without being heavy. For dessert, I selected some sweet and creamy bananas foster with raisins, hot caramel and vanilla ice cream. Other dessert choices were cherry cheesecake, chocolate mousse and fresh fruit.

The lunch menu offers a chef's daily special like garlic lemon chicken scented with fresh rosemary, European-style sandwiches and garden fresh salads. Choose from grilled rib-eye steak, vegetarian fettuccine, sautéed scallops, tuna salad sandwich, Colorado roast beef sandwich and oriental chicken salad. Dinner entrées feature a changing menu of pasta, steak, seafood and chicken such as chicken Marsala, fettuccine Alfredo, New York strip or vegetarian stir fry.

My server was very pleasant, professional and courteous. Classical violin and piano music played throughout the restaurant that Barbara Allyn, an artist from neighboring Rocky Ford, decorated with her paintings. She displays a variety of subjects like Oriental persimmons, a geography of hydrangeas, a landscape called "Montana Mist", a row of relaxing cowboys taking a "Brandin' Break" and a close-up of sea shells on the beach. Completing this motif are a picture of a teapot, lemon and Tabasco Sauce representing "The State of Something Good" and a painting from "The Lazy Hills Ranch". Additional artwork that changes seasonally includes many floral paintings, portraits and outdoor panoramas.

Café Grand'mere is an intimate, one-room restaurant in blues, greens and mauves with a coo-coo clock and a shelf over the front window decked with ceramic pots and hanging plants. The red brick patio on the sidewalk, with bricks from Pueblo, Colorado, extend about four feet into the restaurant. Black-iron tables and chairs are used outside for lunch, weather permitting. An iron fence made locally with iron from Italy enclosed a solid granite waterfalls, red and white begonias, dwarf Alberta spruces and ferns. The top of the patio is covered with a greenhouse shade cloth when in use. Café Grand'mere is a classy American Regional and European Restaurant, a rare find on Colorado's eastern plains.

SPECIAL ONE-TIME OFFER: Buy one entrée at the regular price and receive a complimentary glass of house wine. Valid for every member of your party. Please present to server at time or ordering.
_____ Owner/Manager. _____ Date.

LA JUNTA

Oriental Chicken Salad
(Serves 4 to 6)

Fresh Garden Salad:
Mixed baby greens or assorted salad greens
Fine julienne of carrots
Button mushroom slices
Assorted medium julienne peppers
Thin cucumber slices
Thin onion slices

Noodles:
1/4 bundle of cellophane noodles per serving
1/2 cup vegetable oil

Oriental Chicken:
4 fresh boneless, skinless chicken breasts
1 cup flour
1 teaspoon salt
1/2 teaspoon white pepper

1/4 cup vegetable oil
1/4 teaspoon sesame oil

Garlic, scallions, ginger to taste

1/4 cup dry white wine

1/3 cup prepared oyster sauce

1. Salad Preparation: There is no end to what you can use for this salad. Be creative. Keep it light and use any combinations. Lightly dress with your favorite vinaigrette or Italian dressing.
2. Cellophane Noodle: Heat 1/2 cup vegetable oil in pan just to the point of smoking. Submerge a small amount of the noodles that have been broken apart, allow for expansion and remove quickly. Note: Noodles that do not puff up are not usable. They are too tough. Do not allow your pan to overheat.
3. Chicken Preparation and Assembly: Dredge chicken in flour, salt, and pepper. In a large flat sauté pan, sauté the chicken in vegetable oil to which a few drops of sesame oil has been added. Allow to cook slowly until done. Add garlic, scallions, and ginger, allowing garlic to brown slightly. De-glaze pan with white wine. Add oyster sauce and heat until warm.
4. Slice breasts and place on top of salad greens and vegetable garnishes. Garnish with fried cellophane noodles.

Wine Recommendation: Chardonnay

Recipe by: Ron Charlton, owner and chef

LIMON

Limon was established as a camp in 1888 for the Rock Island Railroad and known as Limon's Camp. It was named after the camp's construction foreman, John Limon. Later, it was called Limon's Junction for the meeting of the Rock Island and Union Pacific Railroads. The present name was adopted in 1909 when the town incorporated. Limon lies on the route of the historic Smokey Hill Trail and the old Butterfield Stage Route. Today, agriculture, tourism and retail trade are the town's major industries.

The deli and bakery that I found prepares fresh, homemade baked goods for your breakfast or lunch pleasure.

Location of Town: Central-east Colorado on Highway 70
Zip Code: 80828. Area Code: 719. Population: 1,831. Elevation: 5,365ft.

J. C.'s Deli and Bakery

197 E Avenue. 775-8836.
Directions: From the west on I-70 take Exit 359. From the east, take Exit 361. Proceed into town on Main Street. Turn south at the signal for E Avenue (the side streets are in alphabetical order). Go one block. The restaurant is on the right on the southwest corner of E Avenue and 2nd Street.

ESSENTIALS
Cuisine: Fresh Pastries, Salads, Pastas, Sandwiches
Hours: Mon-Fri 6AM-4PM. Sat 6AM-11AM. Closed Sun.
Meals and Prices: Breakfast $2-$4. Lunch $3-$4.
Nonsmoking: No
Take-out: Yes
Alcohol: No

Credit Cards: No
Personal Check: Yes, with I.D.
Reservations: Not accepted except for groups over 8 people
Wheelchair Access: Yes
Dress: Casual and business look
Other: Catering on and off premises

HISTORY, PERSONALITY AND CHARACTER
J. C.'s Deli was built and opened in 1991. Julie and Jeff Coonts have been the owners since day one. Julie cooks, bakes and decorates cakes. Jeff also helps with the baking.

LIMON

FOOD, SERVICE AND AMBIANCE

J. C.'s Deli and Bakery has been a popular place with the locals for breakfast and lunch in the 1990s. Just about anyone that I talked to in town told me this. They prepare fresh, homemade pastries, bread, cakes, cheesecakes, brownies and pies. I stopped here for lunch and ordered a very hot and thick cup of homemade ham and bean soup with white kidney and lima beans, carrots, celery, onion and some pepper for spice. My sandwich to accompany the soup was a Monte Cristo — ham, turkey and Swiss on French bread sprinkled with powdered sugar. This was a sweet twist to an old favorite. It came with potato chips and pickles.

For breakfast, J. C.'s offers meats and eggs, a ham and cheese omelet, a croissant, pancakes, biscuits and gravy, French toast and a breakfast burrito. The salad selections feature chicken, chef's, Thai beef, spinach and seafood. Homestyle linguine and spinach fettuccini are the pasta favorites. A healthy choice of sandwiches and subs is headlined by ham, turkey, roast and corned beef, chicken salad, a Reuben, a French dip, a croissant club, meatballs and hot Italian meats and cheese. French fries are also available.

At J. C.'s, you order at the counter and pick up your drinks and silverware on your way to the table. The food is then brought to you. I found the people at J. C.'s seemed to really enjoy being here. They were helpful and full of smiles. A radio station with news and quiet, modern music played in the restaurant. A wooden cart with artificial pink roses is placed at the entrance. On top of the cart is a chalkboard announcing the daily lunch special. Some of their best-liked specials are oven-fried chicken, smothered burrito, chicken fried chicken or steak, meatloaf and chicken and noodles.

Baking accoutrements and posters depicting baking needs deck the stucco walls. The kitchen gear consists of a rolling pin, wheat stalks, a burlap bag and a manual mixer. The posters show breads, baking supplies and a mother baking with a child observing. Complementing this collection is a Ken Davis poster exhibiting eggs in a basket with the caption, "White Eggs Plus" and another titled "Wheat, the Energy Natural". Posters by Bob Coonts (Jeff's second cousin) revealing an American Indian in full headdress and the "Limon Heritage Museum and Railroad Park", just a block down from the restaurant, augment the ambiance. Dolls and a Colorado poster of columbines, the state flower, completed the setting. J. C.'s Deli and Bakery will give you a new start to your day in a refreshing environment.

See bottom of page 161 for restaurant photo.

LIMON

SPECIAL ONE-TIME OFFER: Buy one entrée at the regular price and receive 50% off a second entrée of equal or lesser value. Please present to server at time of ordering. _____ Owner/Manager.
_____ Date.

Oven Fried Chicken
(Serves 4 to 6)

One whole chicken, cut up
1/2 cup margarine

Seasoned flour:
2 cups flour
2 teaspoons seasoned salt
2 teaspoons garlic salt
1 teaspoon pepper
1 tablespoon parsley flakes

1. Line shallow baking pan with aluminum foil for easy clean up. Melt margarine in pan in 400 degree oven.
2. Dip chicken pieces into seasoned flour and place in pan in single layer, skin side down. Bake 30 minutes. Turn skin side up and bake an additional 30 minutes.
3. Serve with mashed potatoes, cream, gravy, roll, and vegetables.

Recipe by: Julie Coonts, owner and cook.

See top of page 161 for recipe photo.

MANITOU SPRINGS

Founded by Dr. William Bell, an English physician, Manitou Springs was originally called Villa La Font or Fountain Village. The town was later renamed Manitou, an Algonquin Indian name meaning "spirit". In 1935, the name was changed to Manitou Springs for the numerous natural mineral springs. Today, town of Manitou Springs is on the National Historic District Register.

The diversified choices here highlight a Polish, German and Russian café and deli, a newly expanded and remodeled restaurant serving Baja Mexican food and an historic inn with Colorado and western cuisine.

Location of Town: Front Range south of Denver
Zip Code: 80829. Area Code: 719. Population: 4,535. Elevation: 6,320ft.

European Café and Deli

935A Manitou Avenue. 685-3556.
Directions: Take Exit 141 from I-25 in Colorado Springs and go west on Highway 24 for four miles. Take the Manitou Avenue Exit and go 1½ miles into Manitou Springs. The restaurant is on the left ½ block past Navajo Avenue.

ESSENTIALS
Cuisine: Polish, German, Russian
Hours: MAY-NOV: 7 days 8AM-8PM. DEC-APR: 7 days 10AM-5PM.
Meals and Prices: Lunch/Dinner $4-$7
Nonsmoking: All
Take-out: yes
Alcohol: No

Credit Cards: No
Personal Check: In-state only
Reservations: Preferred
Wheelchair Access: Yes
Dress: Casual
Other: Deli with meats, cheeses and fresh breads.

HISTORY, PERSONALITY AND CHARACTER

Bozena Jakubczyk opened the European Café and Deli on July 4, 1996. She has been in the restaurant business since 1983 and previously worked at the Heidelburg Restaurant and the Broadmoor in Colorado Springs. Her son, Paul Jakubczyk, assists her. Both manage and cook at the restaurant.

FOOD, SERVICE AND AMBIANCE

I brought one of my tour groups to the European Café and Deli following a tour of NORAD in Cheyenne Mountain, south of Colorado Springs. All the restaurant's sausages, hams and other meat products are prepared from scratch in Chicago. A local bakery provides fresh breads. I ordered the pierogi, a Polish specialty consisting of six large, tender noodle dumplings filled with a delicious mixture of cream cheese, potato, bacon and onion, Russian style. This was the most filling of the entrées and was topped with fried onion, dollops of sour cream and parsley. The pierogis also come stuffed with sauerkraut, meat or potato. On the lighter side was beef goulash in a lot of brown gravy with sliced and spongy dumplings. Mashed potatoes may be substituted for the dumplings. The Polish meatballs are plain in a brown gravy with green peppers spiced with red and black peppers. Their sandwiches are very good and thick with lots of ham and cheese, tuna salad, chicken salad or turkey and cheese. They come on rye or sour dough bread with lettuce, mayonnaise and tomato and a banana and apple garnish. The bratwurst are two links served with well-cooked sauerkraut, bread and potato salad.

Two fresh homemade soups are on the menu every day. The selection varies amongst broccoli, potato, white bean, green pea, vegetable, kapusniak (sauerkraut), chicken, country-krupnik (barley, potatoes, carrots and ham) and others. Botwinka or borscht, a Vienna plate of meats and cheeses, and Romaine salad are also offered. Butter and cheese croissants, French rolls and toast are featured for a light breakfast in the summer and fall.

Our friendly servers rushed around busily to serve all, one or two at a time. The European Café and Deli is a small one-room restaurant. Dolls in dresses holding baskets of flowers adorn the shelves on the wood-panel walls. The white lace at the window tops match the white paper lilies in a large hanging pot. Electric lamps are set on tables with flower-pattern plastic covers. Augmenting this theme is a blue and white painting of aspen, fir trees, a stream and a mountain in a snow filled setting. A statue of Krakow Lajkonik, a Polish traditional man with a black beard in a red coat riding a white horse in a red jeweled cape, stands in the front window. Behind the counter, gourmet coffees, cappuccino, latte and espresso are being prepared. In the summertime, seating is furnished with two tables on the sidewalk. The European Café and Deli introduces bona fide Eastern European dishes and recipes in a complementary style and setting.

MANITOU SPRINGS

SPECIAL ONE-TIME OFFER: Buy one entrée and receive a second entrée of equal or lesser value for free OR receive 50% off one entrée. Please present to server at time of ordering. _____ Owner/Manager. _____ Date.

Stuffed Cabbage
(Serves 5)

1 large head of cabbage

Filling:
1/4 pound ground pork
1/4 pound ground beef
1 cup cooked rice
1/4 onion, minced
1 teaspoon salt
1/2 teaspoon pepper
1/2 teaspoon European vegeta (a spice available in European delis and some markets)
1/2 tablespoon minced garlic

2 tablespoons tomato paste
1 cup water

Sauce:
1 quart water
1/4 teaspoon vegeta
1/2 teaspoon pepper
1/2 teaspoon minced garlic
1 cube chicken bouillon
1 cube beef bouillon
2 bay leaves
4 whole cloves allspice
1 teaspoon dill
1 15-ounce tomato puree
1/2 cup cornstarch (combine with enough cold water to make a thin paste)

1. In a large pot of water, boil cabbage. Remove from pot when leaves begin to soften. Allow to cool and separate leaves. Trim vein portion to allow for wrapping of meat.
2. Combine all ingredients for the filling and mix thoroughly.
3. Place a portion of meat mixture on leaf and wrap to form the stuffed cabbage.
4. Line the bottom of a frying pan with half of the unused leaves. Mix tomato paste with water. Pour this mixture over the leaves on bottom of pan.
5. Place the cabbage rolls in the pan (it is OK to place them on top of each other).
6. Cover the top with remainder of leftover leaves.
7. Cover pan and cook on medium heat for 1 hour.
8. Sauce: Add spices and bouillon to water and cook on medium heat for 20 minutes. Add the tomato puree and cook an additional 5 minutes. Add cornstarch mixture to boiling while stirring the mixture. (This is a thickening agent. If you use too much, the sauce will be too stiff).

9. To Serve: Place 2 stuffed cabbages on a plate and pour sauce on top. Serve with mashed potatoes.

Wine Recommendation: A semi-dry red wine

Recipe by: Bozena Jakubczyk, owner and cook

The Loop
965 Manitou Avenue. 685-9344.
Directions: Take Exit 141 from I-25 in Colorado Springs and go west on Highway 24 for four miles. Take the Manitou Avenue Exit and go 1.6 miles into Manitou Springs. The restaurant is on the left at the corner of Ruxton Avenue.

ESSENTIALS
Cuisine: Baja Mexican
Hours: 7 days 11AM-9PM (10PM Fri/Sat). One hour later each night from Memorial Day Weekend to Labor Day.
Meals and Prices: Lunch/Dinner $5-$13
Nonsmoking: All. Smoking only permitted at bar.
Take-out: Yes
Alcohol: Full Bar
Credit Cards: MC, Visa, Disc

Personal Check: Local only
Reservations: Only accepted for parties of 10 or more.
Wheelchair Access: Yes
Dress: Casual
Other: Children's Menu. Service charge of 15% added to tables of six or more. Charge of .50 for all to go orders. Free refills on coffee, tea, iced tea, soft drinks and lemonade.

HISTORY, PERSONALITY AND CHARACTER

The Loop was originally a high-end steak house, piano bar and illegal gambling hall built in 1889 serving fresh cougar, elk, bear and deer. The first owner was Higginbottom, a famous figure in the Manitou Springs area. His living quarters were upstairs. The Loop derived its name from its location at the intersection of Manitou Avenue and Ruxton Avenue where the old trolley line used to make its loop. This was the end of the line. From 1981 to 1986, El Pardido Mexican Restaurant occupied the building before it returned to The Loop. This time, though, it was a Mexican Restaurant. Mathew Gray has been the owner and manager since October 1, 1991. The Loop has been remodeled many times with the latest addition in 1998 incorporating part of the original restaurant.

MANITOU SPRINGS

Manager Kelly Reynolds, who has been in the restaurant business since the late 1970s, has been with The Loop since 1992. She formerly worked at the Red Lobster in Colorado Springs. Kitchen manager Herron Villeareal began cooking in California in 1986 and has been at The Loop since 1992. He is one of 12 brothers, all cooks! (It sounds as if Mom had lots of help in the kitchen!) Two of Herron's brothers, also cook at The Loop, Ruben and Willie. Ruben has been cooking since 1970 and brings background experience in Mexican, Italian, American and Chinese cuisines.

<u>FOOD, SERVICE AND AMBIANCE</u>

The Loop has a full four-page menu of pleasures from the Baja Peninsula. The main ingredients used in their dishes feature chicken, beef, fish, shrimp, octopus, squid and vegetables. I chose the camarones Acapulco, a plentiful serving of 10 medium-sized gulf shrimps wrapped in crisp and dry bacon and deep fried. The plate presentation was a mound of Spanish rice in the middle surrounded by the bacon-wrapped shrimp, onion and green pepper. Homemade white wine and cream dipping sauce came on the side. A house salad with ranch dressing accompanied the meal. Honey-mustard was also available.

For starters at The Loop, you might try a spinach or chicken quesadilla, the nine layer dip or mini-chimis. Meat eaters will delight in one of their specialties like pollo borracho, chicken in a great seasoning mix sautéed in white wine, or carne Asada, tender sirloin marinated in fresh squeezed lime juice. Seafood lovers should select shrimp Baja sautéed in seasoned butter with onion and bell pepper, snapper Veracruz sautéed in seasoned butter and cilantro with carrots and tomato sauce, pulpos guisados or octopus with onion and bell pepper, or calamari.

Vegetarians will take pleasure in an almost meatless burrito or guacamole enchilada (they both come with beans that are made with lard) and the totally meatless fajita and veggie sandwich. Can't decide? Go for a Loop combination, Baja burrito or order à la carte. For a lighter meal, The Loop offers taco salads, burgers, spicy chili verde, tender roast pork in a delicious Mexican stew, or not as spicy chili rojo. The Loop boasts the "world's largest margarita" for your enjoyment but I will let you be the judge. All the desserts are made fresh at The Loop and includes flan, fried ice cream, sopapillas and sopapillas sundaes.

Service at The Loop was fast, friendly and courteous. A combination of romantic, snappy and slow music sung in Spanish played in the restaurant. The bar to the left of the entrance is divided from the dining area by a stucco wall and glass. An adobe, half-moon shaped fireplace has two mantels filled with wicker baskets and wicker dolls. Next to the fireplace is a piece of wood with a picture of three horses, one tan, one red and one gray, "horsing around". Highlighting the dining room is a very colorful tapestry of a market scene in a Mexican village and a three-dimensional model of an Indian pueblo. Embellishing this theme is an Ansel Adams poster of the Taos pueblo church. Further enhancing the pink stucco walls are turquoise sconces, maracas, a turquoise sombrero, baskets and neon figures of a cactus and a man taking a siesta under a sombrero. Relive a piece of the past in historic Manitou Springs and treat yourself to some exceptional south-of-the-border cuisine at The Loop.

See bottom of page 162 for restaurant photo.

Pulpos Guisdos
(Serves 4)

1 2-pound octopus	2 bell peppers, cut in small pieces
2 onions, cut in small pieces	1 8-ounce can green olives, sliced
1 cup (1 stick) of butter	2 cloves fresh garlic, minced

1. Boil the octopus for 30 minutes or until the skin turns bright purple. Cut into bite-size pieces.
2. Sauté in butter with garlic, onion, pepper, and olives, 3 to 4 minutes or until cooked to desired tenderness.
3. Serve with mixed vegetables.

Wine Recommendation: Inglenook Chardonnay

Recipe by: Ruben Villeareal, kitchen manager

See top of page 162 for recipe photo.

MANITOU SPRINGS

Stagecoach

702 Manitou Avenue. 685-9400.
Directions: Take Exit 141 from I-25 in Colorado Springs and go west on Highway 24 for four miles. Take the Manitou Avenue Exit and go 1 mile into Manitou Springs. The restaurant is on the right at the signal for Pawnee Avenue.

ESSENTIALS
Cuisine: Colorado/Western
Hours: 7 days 4:30PM-9:30PM.
Meals and Prices: Dinner $5-$20
Nonsmoking: Yes
Take-out: Yes
Alcohol: Full Bar
Credit Cards: MC, Visa, Amx, Disc
Personal Check: No
Reservations: Strongly suggested in the summer. Recommended otherwise.
Wheelchair Access: Yes
Dress: Diverse. More dressy in fall and winter, more casual in summer.
Other: Children's menu. Available for banquets.

HISTORY, PERSONALITY AND CHARACTER

The Historic Stagecoach Inn was, quite appropriately, built in stages. The rustic rock and log structure which houses the entrance, parlor and lounge was first built in 1881 as Helen Hunt Jackson's summer cottage. Helen Hunt Jackson was a famous American author whose novel, "Ramona", is still in print today after more than 300 printings in many different languages. The barn-like structure that comprised the main dining room, side porch and kitchen was the first electric company in Manitou Springs. The concrete stump from the 45-foot diameter water wheel used to power the generator is still in Fountain Creek. The foundation structure for the waterwheel was rebuilt in 1998 with plans to complete the waterwheel in 1999.

Following Helen Hunt Jackson, the building became the home of the Manitou Springs Journal. One of the former paper boys for the Journal, A. B. Armstrong, bought both buildings in the 1930s and transformed them into southern Colorado's premier fine dining establishment. He and his family operated the Stagecoach for many decades and were famous for their fried chicken and biscuits with cherry preserves. Famous patrons of the past included President Eisenhower and Pa, Little Jo and Hoss Cartwright.

In the spring of 1994, Gail Haberlin and Rob Stephens, two world class sailors and weary travelers, bought the Stagecoach. They carried out months of extensive renovations to bring it back to its initial charm. The Stagecoach was voted Best New Restaurant in the 1995 People's Choice Award presented by the Colorado Springs Gazette Telegraph. Appreciating comfort and good cheer after a long journey's end, they dedicate their restaurant to travelers everywhere.   Rob also is part owner of the Craftwood Inn in Manitou Springs.

Aaron Mattson manages the front of the restaurant and has been at the Stagecoach since July 1996. He began in the restaurant business in 1984 and was previously general manager of Yakatori Japanese Sushi Bar in Colorado Springs. Aaron also managed Café Express, a vegetarian coffee house in Flagstaff, Arizona, and the AMFAC Resort at the Grand Canyon. Jeff Norcross has been the head chef and kitchen manager since February 1996. He is a graduate of the Culinary Institute of America in Hyde Park, New York, and has been cooking since the early 1990s. Jeff formerly cooked at a seafood restaurant and a T.G.I.F. restaurant in California.

FOOD, SERVICE AND AMBIANCE

I brought a group of people here for lunch on one of my tours. My selection was the New York strip, a good 8-ounce piece flame-glazed just right with a touch of charcoal black on the outside and pink on the inside. It came with two tasty side dishes: crisp broccoli and spaghetti squash sautéed in white wine and seasoned with garlic, basil, salt, pepper and oregano; and Stagecoach mashed potatoes rippled with tiny pieces of skin, parsley, crispy bacon and cabbage. Since our visit, roasted garlic mashed potatoes have replaced the Stagecoach mashers. For dessert, I took delight in a piece of kiwi key lime tart, creamy good and sweet lime-flavored cheesecake topped with slices of kiwi.

The Stagecoach changes its menu each season. To start your evening, you can order buffalo sausage on a skewer, hot crab and artichoke cheese dip, fried calamari or stuffed mushroom caps. For a second course, choose from red bell pepper with chicken and mushroom soup, cowboy red chili with ground buffalo, chicken or sirloin Caesar salad or steak salad. Headlining the main dishes are steaks, chicken, fish and pasta. The Stagecoach uses Colorado Monfort beef and serves prime rib, tenderloin, top sirloin, ribeye and Santa Fe steak. A few of the favorite entrées are sizzling steak with mushrooms, onions and red peppers served on a sizzling platter with burgundy; salmon Wellington; camp fire trout dredged in seasoned cracker meal shrimps; and scallops in a light olive oil and white wine sauce with linguine and vegetable stuffed shells. For a lighter meal try their wild boar, venison or buffalo sausages; pioneer pie made with buffalo; prairie pie prepared with chicken; steak sandwich; Philadelphia cheesesteak sandwich or buffalo burger.

Service was both prompt and courteous. The Stagecoach is adorned in a western motif with artistic contributions from local artists. In the

MANITOU SPRINGS

bar and parlor area stands an original Manitou Springs green stone fireplace with a deer head over the mantel and a picture of "A Raiding Party" of Indians. Two antique Franklin stoves are used to warm patrons, one in the bar, the other in the new café dining addition completed in March 1998. Some of the regional artifacts include deer and elk heads mounted on the walls; a pink stone fireplace with a buffalo head over the mantel and a cowboy hat, boots, whip and brass trough pan on the mantel; and pictures that depict the wild turkey, the fall of the cowboy, Snake Indians, the hold-up, the last of the buffalo and an Indian chief in war dress.

Further enhancing this theme are C. M. Russell prints, Southwestern and Mexican blankets and a poster of Manitou Springs. The dining room upstairs with red cloth curtains was the bedroom first used by Helen Hunt Jackson. For those who prefer dining with a view or outside seating, there is an enclosed sidewalk café in front of the building and a deck over Fountain Creek in the back. Plans are in the works to add a new large outdoor deck onto the west side dining area in the fall of 1998. The Historic Stagecoach is a nostalgic, tasteful place presenting well-prepared food with comfort and elegance.

See top of page 163 for restaurant photo.

Blackened Chicken Alfredo
(Serves 4)

Blackening Spices:
1 tablespoon cayenne pepper
3 tablespoons paprika
1 teaspoon salt
1 teaspoon crushed red pepper
1 teaspoon black pepper
1 teaspoon dry thyme
1 teaspoon dry oregano
1 teaspoon parsley

4 6-ounce chicken breasts
1 quart heavy cream, reduced by 1/2
4 tablespoons Parmesan cheese
Salt
White pepper
2 pounds fettuccini, cooked
Tomatoes
Parsley

1. Mix together blackening spices. Coat chicken lightly on both sides with blackening mix.
2. Cook over high heat in an iron skillet for 2 minutes on both sides (time may vary on different thickness).
3. Heat reduced cream in a large sauté pan. Add Parmesan cheese, salt, and white pepper. When cream is thickened, add cooked fettuccini and toss to coat completely.
4. Portion fettuccini into 4 large pasta bowls. Slice chicken thin on a bias and arrange neatly on top of pasta.
5. Garnish with tomatoes and parsley.

Wine Recommendation: Chardonnay or Sauvignon Blanc

Recipe by: Jeff Norcross, head chef and kitchen manager

MARBLE

Marble was named for the vast marble quarries in the area. The marble from Marble was used for the Lincoln Memorial and the Tomb of the Unknown Soldier in Washington, D.C. The town was founded circa 1890. Marble and silver attracted over 1,000 people to work in the quarries. In the late 1930s, a slow moving mud slide wiped out the town. With the start of World War II, the quarries closed and remained closed for almost half a century, reopening in 1990. Today, marble sculptors from around the world descend upon this small, hidden town each summer to practice their art.

The restaurant that I unearthed in these parts serves home-cooked American food to marble carvers and non-marble carvers alike.

Location of Town: Central Western Slope off Highway 133
Zip Code: 81623. Area Code: 970. Population: 64. Elevation: 7,960ft.

Crystal River Way Station

5590 County Road 3. 963-0795.
Directions: Take Exit 114 from I-70 and go north to the signal. Turn right onto Highways 6 and 24 and go to the next signal. Turn right onto Highway 82 and continue on this road for 11.7 miles to the intersection with Highway 133. Turn right onto Highway 133 and go roughly 22 miles, passing through the towns of Carbondale and Redstone. Between mile posts 46 and 47, turn left onto County Road 3, the road to Marble. Go 5.8 miles. The restaurant is on the left behind the Inn at Raspberry Ridge.

ESSENTIALS
Cuisine: Home-Cooked American
Hours: Memorial Day thru JUN and SEP: Mon-Thu 11AM-5PM, Fri 11AM-8PM, Sat-Sun 8AM-8PM. JUL to Labor Day: 7days 8AM-8PM. OCT to Memorial Day: Fri 5PM-8PM. Closed Sat-Thu.
Meals and Prices: Breakfast $4-$6. Lunch $3-$7. Dinner $10-$15
Nonsmoking: All. Smoking only permitted on deck.
Take-out: Offered for lunch only.

Alcohol: Beer and wine
Credit Cards: No
Personal Check: Yes, with I.D.
Reservations: No
Wheelchair Access: Yes
Dress: Extremely casual
Other: Service charge of 15% added to parties of 6 or more. Box lunches available. On premise catering for parties up to 25 people.

HISTORY, PERSONALITY AND CHARACTER

Crystal River Way Station was originally a motel built in the late 1960s by folks from Louisiana. It later provided rooms and food for the McClure Pass builders. In 1979, it became The Mountain View Inn, a motel, bar and restaurant. In 1991, Miriam and Bob Leone took over the establishment after it had been vacant for four years. Bob is the mayor of Marble. He and Miriam executed an extensive remodeling project converting the building into a dining room with kitchen, three rental apartments and their own living quarters. During the renovation, they pulled several pieces of lead from the pillars. These were evidently remnants of bullets left during Marble's wilder days. The Crystal River Way Station is a source of meals for the marble carvers who come to Marble from all over the world. The name was derived from the fact that the train use to come through this area right below this property.

FOOD, SERVICE AND AMBIANCE

The Crystal River Way Station uses whole grains, fresh vegetables, natural cheeses and locally raised, genetically lean, Saler beef. These foods are handcrafted into lunch specials such as homemade soups and chili, garbanzo bean spread sandwiches, tabbouleh and salad Niçoise. I stopped here for lunch and ordered a good tasting Philly cheese steak. It was non-greasy (which this kind of sandwich can sometimes be) and consisted of very thin slices of tender beef with onions and mushrooms on a fresh, homemade, poppyseed, hoagy-syle roll. Tasty homemade potato salad with the skins left on, onion, chopped celery and sprinkles of paprika accompanied the sandwich.

The Crystal River serves a bottomless cup of coffee with breakfast. Your choices are eggs and meats, omelets, a breakfast sandwich on a homemade Kaiser roll, French toast made with homemade sourdough and Bob's oatmeal. The lunch menu is headlined by sandwiches on homemade sourdough rolls and whole wheat and rye breads, soups, homemade vegetarian or beef chili and salads. Some popular sandwiches are the turkey club, pastrami with sauerkraut and a veggie sandwich with Swiss cheese. Barbecue beef and Hawaiian-style pork are two frequent sandwich specials.

The dinner menu changes nightly with three family recipes each evening that may feature chicken, beef, vegetarian, pasta or pork. The possibilities include spinach and ricotta lasagna made with freshly rolled and cut pasta, black-cherry glazed baked ham, apricot braised pork chops, lemon-herb chicken and old-fashioned Yankee pot roast. Every Thursday night is "Mexican night" with authentic Mexican and Southwestern

MARBLE

fare. Friday is "pizza night" with Crystal River's special versions of Italian peasant pies like garlic-glazed chicken and spinach-ricotta. It is pizza at its finest with homemade, hand-rolled dough.

At the Crystal River Way Station, you place your order and pick up your food at the counter for breakfast or lunch. Dinners offer full service. New age music played in this log cabin decorated with paintings of a wagon train, a gun fight, cowboys on horses and the Sunset Beach Grill. Augmenting this setting are a black-iron pipe stove, a charcoal black sketch of a little girl signed by Abbey and colored-glass artworks of birds, flowers and leaves. A patio out back, partially covered by a slanted wood roof, overlooks a forest of aspen and pines on a steep hill. From a distance, you may hear the marble carvers about 400 yards away along the Crystal River and see their cloud of dust. The Crystal River Way Station is worth the short trip off the main highway for its good home-cooked food, its bucolic panorama and marble carvers.

See page 164 for restaurant photo.

SPECIAL ONE-TIME OFFER: Buy one entrée and receive a second entrée of equal or lesser value for free OR receive 50% off one entrée. Please present to server at time of ordering. _____ Owner/Manager. _____ Date.

Spinach-Ricotta Pizza
(Makes one 16-inch pizza)

Pizza Dough:
1 tablespoon honey or malt syrup
1 cup warm water
2 teaspoons dry active yeast
1/4 cup extra virgin olive oil
3 1/4 cups unbleached flour
1 teaspoon salt

Toppings: (the following are to taste)
Olive oil
Fresh tomatoes, sliced
Salt and pepper
Italian seasoning
Fresh garlic, chopped
Fresh basil leaves, chopped
Fresh spinach leaves, chopped
Ricotta cheese
Grated mozzarella cheese

1. Place yeast in water with honey and oil.
2. Mix flour and salt.
3. Add the liquid mixture to flour and salt. Mix and knead for 3 minutes. Cover with plastic wrap and let rise for 1 hour.
4. Roll out pizza dough and place on pizza screen.
5. Brush with olive oil. Top with tomatoes. Sprinkle with salt, pepper, and Italian seasoning.
6. Scatter the garlic, basil, and spinach. Top with the cheeses.
7. Bake at 425 degrees for about 20 minutes or until crust is brown.

Beverage Recommendation: Red Lady Amber Ale from Idle Spur Brewery in Crested Butte

Recipe by: Miriam Leone, owner

MINTURN

Minturn was named for Thomas Minturn, a Denver and Rio Grande Western Railroad roadmaster.

Mexican food and imaginative decor are found in the restaurant shown here. It prepares casual Tex-Mex cuisine and displays inventive license plates and comical color sketches.

Location of Town: Central Colorado, two miles south of I-70 west of Vail. Zip Code: 81645. Area Code: 970. Population: 1,066. Elevation: 7,840ft.

Chili Willy's
101 Main Street. 827-5887.
Directions: Take Exit 171 from I-70 and go south two miles on Highway 24 to the town of Minturn. The restaurant is on the right as you enter town just past The Scarab Imports.

ESSENTIALS
Cuisine: Casual Tex-Mex
Hours: 7 days 5:30PM-9PM. Closed Mon and Tue in MAY and OCT. July 4th-Labor Day: 11:30AM-9PM. Lunch until 4PM, dinner from 4PM.
Meals and Prices: Lunch $6-$9. Dinner $6-$13.
Nonsmoking: All. Smoking only in the bar.
Take-out: Yes

Alcohol: Full Bar
Credit Cards: MC, Visa, Amx, Disc
Personal Check: Yes, with approval from Tele-Check.
Reservations: Only recommended for groups of 10 or more.
Wheelchair Access: Yes, including bathrooms.
Dress: Casual

HISTORY, PERSONALITY AND CHARACTER

The building occupied by Chili Willy's has a proud and colorful history dating back to the Roaring '20s. It began as a grocery store owned and operated by Cullen and Cooper. In the mid-1920s, they sold the grocery to David D. Williams who added a gas pump, liquor store and sandwich shop. Mr. Williams had to move the building a few feet from its original foundation to make way for Highway 24. He then made additions and remodeled, passing down the business in 1938 to his son, David, who added living quarters, the Valley's first dance hall, a private dining area and a clandestine gambling casino where the kitchen now stands. Running the casino proved more bother than it was worth as the law closed the bar for two six-month periods. The Williams finally converted the casino into a more acceptable storage area.

Following Halloween 1941 when, as rumor has it, a group of unruly members of Camp Hale tore up the dance hall, the Williams replaced it with a café that catered to the miners and their families. Williams Café operated from 1941 until 1973 when the building was sold and the front portion was leased as a liquor store. A pizza restaurant occupied the dining area and bar from 1978 to 1982.

In March 1984, Carol Morley brought her favorite Tex-Mex food, recipes and good ol' fashion hospitality from Texas and opened Chili Willy's for business. Carol's sister, Barbara Zabojnik and Al Brown bought into the restaurant in 1988. All three attended the same high school in Texas and all three are general managers at Chili Willy's. Barb oversees the staff and hiring. Al oversees the bar and kitchen. Carol oversees the entire operation. Head chef Paul Genelin has been cooking at the restaurant since 1994. He has been in the restaurant business since the mid-1980s and previously worked at the Red Lion in Vail.

FOOD, SERVICE AND AMBIANCE

Mexican food fanatics and Texas taste "tantalizers" won't want to miss Chili Willy's when they are in the Vail Valley. Yellow and blue corn tortilla chips are fried daily and brought to your table with thick and spicy salsa supreme. With my taste buds titillated, I delved into a platter of rellenos de camarones with Spanish rice and the best refried beans I ever had! They are prepared with Worchester sauce, cayenne and chili pepper, oregano, garlic, salt and black pepper. You must try them. The rellenos were also excellent, stuffed with shrimp, loaded with Monterey Jack cheese inside, smothered with cheese on top and sprinkled with scallions and peppers. It is served with lettuce and diced tomatoes on the side. No wonder this place is so popular with the locals!

For a starter at Chili Willy's, you might try some nachos, quesadillas, calientitas (Jalapeño poppers) or Texas twisters (onions and jalapeños battered and deep fried). Taco or fajita salads are also available with avocado dressing. Highlighting their house specials are fajitas, enchiladas de camerones (shrimp), chicken and New York strip specials and barbecue baby back ribs. Tex-Mex favorites feature green chili or ranchero sauce on a chimichanga or burrito grande. Vegetarians have their choice of specialties like spinach enchiladas and combo tostados, one with guacamole, the other with chili con queso. Burgers and fries are also on hand for hardcore American food lovers. Spotlighting the sweet stuff are a

MINTURN

sopapilla basket, a Tex-Mex favorite, and deep fried ice cream rolled in a flavored tortilla and served with blueberry, raspberry or chocolate sauce.

Service was fast, friendly and casual. This is a very popular place so expect the noise level to be on the high side. A high wall shelf on orange stucco walls is decked with children's toys, a train picture, movie posters of Mae West and Humphrey Bogart, a Betty Boop doll, ceramic statues of Santa Claus and a Snowman, giant beer bottles, a stuffed armadillo and a pair of long horns. Below this shelf is a row of domestic and foreign license plates. Two of my favorites were "XITE ME" and "JASDIP", an anagram. If you can't figure out what the six letters stand for, ask one of the general managers. Further enhancing the multi-faceted décor are several comical color sketches that display a cowboy from the knees down wearing his Nikona boots. A different wild animal is poised to attack the faceless cowboy in each sketch: a bear, a wolf, a mountain lion, a bald eagle and an armadillo. Rounding out the Wild West ambiance are pink poles painted with chilies and cacti, a street sign for Tijuana, Cuoto and children's crayon drawings.

Chili Willy's has won several honors in the Vail Daily Readers' Poll including Best Margarita every year since 1993, Best Mexican Food in 1997 and Best Place for Kids in 1997. See for yourself why this restaurant has become such a strong mainstay in the Vail Valley.

Special One-Time Offer: Buy one entrée and receive a second entrée of equal or lesser value free (up to $10.00) OR receive 50% off one entrée (up to $5.00). Please present to server at time of ordering.

_____ Owner/Manager. _____ Date.

Refried Beans
(Serves 6)

- 1/2 pound uncooked dry pinto beans
- 1/2 teaspoon salt
- 1/2 teaspoon onion powder
- 1/2 teaspoon garlic powder
- 1/2 teaspoon cumin
- 1/2 teaspoon Mexican oregano
- 1/2 teaspoon cayenne pepper
- 1/2 teaspoon Worcestershire

1. Clean and rinse beans. Cover with water, approximately 2 to 3 inches above beans, and soak overnight.
2. Drain water from beans. Place beans in a stew pot and cover with fresh water (just enough to cover beans). Bring to a boil. Reduce heat to a simmer, cover, and cook for 2 hours.
3. Add remaining ingredients and continue cooking until beans are very soft, approximately 1 hour. Remove beans from heat and let cool.
4. Place beans in a bowl and mash with a potato masher. You may add a little water to reach the consistency you prefer. Place mashed beans in a lightly oiled skillet and reheat. Place in a serving dish or on individual plates and sprinkle with shredded cheese and scallions.
5. Option: For added flavor, you can add 1/4 pound of chopped bacon to the beans while cooking.

Beverage Recommendation: Your favorite Mexican beer

Recipe by: Carol Morley and Al Brown, owners and managers

See bottom of page 163 for recipe photo.

PENROSE

Penrose was established by the Beaver Park Land and Water Company and named for Spencer Penrose, Colorado Springs capitalist and philanthropist.

The family and American country restaurant below serves goose berry pie and other good things in a cherubic and capricious setting.

Location of Town: Central Colorado between Cañon City and Pueblo where Highways 50 and 115 intersect.
Zip Code: 81240. Area Code: 719. Population: 900. Elevation: 5,320ft.

The Goose Berry Patch
660 Highway 115. 372-3910.
Directions: The restaurant is located on the southeast side of Highway 115, 1.6 miles northeast of Highway 50. Coming from Colorado Springs, you must turn left 500 feet before the restaurant just before the highway becomes divided.

ESSENTIALS
Cuisine: Family/American Country
Hours: Wed-Thu 11:30AM-8PM. Fri-Sat 11:30AM-9PM. Sun 8AM-8PM. Closed Mon-Tue.
Meals and Prices: Breakfast $6. Lunch $3-$5. Dinner $7-$11.
Nonsmoking: Yes
Take-out: Yes
Alcohol: Beer and Wine
Credit Cards: MC, Visa
Personal Check: Yes
Reservations: Recommended for weekends and holidays. Accepted otherwise.
Wheelchair Access: Yes, including restroom
Dress: Everything. More casual than dressy.
Other: Special dietary needs accommodated, if possible.

HISTORY, PERSONALITY AND CHARACTER
The present-day Goose Berry Patch Restaurant was built in stages over the past 60 years. Beginning in the late 1930s and early 1940s, there was a simple lean-to that sold cider and fresh produce. This later became the front of the current restaurant. About 30 feet behind the lean-to, the owners lived in a one-bedroom, stucco cottage that later was transformed into a dining area by the contemporary owners. In the 1950s, the lean-to was enclosed and an 8x20 foot kitchen was added to give birth to The Cider Inn, a hamburger place that lasted until 1987. In February 1987, Tim

and Barbara Martin opened The Goose Berry Patch Family Restaurant. In 1989, they connected The Cider Inn with the cottage to make one continuous restaurant. In 1990, Tim and Barbara enclosed the patio in front and expanded the kitchen into this area. In July 1998, they added a 25x35 foot covered patio with screens off the main dining room. Tim and Barbara both manage the restaurant and Barbara does the cooking.

FOOD, SERVICE AND AMBIANCE

The Goose Berry Patch does not serve anything fancy or exotic, just good ol' home cooking. I stopped here and partook of their lunch/dinner buffet, an abundant selection that included their 50-item soup and salad bar. Headlining the buffet are baked and seasoned green beans, chicken fried steak, roast beef, barbecue pork ribs, mashed potatoes with creamy gravy, fruits in a thick sauce, corn, baked ham, linguini with red tomato sauce and meatballs, fried popcorn shrimp and fried chicken. Goose Berry conserve, a combination of apples, raisins, grapes, orange peel and chopped nuts, was on hand to put on their variety of breads. The dessert bar had some tempting options like tapioca, chocolate and rice puddings; rhubarb and cherry supreme pudding with pineapple. Free refills are given on the lemonade. You will get plenty of wholesome food and drink to fill your appetite at The Goose Berry Patch.

The Sunday breakfast buffet features fresh pastries, fruit tray, scrambled eggs, bacon, sausage, corned beef hash, biscuits and gravy, green chili, French toast and pancakes. Additional lunch offerings include homemade soups and chili, salads, burgers and sandwiches. You can order your burger with green chili strips or pineapple and teriyaki sauce. For vegetarians, the Goose Berry also has a black bean burger and a garden burger made with barley and brown rice. Topping the list of sandwiches are breaded fried cod, krab and seafood salad, grilled whole chicken breast, top sirloin and pork cutlet. For dinner, you can choose from an assortment of steaks, seafood and chicken. The crème de la crème of the menu, though, has to be their 25 desserts, almost all homemade, highlighted by fruit and cream pies, bread pudding, a special recipe Gooseberry pie, blackberry or peach cobbler and Bissettis's cheesecakes.

My server was very attentive returning many times to ask how I was doing. The front of the restaurant outside looks like something out of a Mother Goose Nursery Rhyme Book. The overhang has cows at either end with geese, a pig and a rooster in-between. This is a small, red one-story building with white shutters and red heart-shaped indentations. There is an old, red wishing well in front of the restaurant and a small pond surrounded by rocks behind the restaurant.

PENROSE

Inside, the four separate dining areas with white stucco walls and blue doorways and window frames are adorned with several porcelain human and animal doll figures, doll figures carrying or using umbrellas and a doll with a basket next to a wishing well. Embellishing this pattern are wreaths, chili ristras and a straw hat painted to resemble a watermelon. One wall shelf is decked with a little village scene with horse drawn carriages and buildings for a butcher, a baker, a smithy and an inn. A G-scale model train encircled the restaurant with a wall mural background representing the Garden of the Gods, Pikes, Peak, the Eastern Plains, Pueblo Reservoir, the Royal Gorge and the apple orchards which are plentiful in Penrose. The Goose Berry Patch offers decent and healthy meals from their considerate staff in a quaint and whimsical setting.

See bottom of page 261 for restaurant photo.

Special One-Time Offer: Buy one entrée and receive a second entrée of equal or lesser value free (up to $9.95) OR receive 50% off one entrée (up to $4.95). Please present to server at time of ordering.
_____ Owner/Manager. _____ Date.

Gooseberry Pie
(Makes one 10-inch deep dish pie)

5 cups of gooseberries, use frozen; if canned, drain well
1/2 cup rhubarb, cut up
3 cups sugar

1/2 cup flour
1/2 cup cornstarch
1 teaspoon cinnamon

1. Mix together all ingredients.
2. Line pie shell with your favorite pie dough. Put in gooseberry mixture. Cover with top crust.
3. Crimp and sugar crust. Put slits in the top and bake for approximately 1 hour at 350 degrees until bubbly.

Recipe by: Barbara Martin

See top of page 261 for recipe photo.

SAN LUIS

San Luis was named for the patron saint, Saint Louis. It is the oldest town in Colorado, established in 1851. The original site for San Luis was ¾ of a mile south of the present town. San Luis was originally called Culebra, Spanish for "snake" after the Culebra River which winds like a snake through the countryside. Later it was renamed Plaza del Medis, Spanish for "center village", because of its geographical location. Three miles to the north was San Pedro, also known as Upper Culebra or Plaza Arriba. Three miles to the south was San Acacio, known as Lower Culebra or Plaza Abajo.

This Southwestern and Mexican restaurant has been in the same family for over 50 years and is an established institution in this part of the state.

Location of Town: South-central Colorado
Zip Code: 81152. Area Code: 719. Population: 800. Elevation: 7,965ft.

Emma's Hacienda

355 Main Street. 672-9902.
Directions: From I-25, take Exit 50 and head west on Highway 160 for 48 miles to the town of Fort Garland. Turn left (south) on Highway 159 and go 16 miles to San Luis. The restaurant is on the right .1 miles past Highway 142.

ESSENTIALS
Cuisine: Southwest/Mexican
Hours: 7 days 11AM-9PM
Meals and Prices: Lunch/Dinner $4-$6.
Nonsmoking: No
Take-out: Yes
Alcohol: Full Bar
Credit Cards: No
Personal Check: Yes
Reservations: Accepted for parties of 10 or more. Not necessary otherwise.
Wheelchair Access: Yes, but not for restrooms
Dress: Casual
Other: Service charge of 15% for parties of 6 or more. Service charge of 20% for separate checks.
Separate dining room available for private parties up to 80 people.

SAN LUIS

HISTORY, PERSONALITY AND CHARACTER

Emma's Hacienda is housed in a building constructed in the early 1900s. Joe and Emma Espinoza, whose family roots in the San Luis Valley go back four generations, operate the business. The Espinozas bought the building from Richard Cohn who operated a store at this location. On July 4, 1946, the Espinozas opened the El Patio, a bar and restaurant with a pool hall. In 1970, they added a second story to the building, converted the pool hall into a restaurant and renamed the business Emma's Hacienda.

The restaurant continues to be a family operation. Though daughter Joetta Frost took over management of the business in the late 1960s, Emma can still be found in the kitchen on most days overseeing the quality of the food in the restaurant that bears her name, a local landmark. Joe, who served as the town's mayor for three terms, is on hand almost daily to greet guests and visit with local residents.

Today, a new generation of family cooks carries on the tradition. Grandchildren Yolanda and Carlos Deleon have been cooking with Emma since 1987 and 1997, respectively. A second Espinoza daughter, Theresa Lobato, and her two daughters, Mona and Angela, apprenticed under Emma and are working at the restaurant. A third daughter, Margaret E. Lee of Denver and her two sons, Joe A. Espinoza and Albert Espinoza, have also contributed in operating the family-owned business.

FOOD, SERVICE AND AMBIANCE

Folks in the San Luis Valley have long recommended that I include Emma's Hacienda in my guide and I am happy to do so here. Emma's is what you would expect being located in Colorado's oldest town only 19 miles from the New Mexico border: authentic, homemade dishes and recipes from the Southwest and Mexico that have been in the family for four generations. Their homemade chips are served with a hot salsa consisting of a tomato and red chili puree with onion, black pepper and jalapeño seeds. For my entrée, I chose Emma's Special, a combination of red and green enchiladas, taco, beans, rice salad and sopapilla. The taco shells were wrinkled and crisp. Both enchiladas came with cheese and onion. The green enchilada had mild green chili strips. The Spanish rice was enhanced by pieces of green pepper. The beans were topped with cheese and the sopapilla was thick and puffy. Emma's uses mild seasoning so the food is not spicy, except for their salsa.

Emma's lunch and dinner menu offers nachos and stuffed jalapeños for appetizers, several enchiladas and burritos, popular items like stuffed sopapilla with green or red chili and a spicy burrito called the Pancho Villa, menudo and red or green chili. There are also chiliburgers, American burgers and for dessert, bread pudding, homemade pies and sopapilla sundaes with Emma's homemade chokecherry syrup.

Service was friendly and informal. Pictures of American Indians, pueblos and trappers adorn this restaurant that showcases red carpet, red cushion chairs, a jukebox and a circular stairway leading to upstairs dining. This area has the bar and is used for special events, parties or on busy nights. The artwork includes a "Love to see Chili Lovers" poster signed by R. C. Gorman with a picture of a big, green chili, a picture of Sangre Christo Parish and works by Richard Wallender of Denver. There is a photo taken in the early 1900s of Buffalo Bill with local resident Jacobo Sanchez, who rode under the name Jake Sanders. Also displayed is a black and white charcoal by Chipawa Indian David Lundquist of Oklahoma signed in 1981 to "Grandmother" Emma (no relation) depicting a gathering of Indian tribes with various symbols and beautiful headdresses. An artist from Pueblo created a painting of the Manzanares' Home. Feel and taste the spirit of the Southwest when you visit Emma's Hacienda.

SPECIAL ONE-TIME OFFER: Buy one entrée at the regular price and receive a complimentary sopapilla sundae (a sopapilla with vanilla ice cream, homemade chokecherry syrup and whipped cream). One sundae per entrée purchased. Valid for every member of your party. Please present to server at time or ordering. _____ Owner/Manager. _____ Date.

SAN LUIS

Pizza Burrito
(Serves 8 to 10)

1 16-ounce can refritos
1/4 cup of water
2 to 3 tablespoons shortening
1 pound ground meat
8 to 10 flour tortillas
Italian sauce (see recipe)
16 ounces mozzarella cheese, grated
Fresh oregano to taste
Olives to taste

<u>Italian Sauce</u>:
1/4 cup onions, chopped
1 tablespoon olive oil
1 16-ounce can crushed tomatoes
1 8-ounce can tomato sauce
1 cup water
Salt, pepper, garlic powder to taste

1. <u>Italian Sauce</u>: Sauté 1/4 cup onions in olive oil. Add crushed tomatoes, tomato sauce, and water. Add salt, pepper, garlic powder. Bring to a boil and let simmer 15 minutes.
2. Simmer refritos in water and shortening for 15 to 20 minutes. Add water if needed.
3. Grill ground beef.
4. Warm flour tortillas. Fill with refritos and grilled ground meat. Roll and smother with Italian sauce, mozzarella cheese, and fresh oregano.
5. Warm until cheese melts. Garnish with ripe olives.

<u>Wine Recommendation</u>: Cabernet Sauvignon

<u>Recipe by</u>: Emma Espinoza, owner and cook

See top of page 265 for recipe photo.

SILVERTON

First called Baker's Park, Silverton went by several other names, including Reeseville, Quito and Greenville. The name Silverton was chosen in an election in 1875 signifying the silver mines in the San Juan region. Silver mining and the railroad boosted Silverton's population to about 5,000 by 1910. However, as mining declined so did the town's populace. Today, Silverton is a summer tourist town on the northern terminus of the Durango-Silverton narrow gauge train.

Silverton is situated in San Juan County which has the distinction of having the highest mean elevation of any county in the United States. Snowfall averages 200 inches a year. Government studies have shown that the air on top of Molas Pass, just south of Silverton, is some of the clearest and cleanest to be found anywhere in the continental United States.

My high-altitude highlight from this town is an American restaurant with a Southwest flair in a former mercantile.

Location of Town: Western slope on Highway 550.
Zip Code: 81433. Area Code: 970. Population: 716. Elevation: 9,305ft.

The Pickle Barrel

1304 Greene Street.
Directions: Entering Silverton on Highway 550 from either Durango or Ouray, proceed on Greene Street for nine blocks past the visitor center. The restaurant is on the right at the corner of 13th Street.

ESSENTIALS

Cuisine: American with a Southwest flair
Hours: Early MAY-Late OCT: 7 days 11AM-3PM, Thu-Mon 5:30PM-9:30PM. Closed Late OCT-Early MAY.
Meals and Prices: Lunch $5-$6. Dinner $6-$13.
Nonsmoking: All
Take-out: Yes
Alcohol: Beer and wine

Credit Cards: All 5
Personal Check: Yes with I.D.
Reservations: Accepted, not required
Wheelchair Access: Yes, but not bathrooms
Dress: Casual, informal
Other: Children's menu. Service charge of 15% for parties of 6 or more.

SILVERTON

HISTORY, PERSONALITY AND CHARACTER

The Pickle Barrel was originally a mercantile built and owned by Sherwin and Houghton. It was the first commercial masonry building in Silverton. In 1896, Giacomelli and Chino, whose portrait you will see behind the counter on the left, converted the mercantile into the Iron Mountain Saloon. The building was transformed a second time into an ice cream parlor and novelty store with the start of Prohibition in Colorado in 1916. However, that did not stop the owners from installing and using slot machines. They were on wheels for quick transport whenever the authorities arrived. There was also a bottling operation in the basement for bootleg wine and brandy.

The building was closed in 1938. In the late 1940s, it became a liquor store and later returned to an ice cream parlor owned by a woman named Rosie. The building sat vacant from 1950 until 1971 when Fritz Klinke opened a deli called The Pickle Barrel. He has developed it over the years into one of Silverton's longest lasting, finest dining establishments. Fritz knows quite a bit of the history of the area and owns Smedley's Ice Cream Parlor next door with partner Loren Lew. From 1986 to 1995, he also owned and operated The French Bakery in town. Bonnie Stuntebeck is the head chef. She has been with The Pickle Barrel off and on since 1978 and has worked at restaurants in the Milwaukee area during the winter.

FOOD, SERVICE AND AMBIANCE

Linda and I stopped here for lunch when we took the Durango-Silverton narrow gauge railroad train. I had the well-done Parmesan chicken on angel hair pasta in a thick tomato sauce with onions and mushrooms. The sauce had a bitter vinegar taste that I favored. Corn nibblets were served on the side. Linda enjoyed thick homemade chicken noodle soup with celery, carrots, wide egg noodles, plenty of chicken chunks, tarragon and oregano. She also liked the Reuben sandwich on light rye with plenty of corned beef and sauerkraut. Pasta salad came on the side. Other sandwiches available on the lunch menu were breast of turkey, ham and Swiss, club, pastrami, roast beef and Swiss or cheddar cheese. You can also order franks, fruit bowl, burgers or homemade chili. For dessert, try the cheesecake or brownie.

Chef Bonnie creates an eclectic dinner selection, staying away from deep fried foods, doing more things made from scratch and using fresh ingredients. Spotlighting the dinner menu are prime rib, linguini with smoked duck or with chicken in a Cajun cream sauce, Indo chicken over marinated noodles with a peanut sauce, Alaskan salmon, crab stuffed chicken and white bean pistachio burger. Other dinner entrées that you may find on their weekly changing menu are shrimp, crab and scallops in a puff pastry, pistachio crusted chicken, lasagna and black bean burrito. There is a children's menu.

Service is casual. Very quiet classical music plays in the background. This is an old-fashioned, charming restaurant with wood shingle walls, high ceilings and walls made of red bricks, rocks and knotty pinewood planks. The front of the restaurant has three arches. The antique décor includes an old grocery store scale taken from The French Bakery with charge tickets from 1932, a brass cash register, an old coffee grinder, an ice shaver and a can of Wayne Confections. Enhancing the quaint ambiance are several artifacts on top of the salad bar: cans of "Taggart's cookies and crackers", "Reed's butterscotch wafers", "Roods quality candy", "Hickok's marshmallows" and a wooden case of Moose Head beer.

A turn-of-the-century Old English pipe tobacco sign hangs on the wood-shingle wall. Behind the counter and dessert display on the left are a photo of the town of Chattanooga, between Ouray and Silverton, taken in 1889 by W.H. Jackson; a painting of the Lady of Shalot and a 1926 photo of the ice cream parlor and confectionery. You will also find an original calendar regulator clock with pendulum, an 1893 painting of a Colorado Mountain scene by Fritz's grandmother in Denver, several beer signs and pictures of trains on polished wood. There is a red brick fireplace in the rear with a brass sculpture of mushrooms and a spider web made from the head of a 55-gallon drum.

Several celebrities have found The Pickle Barrel including Governor Romer, Michael J. Fox and Christie Brinkley, who was a regular here in 1994. For a nostalgic look at Colorado's colorful past and a creative collection of entrées to choose from, visit the unique Pickle Barrel.

See bottom of page 262 for restaurant photo.

SPECIAL ONE-TIME OFFER: Buy one entrée and receive a second entrée of equal or lesser value free up to $6.00 OR receive 50% off one entrée up to $4.00. Please present to server at time of ordering.
_____ Owner/Manager. _____ Date.

Indo Chicken
with Sweet and Sour Cucumber Relish
(Serves 6 to 8)

Sauce:
- 1/2 medium-size onion
- 3 cloves garlic
- 2 tablespoons rice wine vinegar
- 1/2 cup water
- 1/4 cup soy sauce
- 2 cups peanut butter
- Pinch each of fresh ginger, ground coriander, ground cumin, white pepper and red pepper flakes
- 4 tablespoons fresh chopped cilantro

Marinade:
- 1/4 cup white wine
- 1/2 cup soy sauce
- 1/4 cup rice wine vinegar
- 1/4 teaspoon white pepper

Relish:
- 1 cucumber, peeled and sliced thin
- 1/2 red onion, peeled and sliced thin
- 1/2 cup water
- 1/2 cup sugar
- 1/3 cup rice wine vinegar
- 1/4 teaspoons white pepper
- Dash of salt

- 4 cups of cooked Chinese rice noodles

- 8 6-ounce chicken breasts, boneless and skinless

1. <u>Sauce</u>: Puree onion and garlic in food processor. Add rice wine vinegar, peanut butter and herbs. Puree again. Add soy sauce, water and cilantro. Puree again.
2. <u>Marinade</u>: Mix all ingredients. Pour over Chinese rice noodles. Marinade from 2 to 24 hours.
3. <u>Relish</u>: Place cucumber and onion in a bowl. Heat water, sugar, rice wine vinegar, white pepper and salt in pan. When hot, pour over cucumber and onion mixture. Let sit for 20 minutes. Drain.
4. Salt and pepper the chicken breasts. Char-grill or pan fry in oil.
5. Place 4 to 5 ounces of marinated Chinese rice noodles on plate. Place chicken breast on top of noodles. Lattice sauce over chicken and noodles. Serve with sweet and sour cucumber relish.

<u>Beverage Recommendation</u>: Samuel Smith Pale Ale

<u>Recipe by</u>: Bonnie Stuntebeck, head chef

See top of page 262 for recipe photo.

SNOWMASS VILLAGE

Originally called Snowmass-at-Aspen and later West Village, the town was named for Snowmass Creek which it borders. Snowmass Village was established in 1967 as a ski resort.

I have suggested a potpourri of places to pick, from the only lobster bar in the Aspen Valley, to a casual American bistro with excellent accessibility to skiers, to an American country restaurant specializing in stews and soups to a family steakhouse offering vegetarian and seafood with the largest soup and salad bar in town.

Location of Town: Central Colorado southeast of Glenwood Springs.
Zip Code: 81615. Area Code: 970. Population: 1,449. Elevation: 7,900ft.

The Brothers' Grille

100 Elbert Lane (in the Silvertree Hotel). 923-3520.
Directions: On Highway 82, heading towards Aspen from Glenwood Springs, go 7 miles past the town of Old Snowmass. Turn right on Brush Creek Road. Go 5 miles to Divide Road, then continue another ¼ mile on Brush Creek Road and take your second right. Enter Lower Mall Parking. Park in Lot #6 or the closest available lot. Go across the street and take the first set of stairs to the Main Mall Level. Go about 250 feet to The Silvertree Hotel clock tower. Walk straight past the clock tower, go under the green awning and walk another 30 feet. Enter The Silvertree Hotel on the right. Take the elevator to Level 5 and follow the signs through the hotel to the restaurant.

ESSENTIALS
Cuisine: Casual American Bistro
Hours: 7 days 6:30AM-11PM. Breakfast to 11AM. Lunch 11:30AM-2:30PM. Dinner from 5PM.
Meals and Prices: Breakfast $5-$8. Lunch $6-$9. Après ski $4-$8. Dinner $12-$20.
Nonsmoking: All. Smoking in bar only. No pipes or cigars.
Take-out: Yes
Alcohol: Full Bar
Credit Cards: All 5

Personal Check: Local only with I.D.
Reservations: Recommended for dinner in winter. Not accepted for breakfast or lunch.
Wheelchair Access: Yes, by elevator, once inside the hotel
Dress: Casual
Other: Children's menu. Service charge of 17% added to parties of 6 or more. Box lunches. Room for private parties available.

SNOWMASS VILLAGE

HISTORY, PERSONALITY AND CHARACTER

The Brothers' Grille is in the Silvertree Hotel, formerly the old El Dorado Hotel. The restaurant is owned by Village Property, which also owns the Village Steakhouse in the Wildwood Lodge nearby. Doug Connor is the food and beverage director for Village Property.

Executive chef Shane Bruns is a local resident who is making an impact on his own hometown. Shane worked with the Silvertree Hotel and Wildwood Lodge for five years as the executive sous chef. He started his career with a three-year internship at the Chez Grandmere under Michelle Poumay, a highly decorated Belgian Chef. After his internship, Shane started working throughout the Aspen Valley in four-star properties. He then attended the California Culinary Academy in San Francisco and traveled overseas to Australia.

FOOD, SERVICE AND AMBIANCE

I stopped here for lunch and ordered the mountain man meatloaf sandwich because it was homemade and grilled over an open flame. The meat was lightly charred and tasty with red and green peppers and black pepper spice. It was served open face on Texas toast with garlic mashed potatoes that were lumpy with a few skins left on, just the way I like them. Rich, flavorful, brown onion gravy, which I ordered some extra on the side, was poured over the meatloaf and potatoes. Lettuce, tomato slice and dill pickle garnished the dish. This was a hearty, savory meal for meat and potato lovers.

Breakfast serves up some special delights like smoked salmon hash; Belgian waffle; blueberry and banana pancakes; custard dipped French toast topped with bananas, raisins and cinnamon; and spinach and artichoke hearts benedict. Eggbeaters may be substituted for eggs. The lunch menu features a Caribe' quesadilla made with grilled vegetables and their signature salsa; the Silvertree salad, a local's favorite consisting of greens, grilled muscovey duck breast, roasted almonds, mandarin oranges and goat cheese; pastas; half-pound burgers; blackened prime rib and grilled Rueben. For dinner, you can choose from cowboy chop steak, barbecue baby-back ribs, half-roasted chicken, grilled Rocky Mountain trout and pork porterhouse. A daily selection of cakes, pies and Ben and Jerry's ice cream is available for your pleasure.

Service was conscientious and courteous from the moment I walked into the restaurant. At the entrance to the Brothers' Grille, there is a bar to the left and a wine rack to the right. Over the entrance are antique roller skates, crampons for climbing and skis. Further inside, you will be entertained and amused by actual-size and model-size transportation vehicles hanging from the ceiling; brass, percussion and string musical instruments on the walls and a great vantage point for scanning the town and watching skiers going up and down the mountain. The restaurant directly overlooks one of the chair lifts and skiers can slide right up to the patio and slope-side entrance. The pinewood wall on the right opposite the viewing windows is trimmed with ski photos, old pairs of snowshoes, a sled, a toboggan and several peepholes into the kitchen. Along with the more conventional hanging plants and tiffany ceiling lamps are a model plane, a three-wheel cycle circa 1900 and a child's red wagon stretching overhead.

    The Crow's Nest Room in the rear is host to some unusual photographs of skiers taken underwater, a French horn, a banjo, a couple of drums and several tubas. The Fireside Room to the left of the entrance is a sports room for private parties and has a big screen television and gas fireplace. One side of the room is decorated with fishnets, pictures of fish and a life-size plastic marlin. The opposite side is adorned with saddles, polo mallets, tennis rackets, golf irons and pictures of polo, golf, baseball, biking and rugby. Just beyond the flower boxes on the lower patio, a tent is set up in the summer for banquets. In the winter, ski racks take the place of the tent. An upper patio is used for a grill and barbecue in the summer. The Brothers' Grille is a welcome, inviting place to relax, observe and enjoy some fine American and regional cuisine.

Special One-Time Offer: Buy one entrée and receive a second entrée of equal or lesser value free (up to $25.00) OR receive 50% off one entrée (up to $12.00). NOT valid on holidays or for special events. Please present at time of ordering. _____ Owner/Manager. _____ Date.

Grilled Lamb Chops with Tomato Pearl Couscous
(Serves 8)

Port Demi Glaze:
2 ounces shallots, chopped
2 ounces garlic, chopped
1/2 ounce fresh rosemary with stem
1/2 ounce fresh thyme with stem
3 cups of port wine
2 cups of red wine

1 pint fresh raspberries
4 cups veal stock
1/2 teaspoon of salt
1/2 teaspoon pepper
2 ounces unsweetened butter

SNOWMASS VILLAGE

1. To prepare the port demi-glace, put the first 7 ingredients in a sauce pot and bring to a boil. Then reduce the heat to a simmer. Let reduce by half its volume.
2. Add the veal stock with the salt and pepper and let reduce until the viscosity will coat the back of a spoon. Finish with butter.

<u>Tomato Pearl Couscous</u>:

4 cups chicken stock
1 teaspoon tomato paste
4 cups Israeli couscous
1/4 teaspoon salt
1/4 teaspoon pepper
1 teaspoon fresh parsley chopped
1 teaspoon fresh sage chopped
1 medium tomato chopped

1. Preparing the tomato pearl couscous is a little easier than the sauce. Heat the chicken stock and dissolve the tomato paste. Bring to a boil.
2. Pour the chicken stock mixture over the couscous in a pan. Add the rest of the ingredients, then mix and cover with aluminum foil. Set aside for 15 minutes or until the liquid is absorbed.

<u>Lamb Chops</u>:

16 lamb T-bones
4 tablespoons parsley, chopped
3 tablespoons sage, chopped
1 tablespoon thyme, chopped
1/2 cup whole grain mustard
8 rosemary springs
16 baby carrots, peeled
1 large red beet, peeled
32 asparagus, cleaned and trimmed
1 teaspoon shallots chopped
1 teaspoon garlic, chopped
2 ounce unsweetened butter
1 teaspoon salt
1 teaspoon pepper

1. To prepare the vegetables, blanch the carrots and asparagus to al dente. Melt the butter and sauté the garlic and shallots until aromatic.
2. Add vegetables and season with salt and pepper. Sauté until done.
3. To encrust the lamb, rub the whole grain mustard on both sides of each lamb T-bone and pat on the chopped herbs.
4. Grill to desired temperature.
5. For beet garnish, you will need to have a Japanese slicer. If you do not have one, use a peeler and slice thin pieces and cut julienne.
6. Use rosemary sprigs for each plate for garnish with the beets.

<u>Wine Recommendation</u>: Cote Rotie, Petite Sirah, 1992

<u>Recipe by</u>: Shane Bruns, chef
See page 263 for recipe photo.

Butch's Lobster Bar

At the Timberline Condos. 923-4004.
Directions: On Highway 82, heading towards Aspen from Glenwood Springs, go 7 miles past the town of Old Snowmass. Turn right on Brush Creek Road. Go 5 miles to Divide Road, then continue another ¼ mile on Brush Creek Road and take your first right (the street is Snowmelt Road but it is not marked). Follow the road around to the right for .2 miles. The restaurant is on the left in the Timberline Condos. Park in Lot 13, or the closest available lot, on the right.

ESSENTIALS

Cuisine: Seafood
Hours: Late NOV to Mid-APR: 7 days 5:30PM-10PM. Mid-MAY to Mid-OCT: Thu-Sun 6PM-10PM. Closed Mid-APR to Mid-MAY and Mid-OCT to Late NOV.
Meals and Prices: $14-$27
Nonsmoking: All. Smoking only permitted at bar.
Take-out: Yes
Alcohol: Full Bar
Credit Cards: MC, Visa, Amx

Personal Check: Local only
Reservations: Recommended. Highly recommended in winter.
Wheelchair Access: Yes, but stairs are involved.
Dress: Casual
Other: Children's menu. Split entrées $2 charge. Service charge of 18% may be added to parties of 6 or more. No separate checks. Civic assessment of 2½% added for the SRA (Snowmass Resort Assn.).

HISTORY, PERSONALITY AND CHARACTER

The Timberline Condos were constructed in the late 1960s as a bed and breakfast. The original restaurant was The Timberline, a rib house. From 1988 until 1993, Moguls' American Restaurant reigned. Then, Butch Darden opened Butch's Lobster Bar.

Owner and manager Butch Darden is from Longmeadow, Massachusetts. He trained to be a hard-hat diver and was a lobster man on Cape Cod during the summers in the 1980s. Butch once caught a 19-pound lobster! He started his lobster bar in Aspen in 1987 and moved it to Snowmass Village in 1992. He met his wife, Shari, at the Grand Aspen Hotel. She handles the books at Butch's.

Kitchen manager Peter Krulder began cooking in 1977 at the Ute City Bar and Grill and later worked at The Steak Pit, both in Aspen, before coming to Butch's in 1992. Chef Peter Affolter is a graduate of hotel and restaurant school and has been cooking since 1973. He worked in Swiss kitchens for 2 years, was a former partner of Chefy's in Basalt and cooked at the Aspen Grove Café before starting at Butch's in 1993.

SNOWMASS VILLAGE

FOOD, SERVICE AND AMBIANCE

Butch's Lobster Bar is unique. It is the only lobster bar in the Aspen Valley and they concentrate on seafood at reasonable prices. Live Maine lobster dinners are Butch's specialties. I was traditional and ordered my lobster steamed rather than grilled or stuffed. Grilled may have been more flavorful but not as moist. Stuffed would have included crab meat but lost the distinctive lobster taste. For starters, I had a wonderful bowl of clam chowder made without potatoes but with several pieces of clam in every spoonful. A little bacon and oregano were added to this light, saporous soup. The lobster dinner was delivered on a black, bar server's tray. The meal included a 1¼-pound lobster with claws and tail cracked by the kitchen on request, two new potatoes, corn on the cob, a side of cole slaw, melted butter and a lemon wedge. The presentation was reminiscent of an outdoor clambake with plastic ware and paper dishes. The lobster was smooth in texture, moist and savory.

Butch's is definitely the place to come for lobster if you are in the Roaring Fork Valley. However, there is much more on their menu beginning with two pages of appetizers offering every shellfish imaginable: Cape Cod oysters prepared five ways, Maryland-style crab cakes and soft shell crabs, Nova Scotia mussels, escargot, fried calamari or scallops, lobster bisque and four varieties of clams. Everything is made from scratch at Butch's. Spotlighting the Lobster-alternative entrées are fresh fish, barbecued ribs, Alaskan king crab, top sirloin or filet mignon, five shrimp dishes and daily selections of seafood pasta and chicken. Butch only serves Mexican white shrimp which he considers the best. Several of the recipes are Butch's from Boston and much of the fish is from Seattle. A wine and beer list and homemade desserts are available to enhance your dining experience.

Servers are young and friendly. The ambiance in Butch's is a blend of sea and ski with live lobster tank, sailing maps, model clipper ships, pictures from local folks, ocean photos and scenic views of mountains and village. Vines of philodendron grow through a trellis separating the main dining room in two. A stuffed peacock is perched on the brick fireplace mantel above a globe set on the hearth. The sailing maps came from the Straits of Florida, Newbury Port Harbor and Plum Island Sound, Cape Cod Bay, Provincetown Harbor and Grand Cayman. The tip of Provincetown Harbor from Long Point to Race Point used to be Butch's old diving hole. Photographs from the Florida Keys displaying fishing, dolphins, scuba diving, sandy shores, docks and seaplanes mixed well with the maps. Family photos of a beach house in Ipswich, Massachusetts, from the late 1940s and early 1950s and a photo of Butch's daughter on the fireplace mantel added some homey touches to the dining rooms. Several camera shots of

SNOWMASS VILLAGE

the Aspen and Snowmass Village area taken by locals provide ample contrast to the seafaring décor. Whether you are a landlubber on skis or live for the water, you will find Butch's food and atmosphere to your liking.

See bottom of page 264 for restaurant photo.

SPECIAL ONE-TIME OFFER: Buy one entrée at the regular price and receive a free cup of clam chowder or lobster bisque. Valid for every member of your party. Please present to server at time of ordering.
_____ Owner/Manager. _____ Date.

Shannon's Shrimp
(Serves 2)

12 jumbo shrimps (15 to a pound), peeled and deveined, tails optional
Flour seasoned with salt and pepper
Egg batter
Clarified butter
1 teaspoon whole butter
1 teaspoon minced shallots
1/2 teaspoon finely minced garlic
1 ounce White Vermouth
1 teaspoon Dijon mustard
1/4 cup shrimp stock*
1/4 cup cream
1 teaspoon fresh parsley

*Shrimp Stock:
Shrimp shells
2 quarts cold water
1/2 teaspoon Old Bay Seasoning
1/4 cup white wine

1. Shrimp Stock: Rinse shrimp shells in hot water. Place in a three-quart pot. Add cold water. Bring to a boil. Reduce heat and simmer. Season with Old Bay seasoning and white wine. Simmer for 30 minutes. Strain broth to produce shrimp stock. Boil to reduce by half. Should make about 1 pint.
2. Dredge shrimp in flour seasoned with salt and pepper.
3. Dip shrimp in egg batter.
4. Sauté in clarified butter in pre-heated pan under medium heat. Butter should sizzle when shrimp enters pan. Brown shrimp slightly, flip over and brown on other side. DO NOT OVERCOOK.
5. Remove from pan and set aside.

SNOWMASS VILLAGE

6. Add 1 teaspoon of whole butter in pan. Sauté shallots and garlic until translucent.
7. Deglaze with White Vermouth until reduced by half. Add Dijon, shrimp stock, and cream.
8. Return shrimp to pan. Continue to reduce by half or until bubbly. Add fresh parsley.
9. Serve on top or with rice and your favorite vegetable. May also be served with pasta or mashed potatoes.

<u>Wine Recommendation</u>: A semi-sweet, fruity and spicy Gewürztraminer
<u>Recipe by</u>: Mike Shannon who used to own Shannon's Galley in Aspen in the late 1970s. The recipe was modified by Butch Darden, owner and chef, and Peter Affloiter, chef.
See top of page 264 for recipe photo.

The Stew Pot

62 Snowmass Village Mall. 923-2263.
Directions: On Highway 82, heading towards Aspen from Glenwood Springs, go 7 miles past the town of Old Snowmass. Turn right on Brush Creek Road. Go 5 miles to Divide Road, then continue another ¼ mile on Brush Creek Road and take your second right. Enter Lower Mall Parking. Park in Lot #6 or the closest available lot. Go across the street and take the first set of stairs to the Main Mall Level. Go through the Main Mall about 150 feet. The restaurant is on the right.

<u>ESSENTIALS</u>
Cuisine: American Country
Hours: 7 days 11AM-9PM. Closed Mid-APR thru MAY and Mid-OCT to Mid-NOV.
Meals and Prices: Lunch/Dinner $5-$9.
Nonsmoking: All
Take-out: Yes
Alcohol: Beer, wine and limited cocktails

Credit Cards: MC, Visa
Personal Check: Local only
Reservations: Suggested for parties of 6 or more
Wheelchair Access: Yes, the downstairs part of the restaurant.
Dress: Ski clothes/casual
Other: Children's menu. Service charge of 17% may be added for parties of six or more.

<u>HISTORY, PERSONALITY AND CHARACTER</u>
The building occupied by the Stew Pot was built with the rest of the Snowmass Village Mall in 1968. The building was originally two businesses, a bookstore with posters and a small restaurant. In 1972, The Stew Pot opened

when James "Rob" Robinson was a waiter. In 1973, he moved up to manager and in 1974 he began buying shares of the restaurant. By 1977, Rob bought out the original owners to become the sole owner of The Stew Pot. Manager Julie Benjamin has been with the restaurant since 1992. Chef Rigo Salvidrez has been cooking since 1992 and came to The Stew Pot in 1994.

FOOD, SERVICE AND AMBIANCE

The Stew Pot serves sandwiches, hot and hearty soups and chili, old-fashioned beef stew and salads aimed at "filling the skier's appetite." I selected the stew of the day, green chili chicken. It was a warming bowl of appetizing, mildly hot, thick chicken stock filled with big chunks of chicken and potato, celery, carrot, onion, green and red bell pepper, topped with cheddar cheese, sliced black olives and sour cream. The stew came with a slice of wheat bread made at a local bakery that uses The Stew Pot's recipe.

Spotlighting the sandwich board are honey cured turkey breast, smoked ham and Swiss, tuna or chicken salad, avocado or hummus veggie, hot meatloaf and a veggie gardenburger. There are several salads to choose from such as hummus, chicken, tuna, alpine with turkey, chicken-Mandarin and pasta. If you are in the mood for something with a Mexican flair you can try their chili burrito plate. Detain yourself for one of their delectable desserts from Denver like key lime pie, carrot cake, granny-apple pie, Oreo cookie bash, Snicker's pie or premium ice cream.

Rob employs a youthful staff of quick and courteous servers. Rock music played softly in this two-story restaurant adorned with beautiful and colorful Colorado photographs of the Aspen valley, wildflowers, lakes, waterfalls, mountains and trees. Fresh flowers were set at each table. This is a local's local hangout. For healthy food in a friendly environment or a light dinner, come into The Stew Pot.

SPECIAL ONE-TIME OFFER: Receive 20% off the total food portion of your bill for a party of four or less. Please present to server at time of ordering.
_____ Owner/Manager. _____ Date.

SNOWMASS VILLAGE

Chicken Brunswick Stew
(Serves 6)

6 large boneless chicken breasts
1 medium yellow onion, diced
6 celery stalks, diced
4 carrots, diced
1 tablespoon oil
1/4 cup butter
1 cup white flour
2 cups mushrooms, sliced
2 cups zucchini, cubed
2 tablespoons fresh parsley
2 tablespoon fresh basil
1/2 teaspoon pepper
1/4 cup white wine
2 1/2 cups water
3 large red potatoes, cubed
2 10-ounce cans of creamed corn
1 pint heavy whipping cream
2 tablespoons chicken base or chicken concentrated stock (to personal flavor)

1. Bake chicken breasts at 350 degrees for 20 minutes and set aside. Dice when cooled.
2. Sauté onion, celery, and carrots in oil and butter. Add flour once sautéed. Stir until pasty. Add zucchini, mushrooms and seasonings.
3. Add wine and water to cover.
4. Add potatoes and cover with water again. Cook until potatoes are close to done. Add creamed corn, diced chicken, and heavy cream. Check flavor and add chicken base to your taste.
5. Simmer for 15 minutes to allow all flavors to blend. Serve in soup bowls. Add croutons as a garnish option.

Wine Recommendation: Kendall Jackson Chardonnay

Recipe by: Rob Robinson, owner.

See bottom of page 265 for recipe photo.

Village Steakhouse

40 Elbert Lane (in the Wildwood Lodge). 923-2073.

Directions: On Highway 82, heading towards Aspen from Glenwood Springs, go 7 miles past the town of Old Snowmass. Turn right on Brush Creek Road. Go 5 miles to Divide Road, then continue another ¼ mile on Brush Creek Road and take your second right. Enter Lower Mall Parking. Park in Lot #6 or the closest available lot. Go across the street and take the first set of stairs to the Main Mall Level. Go about 200 feet and take the stairway to your right just past Christy Sports. Walk all the way to the top of the stairs. Turn right and walk about 100 yards. The restaurant is on the left in the Wildwood Lodge. After you enter the lodge, take the first stairway to your right up to the restaurant.

ESSENTIALS

Cuisine: Family Steakhouse Offering Vegetarian and Seafood
Hours: 7 days 5PM-10PM. Closed mid-APR to Memorial Day and Mid-OCT to Thanksgiving.
Meals and Prices: Dinner $15-$26
Nonsmoking: All, including the bar downstairs
Take-out: Yes
Alcohol: Full Bar
Credit Cards: All 5
Personal Check: Local only with I.D.
Reservations: Recommended
Wheelchair Access: Yes, by elevator, once inside the Lodge.
Dress: Casual
Other: Children's menu. Service charge of 17% added to parties of 6 or more. On and off premises custom catering and event coordination. Available for weddings and large groups.

HISTORY, PERSONALITY AND CHARACTER

The Wildwood Lodge was originally called The Victoria when it opened on December 17, 1967. In 1982, a steak and lobster house called Pippins was built in the current location of the Village Steakhouse. In 1993, Village Property Management purchased the lodge and on December 7, 1996, the Village Steakhouse opened.

Restaurant manager Brian MacMillan has been with the Village Steakhouse since February 1997. He has been in the restaurant business since 1982 and previously managed the Brothers' Grill in Snowmass Village from 1993 to 1995 and Josephine's in Denver. Chef Michael Kulick began at the Village Steakhouse in December 1997. He has been cooking since 1991 and is a graduate of Paul Smith College Culinary School in the Adirondacks Region of New York State. Prior to coming to Snowmass Village, Michael cooked at the Harvest House and the Zolo Grill in Boulder, Colorado.

SNOWMASS VILLAGE

FOOD, SERVICE AND AMBIANCE

All entrées at the Village Steakhouse come with the biggest and most complete soup and salad bar in Snowmass Village. The evening that I dined here the soups were tomato basil, creamy with big chunks of tomato and basil leaves, and apple-onion with slices and cuts of both. The mild, sweet apple offset the sharp onion very well. The salad portion of the bar featured all the fixings for a Caesar salad, including anchovies, that I recommend. Highlighting the other 20 or so items are pasta salad, mixed field greens, fresh vegetables, sliced hard-boiled eggs, fresh baked bread, roasted garlic hummus, sun-dried tomatoes and six dressings.

For the entrée, I selected the loin of pork chop with cranberry demi-glace, roasted oranges, new potatoes, fresh asparagus and carrots and a sprig of rosemary. The pork chop was moist, juicy and nicely done with a pink center. This was also a dish of contrasting flavors. The sweet cranberries countered the pungently strong rosemary. An overall attractive platter presentation was enhanced with parsley and red pepper sprinkled on the edges. If cranberry sauce is one of your favorite accompaniments at Thanksgiving, you should try this. For dessert, I delved into a tall piece of Black Forest bread pudding, served warm and topped with bing cherries, whipped cream and a mint leaf. The plate presentation was as appealing as this dish was delicious. It was drizzled with cranberry and vanilla sauce and sprinkled with powdered sugar. Simply scrumptious!

For a tasty appetizer to get you started at the Village Steakhouse, you might try the grilled wild boar and fresh game sausage, spinach herb dip served in a garlic bread bowl, or the sturgeon caviar with three smoked fish. Steaks, of course, are the prime attraction with your choice of New York strip, ribeye, filet mignon, T-bone, porterhouse or slow-roasted prime rib. The seafood selections are tempting, offering pine nut and fresh herb encrusted Rocky Mountain rainbow trout, horseradish crusted and pan roasted Atlantic Coast salmon, and ahi tuna steak. The Village Steakhouse also presents a variety of "other stuff" for your dining pleasure like marinated veal chop, beer mustard grilled chicken breast, a half free range chicken, eggplant pancakes and portobello mushrooms. Some delectable desserts include warm, homemade bread pudding with whiskey sauce — for adults only; Heath bar cheesecake; homemade apple, blueberry and pecan pies; and Ben and Jerry's ice cream.

Service was provided by an energetic and accommodating young fellow. Village Steakhouse is a family place that likes kids, as evidenced by the comical and colorful animal caricatures. Helen Peck Taylor decorated the restaurant with her batiks, paintings and creative, wild animal table scenes. All of the artwork shows wild animals at play, which would appeal to children and nature lovers alike. These paintings and wall hangings portray two bears paddling a canoe, a bear going for a hike, a pink salmon swimming upstream, two goats peering over a cliff, a rabbit riding a horse and a wolf howling at the moon. The sign in front of the restaurant, which is also displayed as a painting inside, depicts a rabbit, raccoon, fox, and deer toasting marshmallows over a campfire while a bear plays a guitar. Complementing the setting are a Southwest-style carpet with a diamond pattern in yellow, maroon, red and green; hunter green tables with blond-color wood edges; and hunter green posts and walls. The Village Steakhouse provides imaginative cooking with fanciful ambiance and is a fun place for children and the young at heart.

Special One-Time Offer: Buy one entrée and receive a second entrée of equal or lesser value free (up to $25.00) OR receive 50% off one entrée (up to $12.00). NOT valid on holidays or for special events. Please present at time of ordering. _____ Owner/Manager. _____ Date.

SNOWMASS VILLAGE

Loin of Pork Chop with Cranberry Port Sauce
(Serves 8)

Cranberry-Port Sauce:
1 cup dried cranberries (or substitute 1 1/2 cups of canned cranberries)
1/2 cup port wine
1/2 cup orange juice
1/2 cup cranberry juice
Cornstarch as needed

Pork Chops:
2 tablespoons oil
8 10-ounce pork chops
1/2 cup pecans, crushed
Salt and pepper
4 oranges
Chopped parsley

1. Place dried cranberries and port wine in a non-reactive sauce pan and simmer until the cranberries are plump and the wine is mostly reduced.
2. Add juices and bring to a simmer. Dissolve approximately 2 tablespoons cornstarch in a little cold water and while the sauce is simmering, add a steady stream until the sauce is glossy and thick enough to coat a spoon.
3. In a large skillet, heat 2 tablespoons oil. Roll the edges of the chops in the ground pecans and lightly season with salt and pepper.
4. Sear the chops in the skillet until both sides are nicely browned. Transfer to a baking sheet or roasting pan and cook in a 450 degree oven until medium in temperature, approximately 8 minutes.
5. Cut the oranges into sixths, oil lightly, and grill until they are warm and lightly browned.
6. Allow the chops to sit for a few minutes before serving, then dress with 2 ounces of the cranberry sauce and garnish with grilled oranges and chopped parsley.

Wine Recommendation: Robert Mondavi Carneros, Pinot Noir, 1995

Recipe by: Shane Bruns, chef de cuisine

See top of page 266 for recipe photo.

SOUTH FORK

      South Fork was an early stage station servicing lumbering and mining. It was named for its location at the confluence of the south fork of the Rio Grande del Norte with that of the main river. Between the town and the headwaters of the Rio Grande, there are 47 tributaries with 500 miles of stream to fish. South Fork hosts the annual Rio Grande Raft Race Championship in June and is the beginning of Colorado's historic Silver Thread Scenic Byway that follows the Rio Grande into the San Juan Mountains and mining towns of Creede and Lake City.

      My chosen restaurant will introduce you to some excellent Texas-style barbecue before or after you head over Wolf Creek Pass.

Location of Town: South central Colorado just east of Wolf Creek Pass where Highways 160 and 149 intersect.
Zip Code: 81154. Area Code: 719. Population: 361. Elevation: 8,200ft.

The Mother Lode
30965 Highway 160. 873-0245.
Directions: From the intersection of Highways 160 and 149, go west on Highway 160 for .6 miles. The restaurant is on the right.

ESSENTIALS
Cuisine: Texas-style Barbecue/Pizza
Hours: JUN-OCT: Sun-Thu 10AM-9PM, Fri/Sat 10AM-10PM. NOV-MAY: 7 days 11AM-8PM.
Meals and Prices: Lunch/Dinner $3-$11. Pizza $4-$15.
Nonsmoking: No
Take-out: Yes
Alcohol: No
Credit Cards: MC, Visa
Personal Check: Local only
Reservations: Accepted
Wheelchair Access: Yes, with assistance
Dress: Casual, ski wear, western outfits
Other: Children's menu. Available for large groups

HISTORY, PERSONALITY AND CHARACTER
      The Mother Lode opened in 1990 as a pizza place. The building that it occupies is relatively new, dating back to the mid-1980s. Current owner/manager Bill C. Hays took over the restaurant in December 1997. He entered the restaurant business in 1996 following a career in agricultural production, "the other end of the food chain". Head chef Scott

SOUTH FORK

Swinehart has been with The Mother Lode since 1998. He started cooking in the late 1970s in barbecue areas in the Phoenix area.

FOOD, SERVICE AND AMBIANCE

The Mother Lode has terrific mesquite ribs smoked on the premises. They are meaty and flavorsome with a spicy, tangy, homemade barbecue sauce and fall off the bone. They made a great combination with corn on the cob, baked potato and toast. I did not try the hand-made pizza, but I did see a few being served while I waited for my barbecue. If looks are any indication, their pizza is as good as their ribs.

Their Texas-style barbecue sandwiches and dinners feature brisket, chicken fried steak, Polish sausage, Texas burger, grilled ham and cheese and chopped pork. Showcasing the other dinner entrées are mesquite smoked steak and chicken. Friday night is all-you-can-eat cat fish. For side dishes, you can choose from French fries, potato salad, cole slaw, barbecue or pinto beans and fried okra. Their house pizza special, the "Wild, Wild West", is a creative blend of barbecue sauces, cheddar cheese, onions and beef. Sub sandwiches completes the menu.

When you enter The Mother Lode, walk up to the counter and place your order. Someone will bring the food to your table. The restaurant has tables made from polished slices of wood, log posts and vegas, an arched ceiling and deer heads at opposite ends of the room. Several picture clocks are hung on the walls portraying John Wayne, a pair of kittens, a white wolf, an Indian on a white horse with buffaloes, and the poem "Footprints" on a sandy beach. Additional adornments include an Indian headdress and pouch with feathers and a wall shelf with canisters and a clock. The adjacent lounge hosts a black-iron, wood-burning stove that shares the same flue with a similar stove in the restaurant just like a double-sided fireplace. Also occupying the lounge is a television, a pinball machine and a pair of old skis. There is a front entrance dining area with two tables. If you are looking for good barbecue or pizza in this part of the state, visit The Mother Lode.

SOUTH FORK

Barbecue Sauce
(Makes about 1 1/2 quarts)

- 1 pound brown sugar
- 1 10-ounce ketchup
- 1 teaspoon dehydrated onions
- 1/4 teaspoon cayenne pepper
- 1/2 teaspoon chili powder
- 1/2 teaspoon paprika
- 1/2 teaspoon garlic
- 1/4 teaspoon salt
- 1/2 teaspoon black peppers
- 1/2 cup mustard
- 1/4 cup Worcestershire sauce
- 1/4 cup vinegar
- 1/8 cup cooking oil
- 1/4 cup lemon juice
- 1/8 cup honey

1. Mix all ingredients in a 3-quart sauce pan.
2. Slow cook for 15 minutes. Pour over chicken, pork, or beef ribs or other meat.

Beverage Recommendation: Your favorite dark beer

Recipe by: Bill C. Hays, owner

See bottom of page 266 for recipe photo.

STEAMBOAT SPRINGS

Steamboat Springs was originally a summer playground for the Ute Indians. The town derived its name from the peculiar puffing sounds emitted by one of its former springs. To the trappers of the 1880s, it produced a sound that resembled a steamboat chugging. This spring was destroyed during construction of the Moffat Railroad, now the Denver and Rio Grande Railroad, in 1908. Steamboat is located in a big bend in the Yampa River with the springs on the south bank of the river. Today, Steamboat Springs is considered by many to be "Ski Town USA" because of the large number of Olympian and National Ski Team members produced here.

Five contrasting restaurants give you the opportunity to taste Steamboat Springs' divergent cuisines. There is a multi-national bistro prepared to "transport" you on a culinary journey, a Mexican restaurant with fascinating Mayan and Southwestern decor, a contemporary French bistro with an outstanding wine list, a brewery and tavern serving New American dishes and a smokehouse preparing their own Texas-style, hickory-smoked barbecue.

Location of Town: Northwest Colorado
Zip Code: 80477. Area Code: 970. Population: 6,695. Elevation: 6,728ft.

Alpine Bistro

521 Lincoln Avenue. 879-7757.
Directions: Entering downtown Steamboat Springs on Highway 40 (Lincoln Avenue) from Rabbit Ears Pass, go 3 blocks past the hot springs pool on the right. The restaurant is on the left between 5th and 6th Streets.

ESSENTIALS
Cuisine: Multi-National
Hours: 7 days 5:30PM-10PM. Mid-MAY to Labor Day weekend: Mon-Sat 11:30AM-2:30PM. Closed Mid-APR to Mid-MAY.
Meals and Prices: Lunch $5-$9. Dinner $12-$21
Nonsmoking: All
Take-out: Yes

Alcohol: Full Bar
Credit Cards: MC, Visa, Amx
Personal Check: In-state with I.D.
Reservations: Highly advisable
Wheelchair Access: Yes
Dress: Casual to formal
Other: Catering available for up to 50 people at the Bistro. Bistro cooking school offered.

STEAMBOAT SPRINGS

HISTORY, PERSONALITY AND CHARACTER

Alpine Bistro was originally a dentist's office built in the 1970s. Three different restaurants also occupied this building: a donut shop; Here Comes the Sun, a breakfast and health food place; and Rosie's Cuban Café. In June 1996, Brent C. Holleman opened Alpine Bistro. Brent is a third generation restaurateur and the former executive chef at Guido's in Aspen. He graduated from the Culinary Institute of America in Hyde Park, New York, in 1984 and did his apprenticeship at the Green Briar in White Sulphur Springs, West Virginia. His experience dates back to 1973 and includes the Pier House and the Boneventure Resort in Florida, the Fairmont Hotel in New Orleans and training in Switzerland, France and the Caribbean. Josh Carter, the dining room manager, has been with the restaurant since June 1996.

FOOD, SERVICE AND AMBIANCE

The Alpine Bistro will take you on "a culinary journey through the world" when you visit. Your "trip for the taste buds" will include Switzerland, India, France, the Americas and the Mediterranean. Their menu changes with each of the four seasons and their "family" will present to you what is seasonally fresh. Fondues are fun and seldom found so I ordered the fondue chinoise, raw bite-size pieces of beef top sirloin, veal, chicken and fresh vegetables that you cook yourself in beef broth kept boiling hot on a burner at your table. Long skewer-forks are used for dipping the meats and vegetables that are ready for consumption in a minute or less. The merriment did not stop here as I could then sink my selections into six different sauces offering a diversity of sensations. The sour cream horseradish had a sharp zing. The rémoulade and Swiss cocktail sauces, prepared with cognac, tomato puree and mayonnaise, were creamy. The mango-curry, my favorite, was sweet. The raita, a popular Indian blend of cucumber and yogurt, was tart and tangy. Finally, the béarnaise was delicately spicy. This was a marvelous mixture of tastes!

Engaging openers include raclette, crab cakes, smoked salmon, shrimp rémoulade and marinated-grilled, stuffed portobello mushroom. For an entertaining international entrée, try pheasant stuffed with apple-sage pâté, Greek lamp chops, veal "Zurich style", seafood curry, Mexican chili brushed red trout, Wiener Schnitzel or Swiss cheese fondue. You can complete your wonderful evening of dining with a gourmet coffee, a liquor or one of their delightful desserts like chocolate decadence, pumpkin cheesecake, chocolate fondue, white chocolate truffle cheesecake or Italian apple torta.

Summertime lunches are highlighted by sandwiches, burgers, salads and entrées. A few of the featured items are shrimp salad Marquesa,

STEAMBOAT SPRINGS

German-style smoked ham, ruby red trout and a pasta of the day. Fresh cappuccino, latte or espresso are also available for your pleasure.

Service was friendly, frequent and informative. Josh explained the sauce to me while the bartender answered most of my questions. New Age music played very quietly in the background. This small restaurant is beautified with posters, framed and under glass, demonstrating the multitudinous variety of squashes, Indian corn, berries, chilies, exotic fruits and edible flowers. Local artist, Milly Judson, exhibited a painting of chili peppers in one corner while framed pictures of Brent and newspaper clippings on the restaurant displayed next to the bar. In warmer weather, you can enjoy the "fruits" of Alpine Bistro on their garden café decked with tables, umbrellas and flowers. No matter what season you arrive in, the hospitable staff at the Alpine Bistro will be happy to introduce their cuisine to you from the four corners of the earth.

Special One-Time Offer: Buy one entrée and receive a second entrée of equal or lesser value free (up to $20.00) OR receive 50% off one entrée (up to $10.00). NOT valid on holidays or for special events. Please present at time of ordering. _____ Owner/Manager. _____ Date.

Filet Mignon "Garlic Sun"
(Serves 6)

24 pieces whole peeled garlic
2 tablespoons virgin olive oil

6 7-ounce filet mignons
Salt to taste

10 black peppercorns, crushed
1 tablespoon shallots, chopped

2 medium sprigs of rosemary, chopped
3 ounces Merlot wine
12 ounces demi-glace or brown gravy
6 ounces Italian gorgonzola cheese

1. Pre-heat oven to 275 degrees and roast garlic in half the oil (about 1 hour).
2. Make an incision in each filet, put one piece of garlic in the middle. Brush with olive oil. Season with salt. Grill to preference.
3. Make sauce-- sauté the rest of the garlic, peppercorns, shallots, and rosemary. Add Merlot. Reduce by half. Add demi-glace. Boil for about 5 to 10 minutes.

4. Place 1 ounce of cheese on top and melt in broiler. Pour about 2 ounces of sauce over filet, with 2 cloves of garlic.
5. Serve with your favorite vegetables and potato.

Wine Recommendation: French Bordeaux or California Merlot

Recipe by: Brent C. Holleman, owner and executive chef.

See page 267 for recipe photo.

The Cantina
818 Lincoln Avenue. 879-0826.
Directions: Entering downtown Steamboat Springs on Highway 40 (Lincoln Avenue) from Rabbit Ears Pass, go six blocks past the hot springs pool on the right. The restaurant is on the right between 8th and 9th Streets.

ESSENTIALS
Cuisine: Mexican
Hours: 7 days 11AM-10PM (lunch until 4PM, dinner from 4PM). Closed Mid-APR to end of APR.
Meals and Prices: Lunch $4-$9. Dinner $7-$15
Nonsmoking: All. Smoking only permitted at the bar.
Take-out: Yes

Alcohol: Full Bar
Credit Cards: MC, Visa, Amx, Disc
Personal Check: Local only
Reservations: No
Wheelchair Access: Yes
Dress: Casual
Other: Children's menu. No separate checks. Senior discount of 20% on food only.

HISTORY, PERSONALITY AND CHARACTER
     The Cantina was originally an ice house and grocery store built in 1932. According to local legend (what the town's old timers say), ice from the Yampa River was cut in blocks with saws and carried in wagons to the ice house. Then saw dust and dirt was thrown on the ice to preserve it for summer. The river rock and cement wall in the back of the building and basement was set in place by Carl Howelsen, a stone master remembered more for bringing ski jumping to the United States from Norway. In the 1960s, the back of the restaurant became Gold Mine Pizza while the downstairs, now used for storage, was the Steinkeller German Beer Hall. Three college buddies opened the Cantina in 1972. Current owners Rogers Israel, James Billys and John Townes bought the restaurant in 1977. Rogers and James

STEAMBOAT SPRINGS

also manage the Cantina. James used to manage the Wobbly Barn in Killington, Vermont. Head chef Scott Schrieber has been with the Cantina since 1995. He was a cook at Hart's Turkey Farm in New Hampshire from 1976 to 1984, on St. Martin in the Virgin Islands from 1987 to 1990 and at L'Apogee in Steamboat from 1991 to 1993.

FOOD, SERVICE AND AMBIANCE

My server started my lunch by serving yellow and blue corn chips with homemade salsa, big chunks of tomato in tomato sauce with jalapeño, onion, garlic and green chilies. From the á la carte menu, I ordered the enchilada in a moderately hot green tomatillo sauce and the chili relleno in a mild red chili sauce. The enchilada was flavorful with seasoned ground beef in a thin, soft corn tortilla topped with sour cream and scallions. The tasty chili relleno was a giant pablano chili, easily six inches long and two inches high, dipped in beer batter and deep fried to a crispy golden brown. These were two complementary yet opposite dishes.

For a lunch or dinner appetizer, you can try Rocky Mountain smoked trout or smoked fresh tuna with jalapeño or ancho-chili mayonnaise or jalapeño poppers. Chili, soup, salads and sandwiches are featured on the lunch menu. Spotlighting this selection are Mexi-toss salad, a local's favorite, Caesar salad, taco salad, Monte Cristo sandwich and turkey wrap. In addition to the chili, soup and salads, the dinner menu offers house specialties like fajitas, stuffed chicken breast and Santa Fe enchiladas. The lunch and dinner Mexican specialties include quesadilla, tamales, chimichanga, taco grandé, huevos rancheros and breakfast burrito. There is a children's menu and, to complete your meal, several homemade desserts like fried ice cream, flan, mud pie, brownie sundae, New York cheesecake, key lime pie, sopapilla and chocolate mousse.

My server was honest, helpful and quick. Old rock tunes played quietly as I gazed at the Mexican, Mayan and Southwest-style decor. Two arched entrances lead to the dining room which is past the bar. The faces of two ceramic sun gods stand watch over the entrances and smile down on the dining room. A locally-made stained-glass artwork showing a Mexican Village scene separate the entrances. Fans and tiffany lamps hang from the ceiling. The red rock wall on the right is adorned with a large embroidered tapestry of a Mexican village, a Mexican hat and paintings of cowboys and horses. Paintings of peasants, photos of El Rapido Tortilla Factory in Tucson, Mexico, watercolors and photos of local men wearing sombreros and photos of old Indian women beautify the left wall. Enhancing this motif is a leather art work of "Cantina Man" and three decorator plates showing flowers and peacock feathers with bright splashy colors.

The front of the house displays a safe from the Mosler Safe and Lock Company that was found in a dry river bed in Wyoming and a Civil War vintage antique mirror over the host's station. However, the most engrossing embellishment and my favorite is the red and orange four-sided figure with legs extended on each side and diagonal lines through the figure. According to Steven "Starsparks" Brick, founder and director of Dreamspell College in Riner, Virginia, this artwork is the Hunab Ku, a sign of the galactic Mayan pyramid and urban architects in use from 1000 BC to 830 AD. It is known as "The One Giver of Movement and Measure". The Cantina has been serving fine Mexican food for over 20 years in one of the more intriguing atmospheres that you will find in Colorado.

See bottom of page 268 for restaurant photo.

Chile Rellenos with Green Tomatillo Sauce
(Serves 6)

Chile Rellenos:
12 5" to 6" fresh poblano chilies
1 3/4 pounds Monterey Jack
    cheese, grated
Masa harina (a lime cured corn
    flour, enough to coat pepper

8 egg whites
8 egg yolks
1 teaspoon salt
8 ounces beer
1 3/4 cups all purpose flour

1. Blanche chiles in hot oven or over char-broiled until showing blisters.
2. "Sweat" chiles by placing in a closed container, peel when cooled.
3. Make small, lengthwise slit in side of chile. Remove seeds.
4. Stuff pepper with cheese. Roll stuffed pepper in masa harina.
5. Whip egg whites until stiff. Mix yolks, salt, beer; adding flour one cup at a time.
6. Mix in 1/2 of whipped egg whites then fold in remaining egg whites.
7. Dip each stuffed coated chile into batter and deep fry until golden brown. Serve immediately with green tomatillo sauce.

STEAMBOAT SPRINGS

Green Tomatillo Sauce:
- 1/2 medium onion, diced
- 3/4 teaspoon garlic, chopped
- 1 fresh jalapeño, diced fine
- 24 fluid ounces whole green mild tomatillo
- 3 whole pickled jalapeños
- 1 cup frozen, mild green chiles, chopped
- 3/4 teaspoon Maggi seasoning (soy sauce)
- 3/4 teaspoon fresh cilantro
- 1 Tablespoon cornstarch
- 2 Tablespoons water

1. "Sweat" onions in thick-bottomed pot until clear; add garlic and fresh jalapeños.
2. Roughly blend drained tomatillos and pickled jalapeños. Add green chiles and blended tomatillos/jalapeños to pot with onions and garlic. Add soy and cilantro.
3. Bring to a simmer, stirring often.
4. Add cornstarch mixed with water to make a slurry. Simmer 5 minutes, stirring continuously.

Beverage Recommendation: Dos Equis Mexican Beer

Recipe by: Scott Schrieber, head chef.

See top of page 268 for recipe photo.

L'Apogée

911 Lincoln Avenue. 879-1919.
Directions: Entering downtown Steamboat Springs on Highway 40 (Lincoln Avenue) from Rabbit Ears Pass, go seven blocks past the hot springs pool on the right. The restaurant is on the left between 9th and 10th Streets.

ESSENTIALS
Cuisine: Contemporary French
Hours: 7 nights 5:30PM-9:30PM or until last seating.
Meals and Prices: Dinner $22-$38
Nonsmoking: All
Take-out: No
Alcohol: Full Bar
Credit Cards: MC, Visa, Amx

Personal Check: In-state with I.D.
Reservations: Recommended
Wheelchair Access: Yes
Dress: Comfortable, from 3-piece suits to ski pants.
Other: Children's menu. Catering and banquet facility available.

HISTORY, PERSONALITY AND CHARACTER

L'Apogée occupies the "Harwig Building" constructed in the early 1880s. It was used as a saddlery store for many years and had several tenants before L'Apogée opened in 1979. Jamie and Sandy Jenny purchased the building in October 1985 and extensively remodeled it into Harwigs Grill and L'Apogée Restaurant. Jamie has been in the restaurant business since 1971, served a three-year apprenticeship in Philadelphia, then came to Colorado in 1975 to manage the restaurant by the gondola. Sandy owned Soupçon Restaurant in Steamboat before joining Jamie at L'Apogée in 1992. Jamie and Sandy both operate the restaurant.

Dining room manager Lee Parker has been with L'Apogée since 1993 and was formerly at Giovanni's in Steamboat. He has been in the restaurant business in Steamboat since 1983. Chef Richard Billingham, who's recipes have appeared in Bon Appetite and Gourmet Magazines, started at L'Apogée in the early 1980s. He left in 1984 to open Ragnar's and Hazie's in Steamboat and traveled to Australia in 1988 where he spent 2½ years opening restaurants. He returned to L'Apogée in 1990.

FOOD, SERVICE AND AMBIANCE

L'Apogée has a nightly menu of specials as well as a regular menu that changes quarterly. I started with the potage du jour, a smooth, roasted bell pepper cream soup topped with croutons and sprinkled with parmesan and parsley. My entrée was the rabbit prepared three ways. First, there was the fresh leg of rabbit rubbed with fresh herbs, oven roasted and

STEAMBOAT SPRINGS

garnished with a sprig of rosemary. Then there was the pan-seared, sautéed tenderloin drizzled with rabbit jus. Finally, the roasted rabbit was shredded with hot house tomatoes and served in a tomato, onion and orange ragout. This was a very lean combination and very moist with roasted rabbit jus. Glazed julienne carrots and a tomato half topped with creamed eggplant and Parmesan cheese complemented the meal.

Chef Richard's menu features freshly prepared salads, classic French onion soup, seafood, meats, wild game, fowl, nightly veal and fruits of the sea selections and tableside preparation. Fresh foie gras is prepared a variety of ways such as foie brûlée topped with brandy brown sugar and caramelized. The veal could be a rib eye cut with a French bread foie gras stuffing, scaloppini lightly sautéed with fresh forest mushrooms or a center cut chop char-grilled. The seafood special might be jumbo prawns rosemary skewered and sizzled tableside or fresh filet of Hawaiian snapper skillet roasted and served with grilled prawns. Other notable choices include twice baked ½ duckling glazed with honey, medallions of south Texas Nilgai antelope and rack of Colorado lamb with a minted lingonberry demi-glace.

L'Apogée has been awarded every year since 1987 with the rare "Best of Awards of Excellence" from The Wine Spectator Magazine. They have also developed a cruvinet wine dispensing system allowing them to serve over forty vintage wines by the glass including some of the finest older bottles. The Harwig Building has a temperature controlled room for white wines on the ground level and a large cellar directly below the restaurant for storing red wines. With Chef Richard's exquisite cuisine and their award-winning wine list of 860 varieties, there never has been a better time or place to complement your meal with a glass or bottle of the "fermented grape". To complete your dining experience, there are several distinguished desserts to choose from like white chocolate bread pudding, warm pineapple tart with rum caramel anglaise, three chocolate mousse made with dark, white and milk chocolates and mild chocolate pyramid filled with milk chocolate, Grand Marnier mousse.

Several punctual, courteous and jovial servers attended my table to host, take my order, serve the dishes and announce the desserts. Candlelit dining is accompanied by a live piano player with a rendition of contemporary jazz and popular tunes. Shell-shaped sconces and white linen on mauve tablecloths with mauve napkins provide the elegance for the evening. Adorning the walls are several modern artworks depicting fishermen in a swamp, a bear in the wilderness and seagulls at the seashore. Crystal and stained-glass windows face the street. In the summer, patio dining is available. L'Apogée is one of those rare restaurants that offers outstanding quality unpretentiously with a commitment to excellence in food and service.

Lapin a ma facon
"Rabbit my way"
(Serves 4)

2 whole rabbits, heads off
1/2 cup kosher salt
1/2 cup fresh thyme leaves
2 oranges, flesh only, chopped

2 tomatoes, seeded, peeled, and chopped
1 cup petite chanterelle mushrooms
Salt and fresh ground white pepper to taste

1. Combine the kosher salt and half the thyme leaves together and rub vigorously into the rabbits. Refrigerate overnight. Next day rinse thoroughly and pat dry.
2. Remove the hind legs and loins. Roast the carcasses in a medium hot oven until golden. When cool, remove as much meat as possible with a fork, shredding it in the process.
3. Place the carcasses in a sauce pot and cover with water. Bring to a boil and reduce to a simmer for 3 hours, adding water if needed. Strain and cool completely.
4. Combine the shredded rabbit meat, oranges, tomatoes, and mushrooms. Season with salt and ground white pepper and the remaining thyme leaves. Set the hash aside.
5. Remove the femur bones from the hind legs, stand upright in an entrement ring and roast in a medium hot oven for about 12 minutes.
6. Meanwhile, lightly dust the loins with flour and pan-sear in butter until golden brown. Add the hash and 1/2 the rabbit jus and simmer over low heat until completely heated throughout.
7. Place the hind leg toward the back of the plate and set the loin around the front, sliced on the bias. Divide the hash onto the plates, drizzle with the remaining jus, and garnish with fresh thyme sprigs.

<u>Wine Recommendation</u>: Robert Sinskey Pinot Noir

<u>Recipe by</u>: Richard Billingham, chef

# Steamboat Brewery and Tavern

435 Lincoln Avenue. 879-2233.
Directions: Entering downtown Steamboat Springs on Highway 40 (Lincoln Avenue) from Rabbit Ears Pass, go two blocks past the hot springs pool on the right. The restaurant is on the left on the southeast corner of Lincoln Avenue and 5th Street behind the Sunglass Hut.

ESSENTIALS
Cuisine: New American
Hours: 7 days 11:30AM-10PM (lunch all day, dinner from 5PM).
Meals and Prices: Lunch $5-$8. Dinner $9-$13.
Nonsmoking: All. Smoking only permitted in tavern.
Take-out: Yes
Alcohol: Full Bar
Credit Cards: All 5

Personal Check: Local with I.D.
Reservations: No
Wheelchair Access: Yes
Dress: Casual
Other: Service charge of 15% may be added for parties of 6 or more. Surcharge of $.50 for substitutions. Take out charge of $.25 per item. No split checks.

HISTORY, PERSONALITY AND CHARACTER
The Steamboat Brewery and Tavern was opened on May 14, 1993 by general manager Joe Walker, executive chef Joel Kunkel and head brewer David Brereton. The brewery in the back can be toured on request. The tavern in front is a casual eating and drinking establishment divided into a dining room and tap room.

FOOD, SERVICE AND AMBIANCE
The menu from the Steamboat Tavern emphasized fresh, made-from-scratch items such as homemade soups and fresh baked breads. The menu is changed every three months to provide variety and to take advantage of seasonally fresh items. I was in the mood for seafood so I ordered some savory homemade Portuguese clam and salmon stew with mushrooms, onion, parsley and herbs in a fish broth. I followed this with a seared, pepper-crusted tuna steak sandwich. It consisted of tender and tasty charred tuna, rare in the middle with fresh basil leaves, lemon aïoli dressing and plenty of chopped black peppercorns on top. Lettuce, tomato and sharp red onion came on the side to add more zing to the peppercorns.
The Steamboat Tavern has some mainstay menu items for all seasons like green chili pork stew, Caesar salad, chèvre cheese and hot crisp fried onions salad, Brooklyn sausage pizza, stromboli Siciliano,

cheeseburger deluxe and classic corned beef brisket Reuben. Various preparations of hummus, fried calamari and turkey are found year-round at the restaurant as well.

Otherwise, you might see fried green tomatoes and field greens, spicy black bean cake sandwich or herb and cracked pepper roasted pork loin in the fall. Winter selections include homemade chicken cannelloni, Santa Fe tequila marinated chicken pizza or Guido's garlic basil fettuccini. Stop here in the spring and you could be dining on roasted asparagus and mascarpone, warm roasted asparagus and Caesar salad wrapped in a spinach tortilla or Catalon-style venison London broil. Sopapilla with wild mushrooms and roasted pablano chilis, chilled Mexican vichyssoise and wild mushrooms in a walnut cream sauce are some of the summer highlights.

To accompany your meal, try one of their fresh brewed beers served from the 310-gallon tanks seen behind the bar. Six beers, mainly ales, are always on tap. If beer is not your fancy, imbibe in their homemade root beer, locally roasted coffee or hot tea, sparkling water or non-alcoholic beers. For a sweet ending to your meal, the Steamboat Brewery presents a springtime chocolate raspberry stout gelato with warm Jamaican rum sauce, a summer season mascarpone and rum cheese cake, pumpkin bread pudding with rum hard sauce for the autumn and Dutch apple pie with zabaglione gelato as a winter warmer.

Service was fast and friendly. Rock and country music played quietly in the background. The dining area is up a few stairs to the left of the entrance. Large windows and glass doors facing 5th Street permit a profusion of light to shine on the cloth beer signs, barmaids' trays and framed beer posters. The Tavern is an open area with a spacious orifice between the dining room and tap room, which has appeal on many levels. There are cribbage boards and backgammon for gamesters, two televisions for sports enthusiasts and a view into the flower shop next door for romantics. The tap room is accented with soft cherry wood and an old-fashion tile floor while high-back cherry wood booths punctuate the dining room. In the summer, you can relax under a big tent outside in the beer garden. The Steamboat Brewery and Tavern is a favorite local's hang out that out-of-town travelers should not pass by in any season.

See top of page 269 for restaurant photo.

STEAMBOAT SPRINGS

<u>Special One-Time Offer</u>: Half price on your first round of beers, beer samplers or homemade root beers. No food purchase necessary. Valid for everyone in your group. _____ Owner/Manager. _____ Date.

Ricotta Stuffed Chicken
(Serves 2)

2 8-ounce chicken breasts with wings attached
1/2 cup ricotta
3 cloves garlic, roasted in olive oil in oven, then chopped
1/2 of a roasted red pepper

1/8 teaspoon thyme
1/8 teaspoon oregano
1 egg
Pinch of salt and pepper
Flour
Olive oil
Parmesan cheese

Cooked fettuccine (12 to 16 ounces)
Marinara Sauce

1. Make an incision in the side of both breasts.
2. Mix ricotta with the garlic, red pepper, thyme, oregano, egg, salt, and pepper.
3. Stuff the chicken with ricotta mixture, flour it lightly, sear it in a pan with olive oil until golden brown.
4. Bake in oven for 20 minutes or until temperature reaches 160 degrees. Do not overcook.
5. Serve over fettuccine with marinara sauce.
6. Garnish with fresh Parmesan.

<u>Wine Recommendations</u>: Hogue Cellars Cabernet Sauvignon/Merlot or Wild Horse Pinot Noir

<u>Recipe by</u>: Joel Kunkel, executive chef

Steamboat Smokehouse

912 Lincoln Avenue (in the Thiesen Mall). 879-RIBS (7427).
Directions: Entering downtown Steamboat Springs on Highway 40 (Lincoln Avenue) from Rabbit Ears Pass, go seven blocks past the hot springs pool on the right. The restaurant is on the right between 9th and 10th Streets.

ESSENTIALS

Cuisine: Texas-style, Hickory-Smoked Pit Barbecue
Hours: 7 days 11AM-10PM. Closed Sun from Mid-APR to late MAY.
Meals and Prices: Lunch $6-$7. Dinner $9-$14.
Nonsmoking: Yes
Take-out: Yes
Alcohol: Full Bar
Credit Cards: MC, Visa, Amx
Personal Check: Yes for checks numbered over 500 with I.D.

Reservations: Not accepted
Wheelchair Access: Yes
Dress: Extremely casual
Other: Children's menu. Service charge of 15% may be added for tables of 6 or more. On and off premises catering with portable smoker. Available for banquets and receptions. Free delivery during ski season. Whole meats, game and fish for sale by special order.

HISTORY, PERSONALITY AND CHARACTER

The Steamboat Smokehouse was originally a livery built in the 1880s. Prior to 1990, the front of the restaurant was a bookstore called Boomtown Books while the back was Blue Bayou, a Cajun Restaurant. The building was vacant for a year before Fritz Aurin, C.S.M. (Certified SmokeMaster) opened the Steamboat Smokehouse in November 1991. Front house manager Drew Coulton started at the Smokehouse in 1994 with experience also dating to the early 1990s. He formerly managed T.G.I.F. and Pizza Hut in Cincinnati. The Steamboat Smokehouse was praised in the Winter/Spring 1998 issue of "Steamboat Magazine" and was recommended as a great family restaurant for Steamboat Springs in the book "Fun Places to go with Children in Colorado" by Marty Meitus and Patti Thorn.

FOOD, SERVICE AND AMBIANCE

The Steamboat Smokehouse slow smokes all of their meats at temperatures ranging from 190°F to 250°F. They have two smokers dating back to the opening of the restaurant, one inside and one outside. The smokers use heat only from solid hickory logs brought up from the Little Dixie area in southeast Oklahoma. No gas or electric heat is used. The brisket and pork take 15 hours in the smoker, the ribs 5 hours and the chicken about

STEAMBOAT SPRINGS

4 hours. Prior to smoking, the meats are rubbed with a mixture of secret herbs and spices that Fritz obtained from his native Texas.

I delved into a combination of meaty pork ribs and lean, not very spicy hot, jalapeño sausage. Two tasty barbecue sauces were served on the side. One was hot, thicker and redder with more tomato flavor. The other was mild, darker and with more chili spice flavor. This is great "off-the-bone" dining. Carry a toothpick when you visit. Mashed potatoes and smoked beans were my side choices. The potatoes were just the way that I like them, skins on, lumpy and with rich brown gravy. The beans were slightly spicy with green and red pepper and onion. The other side options were cole slaw, fries and dinner salad.

The Smokehouse is a family-style restaurant and one of the few in Colorado that serves peanuts in the shell rather than bread or chips and salsa. You discard the shells on the floor after eating the peanuts. For appetizers, the restaurant serves four different kinds of chicken wings, fried okra, jalapeño poppers and bleu balls (chicken cordon bleu). Sliced brisket, pulled pork, pork ribs, turkey breast and jalapeño sausage can be ordered as a sandwich or as a dinner. Additional Sandwich selections include turkey salad, chopped brisket, barbecue Reuben with corned beef, a Memphis special with brisket or pork smothered with cole slaw, turkey breast or a veggie sandwich. A half chicken is available after 5PM. You can enhance your smoked barbecue with draft or bottle beer, wine or margaritas. Other stuff to choose from on the menu are smoked brisket chili, a couple of veggie sandwich alternatives and the Smokehouse salad. For a sweet dessert, you can have deep-dish pecan cobbler, a root beer float or an outrageous brownie sundae.

Service was fast and friendly. My meal on paper plates came out in about five minutes. I listened to country rock music as I sat on a wood bench at a table with a hunter green plastic cover. The rock back wall and the roof timbers are from the original building. The rock was quarried in Steamboat Springs. Busts of wild animals bedeck the walls: deer, buffalo, black bear, long-horn sheep, mountain goat and, my best-liked, a jackalope with a pig's snout hugging a rabbit. Enhancing this ambiance are pictures of wild horses roaming the range and a white horse in a corral. The camaraderie of the Steamboat Smokehouse staff is evident from the party pictures of the crew taken in the restaurant and in the mountains. For hot "out-of-the-smoker" smoked meats served by sociable people in a 19th century locale, come to the Steamboat Smokehouse.

STEAMBOAT SPRINGS

SPECIAL ONE-TIME OFFER: Purchase two dinners and receive a complimentary post peanut viddle (food appetizer). Please present to server at time of ordering. _____ Owner/Manager. _____ Date.

Pecan Cobbler
(Serves 6 to 8)

Cobbler Dough: For an 8x8-inch deep baking dish
1/4 cup lard
1/2 cup butter
1/4 cup Crisco
1 1/2 cups all purpose flour
1/4 teaspoon salt
1/2 tablespoon sugar
1 egg
3 tablespoons cold water

Filling:
3 egg whites
4 whole eggs
1 1/4 cups white sugar
1 1/4 cups light corn syrup
1/3 cup melted butter, cooled
1/4 cup Captain Morgan's spiced rum
1/4 teaspoon vanilla extract
1/4 cup heavy creme
1/8 teaspoon salt
1 3/4 cups pecan pieces

1. Dough: Allow fats to warm to room temperature, about 1 hour.
2. Mix butter and lard, then add other dry ingredients. Mix in Crisco with dough. Add water and mix into dough with rubber spatula by folding and pressing into mixture.
3. Flatten into a square about 1/8 inch to 1/4 inch thick. Wrap in food wrap (Saran wrap) and store in refrigerator for 30 minutes to an hour. If dough has stored longer, allow it to warm at room temperature for about an hour before rolling.
4. Pre-heat over to 350 degrees.
5. For filling: Beat egg whites and whole eggs with a whisk. Whisk in additional ingredients.
6. Baking: Using flour to prevent sticking, roll out dough to at least 12 inch x 12 inch section to cover bottom and sides of pan up to the top. Lay in baking pan with rolling pin or by folding and then unfolding on pan.
7. Fold any overlap behind top of dough and pinch in with finger or fork. Roll bottom with perforating roller or use fork to perforate. Pour pecan pieces in shell. Pour filling into shell.
8. Bake in pre-heated 350-degree oven for 1 hour (set timer for 45 minutes to check) or until knife inserted into middle comes out clean.

See bottom of page 269 for recipe photo.

STERLING

David Leavitt, a surveyor for the Union Pacific Railroad, named Sterling after his hometown in Illinois. He started a ranch in the area and surveyed the Sterling Ditch. The South Platte River and the old Overland Trail pass through this area. Wood carver Brad Rhea has left his mark on the town with numerous carved trees.

The following unique family restaurant serves some good home cooking along with a rare piece of Americana.

Location of Town: Northeast Colorado on I-76
Zip Code: 80751. Area Code: 970. Population: 10,400. Elevation: 3,939 ft.

T. J. Bummer's

203 Broadway Street. 522-8397.
Directions: Take Exit 125 from I-76. Proceed north on Highway 6 going over a high bridge. At the first signal past the bridge, turn right onto 3rd Street (Highway 138). Go six blocks. The restaurant is on the right, ½ block past the next signal.

ESSENTIALS
Cuisine: Family
Hours: 7 days 5:30AM-9PM
Meals and Prices: Breakfast/Lunch $3-$6. Dinner $5-$15.
Nonsmoking: All
Take-out: Yes
Alcohol: No
Credit Cards: MC, Visa, Amx, Disc

Personal Check: Yes, with I.D.
Reservations: No
Wheelchair Access: Yes
Dress: Casual
Other: Senior citizens menu with free coffee or tea. Children's menu. Service charge of 15% added for parties of 7 or more.

HISTORY, PERSONALITY AND CHARACTER

T. J. Bummer's was originally a Country Kitchen Restaurant built in the mid-1970s. The Country Kitchen eventually became just The Kitchen. In 1986, Dan and Karen Rich purchased The Kitchen and opened T. J. Bummer's. The restaurant acquired its name from an 1898 family photo of T. J. and Amanda Bummer, "relatives" of Dan's, hanging on one of the restaurant walls. This is the first restaurant for both Dan and Karen who also opened the J. & L. Café in Sterling in 1994. Karen is the hostess at T. J. Bummer's.

Bruce and Eileen McMahon manage both T. J. Bummer's and the J. & L. Café. Bruce began in the restaurant business in 1960 in Denver. He managed Luby's Cafeteria in Denver and Texas for 11 years before becoming general manager of T. J. Bummer's in 1994. Eileen has been the dining room manager since 1993. She previously worked for her parents' restaurant in Sterling and managed the cafeteria at the Budweiser Brewery in Fort Collins, Colorado, for four years.

John McMahon and Todd J. Rich, the sons of the owners and managers, are the kitchen managers and head cooks. Todd has been cooking in restaurants since 1988 and previously trained as a chef at Yellowstone National Park. He has been with the restaurant since 1991. John has been at T. J. Bummer's since 1993 and formerly was a cook at Denny's and his parents' dinner theater, both in Fort Collins, Colorado.

FOOD, SERVICE AND AMBIANCE

T. J. Bummer's motto is "Friendly — not fancy". Dan and Karen also "expect and demand premium service from [their] wait staff". I found all of this to be true on my visit. Headlining their dinner menu are chicken, steak and seafood. The recipe for coating the shrimp is their own and they prepare many of the sauces in house. I went with the top sirloin pepper steak, southwest style, with the soup of the day, chili cheese. The soup was very hearty, chock full of tomatoes with ground beef, kidney beans, bell peppers, onions and celery. The flavorsome, juicy and tender pepper steak was prepared medium-rare just the way I like it, topped with a blend of special seasonings and a whole green chili, seeds and all, marinated in pepper juice. All of T. J. Bummer's steaks "are aged to perfection, hand cut and cooked to your specifications." A baked potato and dinner roll accompanied the meal. Cornbread muffins are also available.

Highlighting the "served all day" breakfast menu are homemade muffins, omelets, biscuits and gravy, pancakes, chicken fried hamburger steak, German sausage, breakfast burrito with award winning green chili (1st place in the Sterling Green Chili Cookoff), French toast, Belgian waffle, sirloin and ground steak. A variety of burgers, sandwiches and salads are featured on the lunch menu including a pattymelt, turkey club, sirloin steak sandwich, taco salad and California chicken chef salad. They also serve shrimp or chicken baskets. Spotlighting their signature dinner entrées are great prime rib, barbecued baby-back ribs and chicken-fried chicken breast (the biggest seller in the house). For dessert, try one of their fresh baked fruit pies, New York style cheesecake, hot fudge cake, sundaes, strawberry shortcake or apple dumplings.

STERLING

Their staff is well-trained and proficient. They provide service with great dignity. A variety of pop tunes played very faintly in the background. Those old enough to remember and those who just like antiques and nostalgia will love this place. The windmill in front of T. J. Bummer's is an introduction of things to come when you pass through their doors. In the foyer, you will discover an old radio with big dials, a phonograph speaker for a public address system, a Crescent radio receiver by Sears, Roebuck & Co., Zane Grey novels, a Mae West poster and the front grill from an old Ford.

Just inside the restaurant, you will see an old red telephone booth (I half expected Dr. Who to jump out at any minute), a fireplace and a big red Mobile gas pump, converted to a fish tank, with the red flying horse emblem on top. Further investigation revealed a metal box for "Iten's Fairy Crackers" on top of a barrel labeled "Sincerity Brand Crackers, Cakes and Biscuits". Advertisements for Cactus Tire Boots and Patches, Chevrolet Automobiles ("So smooth, so powerful"), Ayer's sarsaparilla and Town Talk Bread accentuate this melange.

There's more! Jars of fruits and vegetables — carrots, tomatoes, pickles, peaches and cherries — canned by Dan adorn the shelves. Hanging from the ceiling are a Quaker State Motor Oil sign, a figure of Snoopy dressed as "The Red Baron", a rifle, a red antique child's tractor, a crate for Sunflower Shoes, an old tricycle, a Jack Daniel's Whiskey sign and lamps. Posters of Hollywood stars from the 1930s and 1940s — Judy Garland, Abbott and Costello, Charley Chaplin, W. C. Fields, Laurel and Hardy, and The Marx Brothers — amplify the romantic setting. The rear left booth has an old 1934 radio and there is a California license plate celebrating the 1939 World's Fair. Finally, neon figures of a pink pig and a green chili complete this extraordinary collage.

Dan, Karen and their staff take great pride in what the locals affectionately refer to as "Bummer's". The folks here allude to their restaurant as "world famous" and perhaps it will be one day. Dan states that travelers from across the country and Canada are frequently surprised and awed when they discover Bummer's. Karen, who asks that "you come and see us", says "we hear high praise from travelers almost on a daily basis". Stop at T. J. Bummer's and enjoy some super fare served by a staff that will rival those in many higher-priced establishments. You will be treating yourself to a unique slice of Americana that should not be missed.

SPECIAL ONE-TIME OFFER: Buy one entrée and receive 50% off a second entrée of equal or lesser value. Discount valid for one second entrée only. Please present to server at time of ordering. _____Owner/Manager. _____Date.

Baby-Back Ribs with Barbecue Sauce
(Makes 3 to 4 Quarts)

Select imported Danish baby-back ribs, in slabs weighing 1 1/4 pounds or less

1/2 cup chopped onion
1/4 cup olive oil or salad oil

3 14-ounce bottles of catsup
1 1/2 14-ounce bottles of water
1/3 cup of vinegar
1/3 cup of Lea and Perrins
1/4 cup of Liquid Smoke
1/3 cup of Brer Rabbit Molasses

1/3 cup yellow mustard
2 tablespoons salt
1 teaspoon black pepper
1/8 teaspoon cayenne pepper
2 tablespoons Durkees hot sauce
1/4 teaspoon garlic powder

1/3 cup of brown sugar

1. <u>Sauce</u>: Sauté onions in oil until transparent. Add the rest of the ingredients (except brown sugar and ribs).
2. Bring to a boil and simmer for one hour. Then add brown sugar.
3. Bring 3 gallons of water to a boil with 2 cups of salt and 1/2 cup of black pepper.
4. Place slabs of ribs in boiling water and bring back to a boil for 30 minutes.
5. Remove from water and baste with sauce.
6. Cook for 4 1/2 hours in regular oven at 250 degrees..
7. Take slabs out of the slow cooker as needed and finish for 4 to 5 minutes on each side on a charcoal broiler.
8. Serve with side dishes.

<u>Beverage Recommendation</u>: Your favorite cold beer

<u>Recipe by</u>: Bruce McMahan, manager

See top of page 270 for recipe photo.

Gooseberry Pie from The Goose Berry Patch in Penrose.

The Martin family in front of The Goose Berry Patch in Penrose.

*Indo Chicken with Sweet and Sour Cucumber Relish from The Pickle Barrel in Silverton.
Photo by Bonnie Stuntebeck.*

*The Pickle Barrel in Silverton.
Photo by Herb Barnett.*

*Grilled Lamb Chops with Tomato Pearl Couscous from
The Brothers' Grille in Snowmass Village.
Photo by David J. Gruber.*

*Shannon's Shrimp from Butch's Lobster Bar in Snowmass Village.
Photo by David J. Gruber.*

*Butch, with a picture of his daughter Lauren on the mantel,
at Butch's Lobster Bar in Snowmass Village.
Photo by David J. Gruber.*

*Pizza Burrito from Emma's Hacienda in San Luis.
Photo by Joetta Frost.*

*Chicken Brunswick Stew from The Stew Pot in Snowmass Village.
Photo by David J. Gruber.*

Loin of Pork Chop with Cranberry Port Sauce from
the Village Steakhouse in Snowmass Village.
Photo by David J. Gruber.

Barbecue Sauce from The Mother Lode in South Fork.
Photo by Bill Hayes.

Filet Mignon "Garlic Sun" from The Alpine Bistro in Steamboat Springs.

Chili Rellenos with Green Tomatillo Sauce from The Cantina in Steamboat Springs. Photo by Ken Proper.

The Cantina in Steamboat Springs. Photo by Ken Proper.

*The Steamboat Brewery and Tavern in Steamboat Springs.
Photo by Joe Walker.*

*Pecan Cobbler from the Steamboat Smokehouse in Steamboat Springs.
Photo by Fritz Aurin.*

Baby-Back Ribs with Barbecue Sauce from T. J. Bummer's in Sterling. Photo by Dan Rich.

Peggy's Marinated Cole Slaw from Smokin' Moes in Winter Park. Photo by Cyndie Saffell.

Cervena Cold Smoked Roast of Red Deer from
The Tyrolean in Vail.

The Tyrolean in Vail.

Steamed Seafood Basket à la Fireside from Alys' Fireside Café in Walsenburg. Photo by Alys Romer.

Alys' Fireside Café in Walsenburg. Photo by Alys Romer.

*Chicken Picatta from the Alpine Lodge Restaurant in Westcliffe.
Photo by David Leugers.*

*The Alpine Lodge Restaurant in Westcliffe.
Photo by David Leugers.*

*Chicken La Bomba from The Hideaway in Winter Park.
Photo by Geoffrey Schober.*

*The Hideaway in Winter Park.
Photo by Geoffrey Schober.*

Benjamin James Bennis with Cosmo the Corgi in City Park, Denver. Photo by Linda P. Viray.

VAIL

The valley of Gore Creek, where Vail now stands, was first settled in the 1880s by silver prospectors. Unsuccessful at silver mining, they developed homesteads instead and raised cattle and grew crops. Vail and Vail Pass to the east were named after Charles D. Vail, Colorado State Highway Engineer in the 1930s. The town of Vail is relatively new having been established in 1959 and incorporated in 1966. Vail ski area opened in 1962.

My prime choice among the many restaurants in this town spotlights a creative European and American place that is both sophisticated and amiable offering many ethnic delights.

Location of Town: West of Denver on I-70 between Copper Mountain and Avon
Zip Code: 81657. Area Code: 970. Population: 3,659. Elevation: 8,160ft.

The Tyrolean

400 East Meadow Drive. 476-2204.
Directions: Take Exit 176 from I-70 and proceed to the round-a-bout south of the highway. Head east on South Frontage Road for ¼ mile and turn right into the Village Parking Structure. Try to park your vehicle towards the east end of the parking garage. Exit the garage on foot. You will be on East Meadow Drive. Proceed to your left (east). The restaurant is at the end of the road on the right.

ESSENTIALS
Cuisine: Creative European/American
Hours: Late MAY to late APR: 7 days 6pm-10pm. Closed late APR to late MAY.
Meals and Prices: Dinner $16-$34
Nonsmoking: All. Smoking only permitted at the bar.
Take-out: Yes, with à la car, only at off-peak times.
Alcohol: Full Bar

Credit Cards: MC, Visa, Amx
Personal Check: No
Reservations: Recommended in ski season, appreciated at other times
Wheelchair Access: Yes
Dress: Casual, but no ski boots
Other: Children's portions available. No substitutions. Service charge of 18% added to parties of 6 or more. Available for small private parties.

VAIL

HISTORY, PERSONALITY AND CHARACTER

The Tyrolean, named after the Tirol Province in Austria, is in a section of a lodge and restaurant designed and built by Austrian craftsmen in 1967. Austrian Pepi Langegger purchased the original restaurant, The Blue Cow, in 1972. In 1976, he added game items to the menu and changed the name to The Tyrolean. During 1981, a new exterior building was added and the interior underwent complete remodeling and redecorating. Pepi attended hotel and restaurant management school while in Austria. He also owns The Golden Eagle Inn in Beaver Creek and the Twin Creek Game Ranch for elk and fallow deer in Silt, Colorado.

His son, Sigmund, attended hotel and restaurant management school at Denver University, spent one year at the Four Ways Inn, a five-star resort in Bermuda and has managed The Tyrolean since 1991. Head chef Scott Elliott also hails from a restaurant family and attended Newbury College in Brookline, Massachusetts. He started as a line cook at The Tyrolean in 1991. Sous chef Andy Exell has been with the restaurant since 1995 having previously cooked at The Trellis in West Virginia.

FOOD, SERVICE AND AMBIANCE

The cuisine at The Tyrolean consists of several ethnic influences: Austrian, German, Italian, Greek, Mediterranean, American and southwestern. I decided to combine Italian with wild game and ordered the smoked pheasant with spinach tortellini sautéed with sundried tomatoes, tart artichoke hearts, roasted red peppers, roasted elephant garlic and herbed natural au jus. Fresh oregano springs and Reggiano Parmigiano, the "good stuff from Italy", was sprinkled on top. It was a scrumptious dish that I absolutely loved: a marvelous combination of tastes and flavors. This bowl of delectable edibles was also colorful and bright thus living up to their motto: "Each entrée is created to appeal to the eye as well as the palate". Accompanying the meal was fresh, hot baked bread straight out of the oven with a crispy crust and soft dough.

The Tyrolean's varied menu offers something for everyone: seafood, fowl, veal, beef, pasta, vegetarian and game specialties. They prepare all of their stocks from scratch and cream is seldom used and only in small quantities to "tighten" some sauces. A few of their delicious sounding appetizers are applewood-smoked trout, wild boar quesadilla and grilled quail with arugula. In the winter, Beluga caviar, considered the best and prized for its soft, pea-sized eggs, is added to the list of appetizers. For a second course, you can choose from southwestern onion soup gratin, the soup du jour, English cucumber and sweet onion salad or a field greens salad.

A sampling of their entrées that are offered during the summer, winter and off-season includes honey and Dijon roasted free range chicken, pine nut crusted Rocky Mountain trout, wiener schnitzel, pan-seared filet mignon, mushroom-crusted shrimp and grilled elk loin steak. Some of the winter items Chef Elliott adds to the menu are fresh fish Lyonaise, roasted rack of New Zealand lamb, roasted vegetable lasagna and daily game specials. To complement your meal, you can choose from their award winning list of 225 bottles representing a well-balanced selection from different regions, styles and price ranges.

Service was neat, professional and conscious of detail. My setting was cleaned with a crumber when my meal was finished and my server shielded the cup from me with his towel when he poured the coffee. Nice touches! Combinations of light jazz, classical, instrumental piano and harp and new age music played softly in the background.

The Tyrolean prides itself on preserving the original architecture that was present when men in laderhosen would dance and play the accordion. You enter the restaurant through a front door made of solid oak with wrought iron. To the right of the entrance facing the patio are stained-glass windows covered with wrought-iron bars. I had a corner booth and sat below an expertly taken photograph by Marty Stouffer of a mountain lion chasing a big horn sheep.

The two distinguishing interior design features in the restaurant are the carved stucco artworks by Horst Essl and the two substantial sleds hanging by wrought-iron chains from the vaulted ceiling. Essl's works involved quick-drying stucco that had to be molded, shaped and painted within an eight-hour period. His art can be seen at the entrance under The Tyrolean Inn sign where there is a stucco carving of four male big horn sheep and in the restaurant where he sculpted an elk herd, mallard ducks, pots and flower patterns. Electric lanterns hang from the unique sled chandeliers that have been with the restaurant since 1972.

Further enhancing the rustic, old-world décor are bald and golden eagle replicas, an elk bust, sketches of mountain lions and elk facing off and the head and antlers from the 7th biggest mule deer ever killed in Colorado: non-typical with 24 points. The upstairs dining room that is sometimes used for semi-private parties has lodge-pole pine beams adorned with brass ladles, pots, soup spoons, buckets and dried flowers. The Tyrolean renders fabulous food with warm, friendly, down-to-earth service in an authentic Austrian atmosphere.

VAIL

See page 272 for restaurant photo.

Cervena Cold Smoked Roast of Red Deer
(Serves 6)

2 1/4 pounds Cervena Red Deer, top round, cut to 6 ounce roasts
6 ounces hickory wood chips
1 1/2 pounds frozen game bones, broken up
1 1/2 Granny Smith apples, cored and quartered
1 D'Anjou pear, cored and quartered
Mirepoix
2 medium onions, peeled and chopped
1 medium carrot, peeled and chopped
1 medium turnip, peeled and chopped
2 stalks celery, chopped
1 cup cranberry juice
1 quart demi-glace
1 quart water
1 cup Merlot (red wine)
7 juniper berries, crushed
1 bay leaf
5 parsley stems
3 sprigs fresh thyme
2 teaspoons arrowroot
2 teaspoons water, cold
1/2 cup dried cranberries
Salt and pepper

1. Preheat oven to 500 degrees.
2. Place 3 ounces of hickory chips in a bowl full of water to soak for 10 minutes. Hold on paper towels to soak up any excess water on the outside of the wood. With the rest of the chips, in a smoker, get a small hot fire started and add some of the wet chips (this should knock the fire down to coals).
3. Ventilate the smoker well and place the bones, apples, and pears on the rack. Cover and smoke for 8 to 10 minutes. Open cover and remove the bones and fruits.
4. The coals should still be hot. Add the rest of the soaked wood chips and close all of the ventilation to the smoker.
5. Place the Cervena red deer roasts on the rack. Cover tightly and smoke until the coals are dead, about 10 minutes.
6. Reserve the roasts covered in the refrigerator until ready for service. Place the bones in a small roasting pan and roast in the oven for 10 minutes.
7. Add the Mirepoix and smoked fruit and roast for 10 minutes more or until the onions start to caramelize. Remove from the oven.

8. While the pan is still hot, add the red wine and mix thoroughly. Scrape the bones and Mirepoix out of the roasting pan and into a medium sauce pot.
9. Cover with cold water, demi-glace, and cranberry juice, and bring to just a boil.
10. Turn back to a simmer and add the juniper berries, bay leaf, parsley stems, and thyme springs. Simmer for one hour.
11. Strain through a fine chinois into a large measure. You should have about 6 cups leftover.
12. Rinse the chinoise and place 4 folds of cheesecloth into it. Restrain the stock into a medium sauce pan and boil for 15 minutes. Add the cranberries and cook for 5 minutes.
13. In the meantime, add the cold water to the arrowroot and mix thoroughly. While whisking rapidly, add the arrowroot to the boiling glace and cook for one minute.
14. Remove from heat and season with salt and pepper. Cover and hold somewhere warm for service.
15. Turn the oven down to 400 degrees and heat a large sauté pan on the stove until extremely hot.
16. Season the roasts on all sides with salt and pepper and add a small amount of oil to the pan. Sear the roasts on all sides until slightly darkened.
17. Place roasts into the oven and cook for 8 minutes or until medium rare. DO NOT OVERCOOK.
18. Pull from oven and let rest for 5 to 8 minutes. Cut each roast into 3 medallions and serve with a spoonful of the sauce under each one.

<u>Wine Recommendation</u>: 1995 Fiddlehead Cellars Pinot Noir from Oregon or 1989 Nuits St. George, Clos Des Porrets, Henri Gouges

<u>Recipe by</u>: Scott Elliott, executive chef

See page 271 for recipe photo.

WALSENBURG

Walsenburg started as a little Mexican settlement called La Plaza de los Leones, for Don Miguel Antonio Leon, an early settler. In 1870, Fred Walsen opened a general store and became a community leader. When the village was incorporated in 1873, the name was changed in his honor. Postal authorities briefly changed the name to Tourist City in 1887, but indignant citizens demanded the return of the old name. In the 1930s, the town nicknamed itself "The City Built on Coal" for the massive coal deposits and numerous coal camps in the area.

A gourmet chef creating an international eclectic cuisine is a rare find in most small towns but that is exactly what you will get at Alys'.

Location of Town: South-central Colorado off I-25.
Zip Code: 81089. Area Code: 719. Population: 3,300. Elevation: 6,182ft.

Alys' Fireside Cafe

606 Main Street. 738-3993.
Directions: From the north on I-25, take Exit 52 and follow Highways 85 and 87 west for two miles to where it becomes Main Street. The restaurant is on the left just past 6th Street. From the south on I-25, take Exit 49 and follow Guerrero Avenue until it turns into Main Street. The restaurant is on the right ½ block past the signal for 7th Street.

ESSENTIALS
Cuisine: International Eclectic
Hours: Mon-Fri 11:30AM-2:30PM. Wed-Sat 6PM-9PM.
Meals and Prices: Lunch $5-$7. Dinner $11-$17.
Nonsmoking: No
Take-out: Yes
Alcohol: Full Bar
Credit Cards: MC, Visa, Disc
Personal Check: Yes, with I.D.

Reservations: Appreciated
Wheelchair Access: Yes, including restrooms
Dress: Jeans to dressy
Other: Delivery available from Restaurant Runners. Banquet and special group facility downstairs. Live entertainment on weekends and special occasions.

HISTORY, PERSONALITY AND CHARACTER
Alys' was originally a turn-of-the-century saloon and gambling hall. In the 1920s, Babe Shosky ran a restaurant and bar that catered to boxing and sports enthusiasts. Babe, a boxing fanatic himself, was good friends

with the legendary "Manasa Mauler", Jack Dempsey. Rumor has it that Babe lost the restaurant/bar in a poker game in the mid-1970s. The new owner opened the Fireside Café and brought in the two huge stone fireplaces. He died of a heart attack and the building closed down from 1982 until 1994 when Alys Romer, no relation to the Governor, opened Alys' Fireside Café. Alys is a gourmet chef from New Jersey who spent 23 years traveling all over the world, eating at the finest restaurants while doing product development for United Fruit Company, Lipton Soups and international flavor and fragrance companies. In addition to preparing her nightly changing dinner selections, Alys teaches cooking classes in the winter. Vicki Hambrick has been the dining room manager since 1994 following a career in Denver restaurants.

FOOD, SERVICE AND AMBIANCE

The evening that I visited the offerings were prime rib, coho salmon, chicken with saffron rice, paella, 16-ounce T-bone, garlic-basil ravioli with rosé Alfredo sauce, shrimp scampi and rack of lamb with a red pepper cup filled with minted peas. Other favorites that you might find on the menu are fresh Maine lobster (flown in live), Alaskan king crab legs, a steamed seafood basket, pheasant and Malaysian curry fish or chicken. I went with the paella served on a bed of lettuce in a steamer basket (wooden bowl) filled with green beans, red and yellow peppers, shrimp, oh so tender scallops, mussels, pink salmon, peas, chorizo and lobster cut into small pieces. All of these wonderful items added up to one savory meal that would put a smile on even the most discerning palate. A full bowl of "sprightly" greens, croutons, tomato, carrot, and cucumber in a light homemade balsamic vinaigrette dressing preceded the entrée.

They also make blue cheese and raspberry vinaigrette dressings and serve honey-Dijon and Italian as well. You can accompany your meal with one of their domestic or imported beers or wines. For dessert, I delighted in a piece of chocolate whiskey pudding. It was like chocolate pudding with a brownie crust flavored with whiskey and topped with whipped cream, a mint leaf and sweet pea petals. Scrumptious! This delicious dessert is a must for chocolate lovers. Other tempting selections include wild berry torte, cheesecakes, carrot cake, chocolate layer cake, bread pudding and tiramisu.

Soups, salads and sandwiches are the agenda for lunch. You can match a cup of New England clam chowder, minestrone, turkey or cream of carrot soup with a turkey club, French dip, ham and cheese, Italian deli, grilled veggie or fresh buffalo mozzarella sandwich.

WALSENBURG

My server was helpful, informative and enjoyed working as a part-time waitress. Tapes of modern and pop music mixed with new age instrumentals played during the evening. International as well as local art works enhance the left side of the dining room while the right side is adorned with a mirror that runs the full length behind a beautiful 27-foot oak and mahogany bar built in 1933. In the middle of the back bar is the lit-up outline of a pink flamingo. Other artworks, several from Alys's father in New York City who is an art collector, include portraits, sketches and an intriguing and humorous three-dimensional sculpture of an actor just about to enter, or exit, from behind a curtain. A huge stone fireplace erected with stones from nearby Cuchara in the 1970s stands at the far end of the dining room. A second stone fireplace is downstairs in the banquet room. Definitely turn off in Walsenburg when traveling the south I-25 corridor, ignore the sullen exterior with the neon sign and enter a world of gourmet cooking and fine dining unlike any you would expect in this part of the state at Alys' Fireside Café.

Special One-Time Offer: Buy one entrée and receive a second entrée of equal or lesser value free (up to $16.00) OR receive 50% off one entrée (up to $9.00). NOT valid on holidays or for special events. Please present at time of ordering. _____ Owner/Manager. _____ Date.

See bottom of page 273 for restaurant photo.

WALSENBURG

Steamed Seafood Basket a la Fireside
(Serves 1)

3 ounce lobster tail, partially pulled from shell, as a centerpiece
3 New Zealand green lipped mussels
3 shelled and deveined shrimp
3 sea scallops
1-inch x 2-inch piece of Sea bass, sliced
Small slice of salmon

2 tablespoons frozen green peas or green beans
10 Haricots Verts (green string beans)
6 carrots, julienne
1 strip red pepper
1 strip green or yellow pepper
Salt and pepper
Lemon peel, chopped
Sprig of fresh dill or dried dill weed
Parsley sprigs
Redleaf lettuce, purple cabbage or kale
Optional: ginger or lemon grass instead of dill for a more Oriental dish

1. Use individual bamboo steamer. Line the inside of basket with red leaf lettuce, purple cabbage, or kale. Use about 1/2 cup cooked rice or pasta. A flavored rice or saffron rice, or pasta such as calamari or spinach pasta, or other interesting flavors that would complement the seafood may be used.
2. Put all seafood in the basket. Top with peas, beans, carrots, and peppers.
3. Sprinkle with salt, pepper, lemon peel, and dill.
4. Or go Oriental with a little ginger or lemon grass instead of dill.
5. Add parsley sprigs and steam without steamer lid in a pasta pot.
6. Place baskets on pasta steamer insert.
7. The water should not come above the holes in the pasta strainer. Steam about 10 minutes or until seafood is flaky.
8. Serve with drawn butter and lemon wedges.
9. A nice green salad makes a terrific complement to this meal.

Wine Recommendation: Hess Collection Chardonnay

Recipe by: Alys Romer, owner and chef

See top of page 273 for recipe photo.

WESTCLIFFE

Westcliffe is located in the Wet Mountain Valley, one of Colorado's most majestically scenic areas, set between the Wet Mountains and the Sangre de Cristo Mountains. Originally called Clifton, the town was renamed by Dr. W. A. Bell for his birthplace, Westcliff-on-the-Sea England. Dr. Bell, along with General William J. Palmer, entered the Wet Mountain Valley in 1870 in search of a southern route for their Denver and Rio Grande Railroad. They settled on Westcliffe for the terminus of their railroad. When the rich mines of nearby Silver Cliff began to dwindle, Westcliffe, one mile to the west, sprang to life.

The following is a review of a true "off-the-beaten-path" restaurant with a Colorado high-country meat and potatoes menu.

Location of Town: South-central Colorado on the eastern edge of the Sangre de Cristo Mountains.
Zip Code: 81252. Area Code: 719. Population: 312. Elevation: 7,888ft.

Alpine Lodge Restaurant

6848 County Road 140. 783-2660,
Directions: From Pueblo, take Highway 96 to the west for 52 miles into Westcliffe. At the east end of town, turn left onto Highway 69 (Antler's Liquor and Motel is on the far left corner). Go south for 2.8 miles. Turn right onto County Road 140 or Schoolfield Road and head west again. (From the intersection of Highway 69 and County Road 140, there are signs leading you to the Alpine Lodge.) Go 4½ mile and turn left at the 'T' continuing on Country Road 140. Follow the winding, gravel road for another 2½ miles and turn left at the Alpine Lodge sign.

ESSENTIALS
Cuisine: Colorado High Country Meat and Potatoes
Hours: Mid-APR to Mid-OCT: Thu-Sat and Mon 5PM-9PM, Sun 2:30PM-8:30PM. Call for Tue/Wed hours. Mid-OCT to Mid-APR: Thu-Fri 5:30PM-8:30PM, Sat 5PM-9PM, Sun 2:30PM-7:30PM. Closed Mon-Wed.
Meals and Prices: Dinner $5-$19

Nonsmoking: Yes
Take-out: Yes
Alcohol: Full Bar
Credit Cards: MC, Visa
Personal Check: Yes
Reservations: Recommended
Wheelchair Access: Yes, with portable ramp.
Dress: Casual

Other: Available for receptions, catering, club dinners and banquets. Five 2-bedroom cabins with small kitchens available at moderate prices.

HISTORY, PERSONALITY AND CHARACTER

The Alpine Lodge Restaurant was originally a cabin built in the 1950s. It was converted to the Alpine Lodge Restaurant in the mid-1960s. In 1990, David and Marian Leugers purchased the restaurant. They both manage the restaurant's operations. Marian, who has been cooking and operating restaurants in Cañon City since the late 1970s, does the cooking at the Alpine Lodge Restaurant.

FOOD, SERVICE AND AMBIANCE

The Alpine Lodge Restaurant specializes in steak and seafood so I ordered the charbroiled New York strip with green chile and cheese enchiladas with red chile while Linda went with the sautéed shrimp. I chose the very thick and creamy clam chowder with spices and big slices of carrots and potatoes. Linda selected the salad bar highlighted by pistachio (her favorite) marshmallow salad with sliced almonds, pineapples and cherries that she found cool and delicious. The charbroiled strip was a meaty, mouth-watering piece topped with mild green chile and cooked just right for me, medium-rare. The cheese enchilada came with spicy red chile sauce topped with tomatoes and lettuce. Linda's shrimps were very moist, not tough or overcooked, and served with white rice and julienne carrots. We both appreciated our dishes and did not leave room for dessert.

Other charbroiled steak dinners with sautéed mushrooms for your pleasure include T-bone, filet mignon, rib-eye, top sirloin and tenderloin of bison. Some savory seafood entrées on the menu are charbroiled orange roughy, beer-battered shrimp, cornmeal breaded rainbow trout and fish and chips. The menu also offers diversified alternatives like pork chops, ham steak, fried chicken, bluecorn enchiladas and ravioli with red sauce.

New Mexican dinners that feature tacos, chili rellenos, burros, shrimp and big combinations are presented on special nights. Barbecue is a regular Thursday night special and prime rib is on the menu every night during the summer and on Fridays and Saturdays during the winter. Specials are served every evening. Appetizers, burgers and sandwiches are available before dinner or as a light meal. For dessert, you can try one of their homemade pies such as blackberry, blueberry, pecan or gooseberry, chocolate mousse, flan or cheesecake.

WESTCLIFFE

Our host/owner David was very attentive, hospitable and likeable. Taped light jazz played quietly throughout the evening. Intermittently through the year, typically on Fridays and Saturdays, they will have live music including jazz, combos or solo acts. Every third weekend of the month the Alpine Lodge Restaurant has a "Celebration of the Spoken Word". Friday evenings are an open poetry forum for any poet. On Saturday evenings, the Alpine Lodge Restaurant's "House Poet", Lou Malandra from Littleton, Colorado, gives a reading.

The Alpine Lodge Restaurant is a rustic, two-story restaurant and lounge with a rock, wood-burning fireplace and wagon wheel chandeliers. The walls and banisters are made of unfinished, course knotty pinewood. Several paintings by regional artists of the surrounding area embellish the walls portraying a black bear, American Indians and cattle-rustling cowboys on a chase. The pictures also illustrate aspen-covered mountains, valleys and streams. The Alpine Lodge Restaurant, probably more than any other restaurant in this book, exemplifies the true "Colorado Restaurant Off The Beaten Path". Now that you know about it, make sure to include this hidden treasure in your travel plans.

See bottom of page 274 for restaurant photo.

<u>Special One-Time Offer:</u> Buy one entrée and receive a second entrée of equal or lesser value free (up to $12.00) OR receive 50% off one entrée (up to $6.00). NOT valid on holidays or for special events. Please present at time of ordering. _____ Owner/Manager. _____ Date.

Chicken Picatta
(Serves 4)

4 chicken breasts, pounded
2 cups flour
1 tablespoon salt
2 teaspoons black pepper
1 1/3 cups clarified butter
8 ounces mushrooms, sliced

2 tablespoons minced garlic
1/2 cup lemon juice
4 cups cooked rice
4 lemon slices
4 teaspoons fresh chopped parsley

1. Dredge pounded chicken breasts in flour, salt, and pepper mixture.
2. Heat clarified butter over medium heat in an electric skillet and brown chicken breast until gold brown on each side.
3. Turn down heat to medium-low and add garlic and mushrooms. Sauté with the chicken breast until mushrooms are limp.
4. Carefully pour the lemon juice over the chicken and stir. Turn off heat.
5. Place each chicken breast on top of one cup of cooked rice and pour mushrooms, garlic, and lemon sauce on top.
6. Garnish each with one lemon slice and 1 teaspoon fresh parsley. Add your favorite vegetable.

Wine Recommendation: Colorado Cellars Alpenglow Reisling

Recipe by: David Leugers, owner

See top of page 274 for recipe photo.

WINTER PARK

Winter Park was originally a construction camp for the Moffat Tunnel whose west portal is located here. Appropriately, the town was named West Portal. Skiing dates back as far as 1925 when there was a 25 cents rope tow. Several years and two fires later, the world's first double chair lift was completed in 1947. The town's name was changed to Winter Park with the assistance of then Denver Mayor Benjamin F. Stapleton and many sports enthusiasts. They were trying to publicize the town as one of the finest winter sports centers in the country. Today, Winter Park is home to a handicap ski clinic and host of the Special Olympics.

Depicted for your perusal are three of Winter Parks finest: a Mexican restaurant serving octopus and cactus, a mountain eclectic and international restaurant with an old world essence and a hickory-smoked barbecue place with their own smoker and a lot of character.

Location of Town: North-central Colorado on Highway 40
Zip Code: 80482. Area Code: 970. Population: 528. Elevation: 9,040ft.

The Hideaway
78259 Highway 40. 726-1081.
Directions: Located on the east side of Highway 40 at Kings Crossing Road on the north end of town.

ESSENTIALS
Cuisine: Mountain Eclectic/International
Hours: JUN to Mid-APR: 7 days 5pm-10pm (11pm Fri/Sat). Mid-APR to Mid-NOV: Tue-Sat 11am-4:30pm, Sun 8:30am-2pm, Fri-Sat 5pm-11pm, Sun 5pm-10pm
Meals and Prices: Lunch $4-$11. Dinner $11-$23
Nonsmoking: Yes
Take-out: Yes
Alcohol: Full Bar
Credit Cards: MC, Visa, Amx, Disc
Personal Check: In-state with I.D.
Reservations: Recommended
Wheelchair Access: Yes, including the bar and restroom
Dress: Mountain casual
Other: Service charge of 17% added to parties of 6 or more. Available for large parties, receptions and weddings. Hideaway Catering available on and off premises. Room service delivery available within Winter Park.

WINTER PARK

HISTORY, PERSONALITY AND CHARACTER

The Hideaway Olde World Lodge, Bistro and Pub occupies a building that was originally a corporate retreat for Burlington Northern executives from 1962 to the late 1960s. From the late 1960s until the mid-1980s, this place was the Sitzmark Dude Ranch. Then it laid vacant until the late 1980s when it was converted into the Lord Gore Restaurant, opened only in the winters through the 1996-97 ski season. In August 1997, The Hideaway moved to this location from Park Place Plaza one block to the south, complete with a top to bottom, end to end total renovation.

Chief executive chef and general manager Geoffrey Schober has been in the restaurant business since 1969. He assisted in opening the original Hideaway in Winter Park in 1972 above Hernando's former location. The Hideaway closed in the 1980s but reopened with a new logo and style in October 1991 in the Park Place Plaza. Geoffrey graduated from the Hotel Fach-Shule School in Lucerne, Switzerland, and was a corporate supervising chef for the Hilton Hotel Corporation for nine years. After moving to Winter Park, Geoffrey assisted in the opening of the original Chalet Lucerne and L. C. Benedict's (now The Last Waltz). His general partner, Ed Raegner, worked at The Depot in Telluride, Colorado, in 1992 before coming to Winter Park in 1994 to be the bar manager at The Hideaway. Ed's first generation Irish family comes from a long background in hotel operations. His family operated an inn in Dublin, Ireland, as well as a hotel in New York City.

Sous chef Mark Consiglio, known as "The Counselor", is a graduate of the Culinary Institute of America in Hyde Park, New York, and has been a chef since 1992. He was an apprentice at the famed Depui Canal House in New York State and has been at The Hideaway since 1995. Dining room manager Jeff Hamburg has been in the restaurant business since 1988 and joined The Hideaway in November 1997. He was formerly the restaurant manager at Restaurant on The Ridge in Fraser. Andrea Hurst, catering manager/special events coordinator, joined the Hideaway to spearhead its on/off property catering operations into one of the most revered in the county. They specialize in weddings, family reunions and off property catering.

FOOD, SERVICE AND AMBIANCE

Linda and I stopped here for the Sunday brunch buffet highlighted by made-to-order omelets and light and fluffy waffles with bananas prepared by the chef while you watch. Other specialties on this feast include salads with a house emulsified vinaigrette dressing, fried potatoes with peppers and onions, apple-rhubarb cobbler, raisin torte with raspberry

WINTER PARK

sauce, soft and chewy fudge nut brownies, and sticky cinnamon buns. All together, the meal was fresh and filling as well as sweet and delicious.

Some bistro temptations to get you started at dinner are the five onion bisque, truly Thai spring rolls direct from Bangkok, artichoke and mushroom fritters and fantastic Caesar salad. As another prelude to your entrée, you can select from Hideaway's salads and specialties such as tenderloin empanadas, wild game or seafood bouillabaisse. Pasta, seafood, beef and fowl are featured for dinner as well as authentic Swiss fondue. Two of the favorites are mesquite flame-broiled prime aged beef and crispy duck. Friday and Saturday nights, the Hideaway serves a bountiful seafood buffet. For a summer-time lunch in the pub or on the sundeck, you can choose from the mesquite-grilled backyard burger; Indonesian fish, chicken, beef or vegetarian kabobs; roasted corn chowder or one of their daily luncheon specials. Accompany your meal with a selection from their wine list, one of the most unique in the state.

Easy listening rock and blues music played while we made our buffet selections. Geoffrey Schober and company demonstrate a worldly and wilderness setting at The Hideaway. Forty flags of American states and foreign countries hang along the front of the building. When you reach the front door of the bistro, you will notice a custom stained-glass picture of a wolf in the forest. Robbie Anderson, acclaimed wood carver and friend of Geoffrey from Pennsylvania, created the incredible woodwork in the bistro and Olde World lodge upstairs and the enchanted pub downstairs. Bunches of grapes and grape leaves carved on the balcony in the bistro exhibited a truly European atmosphere. A one-of-a-kind antler chandelier hangs from the vaulted ceiling in the center of the dining room. Rosemary mahogany is used throughout the restaurant. A three-dimensional carving at the aspen-looking white bar depicts sheep on a mountain ledge with elk, trees and mountains in the background. Adjacent to the bar is a comical cartoon caricature of a kitchen filled with chefs and food everywhere. It was dedicated to Geoffrey by Paul Bocuse, the world-renowned, five-star Michelin chef known as the godfather of French cuisine.

At the top of the stairs leading to the balcony is a photograph of Lake Granby catching the sunlit reflection of the mountains. Adorning the balcony dining area are John Scott photographs of wagon wheels and flowers, cowboys and bulls, and Indians crossing a river.

The Hideaway Pub downstairs is a custom artist's rendering of an enchanted pub with woodwork resembling the charm of a mountain forest merged with the style of a New Orleans bistro. It offers billiards, darts, foosball, air hockey, video games and live entertainment. The back wall has the appearance of red brick partially covered with slate. The concrete building supports are pasted with papier mâché to resemble petrified wood stumps. There is a three-piece burgundy couch pit at the end of the pub facing the fireplace. Robbie also originated the three-dimensional woodworks behind the bar. One reveals deer in a clearing with trees painted in the background. The other shows elk with a mountain backdrop. He also carved the trees, logs and green leaves on the doors along the custom back bar. The new Hideaway has a fresh and original ambiance to serve their tried and true regional and international eclectic cuisine, a genuinely don't miss olde world experience!

See bottom of page 275 for restaurant photo.

SPECIAL ONE-TIME OFFER: Buy one entrée at the regular price and receive 50% off a second entrée of equal or lesser value. Offer NOT valid for market priced items. Please present to server at time of ordering. _____ Owner/Manager. _____ Date.

Chicken La Bomba
(Serves 4)

4 chicken breasts, skins on, double breast on bone, unsplit (special order from butcher)
1 cup vinaigrette dressing
1 cup peeled garlic
1/2 cup nonpareil capers
4 sprigs fresh thyme
1 quart fresh or canned chicken stock
1 pint imported balsamic vinegar
1 bunch fresh parsley, finely chopped
1 cup pitted calamata olives
1/2 cup brine from olives

1. Marinade the double breasts for 4 hours in the vinaigrette dressing.
2. Roast at 275 degrees for 1 1/2 to 2 hours (or until internal temperature is at 145 degrees). Remove from bone.
3. Sauce: Combine garlic, capers, leaves from two of the thyme sprigs, chicken stock, balsamic vinegar, parsley, olives, and brine in a 2-gallon stock pot. Reduce to 1 1/2 pints.
4. To serve, reheat breasts on an open flame broiler or oven. Place one breast on each plate. Top with 6 ounces of sauce. Garnish with half sprig of thyme. Serve with vegetables and potatoes of your choice.

Wine Recommendation: Poligny Montrachet

WINTER PARK

Recipe by: Geoffrey Schober, C.E.C. and owner

See top of page 275 for recipe photo.

La Taquería
73287 Highway 40 (in the Park Place Center). 726-0280
Directions: Located on the east side of Highway 40 at High Country Road in Park Place Plaza in the center of town.

ESSENTIALS
Cuisine: Mexican
Hours: 7 days 2PM-11PM. Closed MAY until Memorial Day Weekend.
Meals and Prices: Lunch/Dinner $5-$11
Nonsmoking: All. Smoking only permitted at the bar.
Take-out: Yes
Alcohol: Full Bar
Credit Cards: MC, Visa, Amx, Disc

Personal Check: Yes, with I.D.
Reservations: No
Wheelchair Access: Yes
Dress: Casual, some ski wear
Other: No separate checks. Service charge of 17% added to parties of 6 or more. Service charge of $2 for split plates. Available for catering, in-house and out, and large groups.

HISTORY, PERSONALITY AND CHARACTER
   La Taquería occupies a place that was originally a '50s-syle diner. It later became a hamburger place called Oldies But Goodies before it was transformed into La Taquería in October 1995. Current owners Mike Ayre and Ian Gough have owned La Taquería since October 1997. Mike has been in the restaurant business since 1992, was formerly general manager at Smokin' Moe's in Winter Park and spent a tour on Turks and Caicos in the Caribbean. Ian started in restaurants in 1989, was manager for five years at Beaver Village in Winter Park and also worked at Smokin' Moe's. Mike and Ian both manage and cook at La Taquería.

FOOD, SERVICE AND AMBIANCE
   Always in the mood to try something different, I ordered the cactus quesadillas. First, my server brought some chips and tasty homemade salsa, thick with tomatoes, moderately hot and flavored with onions and hot peppers. With my taste buds 'south of the border' stirred up, it was time for my 10-inch quesadilla pie filled with cactus leaves, American cheese and sweet mild chilies. Dollops of sour cream and guacamole topped the pie.

The cactus was similar to okra in texture but actually had a flavor and was sweeter and better. You should definitely try these.

La Taquería serves fresh, authentic Mexican food from their guacamole taco salads to the apple chimichanga à la mode. Some Mexican favorites to start your meal are chicken fajita salad, jalapeño poppers and nachos grande. La Taquería serves some fascinating fajitas with pork tenderloin and pineapple, fresh fish or veggies and cactus. For a lighter meal, you can choose from a jumbo soft taco, Tijuana chicken sandwich, a Mexican burger or regular American burger. The list of engaging entrées includes super burritos with fish or buffalo, Colorado mountain chili, Mexican pizza and kabob, chili rellenos, flautas and red snapper in tequila cream sauce. Fried ice cream, chocolate tacos, raspberry burrito and hot fudge nachos highlight the desirable desserts.

Service was efficient, quick and casual. Water is served in mason jars and each table has a paper towel roll. Blues rock music played at a moderate pitch. This is a one-room restaurant divided by a trellis draped with a Mexican rug. The sunset cloud-color walls are decorated with Ansel Adams posters of "The Mural Project 1941-1942" depicting Taos Pueblo Church in New Mexico and cactus. Further enhancing this Mexican habitat are a great chili poster, both a sun-god and moon-god sculpture, a painting of an Indian pueblo, hanging chili ristras and dried corn, and a poster advertising a bullfight in Plaza de Toros, Cancun. For some distinctive and genuine Mexican dishes, visit La Taquería when you are in Winter Park.

<u>Special One-Time Offer</u>: Receive a free house margarita with a $10.00 purchase or more. One per person. Please present to server at time of ordering. _____ Owner/Manager. _____ Date.

WINTER PARK

Spicy Tomato Tortilla Soup
(Serves 8)

1 onion, diced
1/2 green pepper, diced
1 can tomatoes, diced
1 cup green chilies, diced
1/2 cup jalapeños
1 tablespoon garlic powder
1/2 tablespoon chili powder
1/2 tablespoon crushed red pepper
1/2 tablespoon black pepper
1 tablespoon salt
1/2 cup pineapple chunks
1 cup tortilla chips, broken into pieces
1 cup water

1. Sauté onions and peppers. Add rest of ingredients.
2. Bring to a boil. Simmer for 1 hour.
3. Mix in a blender to smooth consistency. Pour into soup bowls. Top with grated cheese and serve with warm flour tortillas

Recipe by: Mike Ayer and Ian Gough, owners and cooks

Smokin' Moe's

47 Cooper Creek Way, Suite 131. 726-4600.
Directions: Located on the west side of Highway 40 on the Garden Level of Cooper Creek Square just north of Vasquez Road as you first enter downtown Winter Park from the south.

ESSENTIALS
Cuisine: Hickory Smoked Barbecue
Hours: 7 days 11am-10pm(11pm Fri/Sat). Closed mid-APR to mid-MAY and mid-SEP to mid-OCT.
Meals and Prices: Lunch/Dinner $5-$16
Nonsmoking: Yes
Take-out: Yes
Alcohol: Full Bar
Credit Cards: All 5
Personal Check: Grand Country only with I.D.
Reservations: Recommended for parties of 6 or more
Wheelchair Access: Yes
Dress: Winter Park casual
Other: Children's menu. Service charge of 17% added to parties of 6 or more. No separate checks. Catering in house and out-of-house with mobile smoker for parties from 10 to 1,000. Available for birthdays, weddings and other special occasions.

WINTER PARK

HISTORY, PERSONALITY AND CHARACTER

The space occupied by Smokin' Moe's in Cooper Creek Square was originally the Stampede Night Club from 1985 until 1992. The place was vacant for about a year before the Chili Moon Restaurant moved in from 1994 until 1996. In June 1996, Doug and Stephanie Camozzi opened Smokin' Moe's. They have also owned the Divide Grill in Winter Park since 1993. Doug has been in the restaurant business since 1975. He was previously part owner and manager of the Avenue Bar and Grill in Denver and manager of the Bay Wolf in the Cherry Creek section of Denver. Stephanie is a graduate of Club Med of North America. She worked in the travel and resort industry prior to working in restaurants beginning in 1990. She formerly managed the Divide Grill. Doug and Stephanie were also consultants for restaurants in the Turk and Caicos Islands in the Caribbean. General manager Bill Anderson, a native Texan, began at Smokin' Moe's in 1997 after working four years at the Divide Grill.

FOOD, SERVICE AND AMBIANCE

Smokin' Moe's presents carefully selected meats that are slowly smoked in their authentic smoker over hickory wood from Osage County, Oklahoma. Doug calls it "traditional Texas-Oklahoma style barbecue". I ordered the hickory-smoked barbecue baby-back ribs, a half rack of thick, meaty ribs with hickory smoke flavor. It was a plentiful serving for lunch. For one of my two side dishes, I selected savory smoked and baked beans with several (I counted nine) pieces of bacon. (That in itself is a tale for "Beyond Belief: Fact or Fiction"). My second side dish was creamy coleslaw sweetened with honey. Homemade Texas toast accompanied the meal. You can make a trip to the chuck wagon table and help yourself to onions, jalapeños, cherry peppers, pickled okra, pickled chips, banana peppers and pepperoncini. Two barbecue sauces are offered tableside: Smokin' Moe's mild sauce sweetened with sugar, molasses and corn syrup; and Selmon Brothers hot barbecue sauce spiced with salt, garlic and other ingredients. One sweet sauce, one tangy, both perfect with smoked ribs.

Smokin' Moe's serves a full fare of smoked meats including St. Louis pork ribs, beef brisket, Polish sausage, fat-free turkey sausage, pork chops and chicken. For the purist, there is a 10-ounce sirloin and for the vegetarian, a plate with baked potato, corn on the cob and two sides like spicy pintos, wedge cut fries, macaroni salad or potato salad. For the adventuresome, smoked armadillo is available in season. (Not really. That is just a little Texas humor). As an appetizer, you can choose a big bloomin' onion, smoked Okie baloney or cheddar stuffed jalapeños. If you are in the mood for something lighter, pick a sandwich with pork, brisket, ribs or baloney; a burger or a salad. Make your way to the end of the dinner trail with a choice between peach cobbler, Moe's apple pie, banana cream pie and vanilla or cinnamon ice cream.

Service was prompt and courteous at Smokin' Moe's. Country music and many families filled this restaurant. Smokin' Moe's has an atmosphere and character all its own. It goes all out beginning with the photo history of Moe's family on the wall just inside the entrance. You will notice a strong resemblance between several family members. Just beyond the photographs before you reach the host's stand, their mascot Moe will greet you from where he is perched on the wall shelf. The tables are covered with large sheets of brown artist's paper. A handy roll of brown paper towels is set on each table enough for the messiest of barbecue gourmands. The condiments are housed in IBC cream soda six-pack containers. Forks and knives come in mason jars. The middle section of the dining room is under a "starry sky" ceiling. The interior wall is made of logs and decorated with brass-bed head and foot boards, old rodeo photos and a rope.

Enhancing the ambiance are several horse saddles, carriage gear and an old-looking photo from the Pleasure Parlor in Greeley, Colorado, dated 1892 (a place where the nostalgic can relive the past). A private dining room in the back resembles a jail cell with bars and a wall textured to look like a rock wall. Just outside the jail cell dining room is a barrel filled with peanuts in the shell and a stack of buckets to take them back to your table. A row of wagon wheels on an unfinished wood ledge and saloon-style swinging doors separates the dining room from the bar and pool table in the rear. Visit Smokin' Moe's, learn the "legend" of Moe, delve into some fresh smoked meats and you will soon be asking for "Moe".

Special One-Time Offer: Buy an entrée of $10.00 or more and receive a complimentary homemade peach cobbler. Valid for up to four people. Please present to server at time of ordering.
_____ Owner/Manager. _____ Date.

Peggy's Marinated Cole Slaw
(Serves 8 to 10)

1 large crisp head of cabbage	2 teaspoons sugar
2 large Bermuda onions	1 teaspoon dry mustard
1 large sweet green pepper	1 teaspoon celery seed
1 cup sugar	1 teaspoon salt
	1 cup apple cider vinegar
	3/4 cup vegetable oil

1. Slice cabbage, onion, and pepper. Place in a large enamel bowl or old-fashioned crock bowl and mix.
2. Sprinkle sugar over the top and set aside. Do not mix in a metal container.
3. In a sauce pan, combine the rest of the ingredients. Bring to a boil and pour over the cabbage mixture. Toss well and cover immediately. Refrigerate and let stand for 4 hours. Mix thoroughly. Store in refrigerator.
4. Best to let stand for 2 or 3 days and will keep for several days.

This is a recipe from a neighborhood friend. We used to make it in my great-grandma's crock, circa 1920. The longer that it marinates, the better it tastes.

See bottom of page 270 for recipe photo.

WOODLAND PARK

Formerly known as Summit Park and Manitou Park, Woodland Park was named for the abundance of pine and spruce trees.

It is hard to find fault with a restaurant dedicated to Grandma, as you will soon find out.

Location of Town: On the front range southwest of Denver
Zip Code: 80866. Area Code: 719. Population: 4,610. Elevation: 8,437ft.

Grandmother's Kitchen

212 East Highway 24. 687-3118.
Directions: Take Exit 141 from I-25 on the south side of Colorado Springs. Go west on Highway 24 for 18 miles to Woodland Park. Go .4 miles past the signal for Baldwin Street (the 2nd signal as you enter Woodland Park). The restaurant is on the right.

ESSENTIALS
Cuisine: Country Family
Hours: Tue-Sun 6AM-2PM (Breakfast until 2PM, lunch from 11AM). Closed Mon.
Meals and Prices: Breakfast $3-$6. Lunch $4-$6.
Nonsmoking: Yes
Take-out: Yes

Alcohol: No
Credit Cards: MC, Visa
Personal Check: In-state with I.D.
Reservations: No
Wheelchair Access: Yes
Dress: Casual
Other: Senior discount of 10% for those 65 or older.

HISTORY, PERSONALITY AND CHARACTER

The kitchen area of Grandmother's Kitchen was originally a small hot dog stand. The front dining room and a back room were added later and the building was used as an arcade, a flower shop and a drive-through hamburger stand through the 1960s and 70s. Grandmother's Kitchen opened in 1988 and in January 1991, Thor and Jerri Furnes bought the restaurant. Thor is also the manager and head cook.

FOOD, SERVICE AND AMBIANCE

I stopped here for breakfast one fine spring morning and was treated to their country scramble, a tasty and fresh concoction of crinkle potatoes, mushrooms, green peppers, onions, ham and melted American cheese. Other breakfast options are omelets, hot cakes, breakfast sandwiches, burritos, steak and eggs and homemade waffles. Lunch featured sandwiches, burgers, some specialties and a lighter fare. The sandwich selection includes a Reuben, hot beef or turkey, tuna melt, Monte Cristo, French dip, barbecue beef, chicken salad, BLT, Philly beef and cheese, meatloaf and a veggie croissant. A Frisco burger on sourdough bread with Thousand Island dressing is offered. The other choices are chicken fried steak, Grandma's beef stew, pot pies, soup, chili and taco or chef salad.

Service was friendly, down-to-earth and very efficient with the coffee pot (a critical factor in my mornings!). Grandma is evident everywhere in this quaint, country-style, one-room family restaurant. A cut-out, wood poster of Grandma with gold curly hair wearing a gardening cap and holding flowers greets you at the entrance. In the back is a wood clock painted red with the word "Godmothers" inscribed on it. The dining room is garnished with wreaths, dolls, wood ducks and kettles. Pictures of a cow, a family sitting down to dinner, and jars of jam, jelly and apple butter enhance the bucolic background. Blue is the predominant color here. Tiny hearts and little farm houses are painted on blue walls that match the chairs, tables, wall shelves and trellises. Grandmother's Kitchen is the ideal place for Mother's Day, Grandparent's Day or anytime you are in the mood for home-cooked food in a very down-home setting.

Grandma's Beef Stew
(Serves 6)

1 pound lean beef, cubed
4 carrots, sliced
2 onions, chopped
1 15-ounce can stewed tomatoes
   with juice
1 cup peas

1 cup cut green beans
1 cup mushrooms, sliced
1 package of brown gravy,
   prepared
4 medium potatoes, cubed
Dash of thyme and oregano

1. Brown beef for 15 minutes with tomatoes and juice.
2. Add remaining ingredients and simmer for 1 to 1 1/2 hours or until vegetables are tender.
3. Add brown gravy for taste. Serve in a bread bowl.

Recipe by: Thor Furness, owner and head cook

RECIPE INDEX

BEEF

Espresso-Blackened Tenderloin of Beef, Au Poivre, with Rich Mashed Potatoes and Yam Frites. Renaissance, Aspen, **19**

Beef Wellington. The Wellington Inn, Breckenridge, **85**

Thai Banderillas with Peanut Sauce. Backcountry Gourmet, Crested Butte, **99**

Double Peppered Flank Steak. Back Street Steakhouse, Grand Lake, **173**

Filet Mignon "Garlic Sun". Alpine Bistro, Steamboat springs, **242**

CHICKEN

Vol Au Vent. Le Rendezvous, Durango, **114**

Jamaican Jerk Chicken. The Columbine, Evergreen, **127**

Oven-Fried Chicken. J. C.'s Deli and Bakery, Limon, **193**

Indo Chicken with Sweet and Sour Cucumber Relish. The Pickle Barrel, Silverton, **222**

Ricotta Stuffed Chicken. Steamboat Brewery and Tavern, Steamboat Springs, **252**

Chicken Picatta. Alpine Lodge Restaurant, Westcliff, **289**

Chicken La Bomba. The Hideaway, Winter Park, **293**

DESSERT

Rice Pudding. The Wayside Inn, Berthoud, **35**

White Chocolate Sundried Cherry Bread Pudding with Berry Sauce and Vanilla Bean Cream. Top of the Word, Breckenridge, **81**

Hazelnut Ice Cream Cake with Chocolate Rum Sauce. Soupçon, Crested Butte, **108**

Roasted Strawberry and Cherry Meringue Pie. Blue Creek Grill, El Jebel, **124**

Montana Huckleberry Pie. Keys on the Green, Evergreen, **130**

Cream Cheese Peanut Butter Pie. Daily Bread, Glenwood Springs, **141**

Coconut Cream Pie. Country Peddler, Granite, **179**

RECIPE INDEX

Gooseberry Pie. The Goose Berry Patch, Penrose, **214**

Pecan Cobbler. Steamboat Smokehouse, Steamboat Springs, **255**

LAMB

Grilled Australian Lamb Sirloin with Goat Cheese, Caramelized Onion Crostada, and Balsamic Mint Jus. Seasons, Durango, **120**

Grilled Colorado lamb Chops with Garlic and Raspberry Sauces. Uptown Bistro, Frisco, **137**

Colorado Lamb Chops. Great Northern Tavern, Keystone, **183**

Grilled Lamb Chops with Tomato Pearl Couscous. The Brothers' Grill, Snowmass Village, **225**

MEXICAN

Crawfish Chili Rellenos with Tabasco Buerre Blanc on top of a Roasted Corn and Black Bean Relish. Swan Mountain Inn, Breckenridge, **76**

White Bean Chili. Dos Hombres, Glenwood Springs, **144**

Yucatecan Soft Shell Tacos. Los Desperados, Glenwood Springs, **147**

Shrimp Enchiladas with Jalapeño Cream Sauce. E. G.'s Garden Grill, Grand Lake, **176**

Fish Tacos. Su Casa, Keystone, **186**

Refried Beans. Chili Willy's, Minturn, **211**

Pizza Burrito. Emma's Hacienda, San Luis, **218**

Chili Rellenos with Green Tomatillo Sauce. The Cantina, Steamboat Springs, **245**

PASTA AND PIZZA

Feta Fettuccine. Blue River Bistro, Breckenridge, **59**

Rasta Pasta. Rasta Pasta, Breckenridge, **72**

Spinach-Walnut Fettuccine. Double Diamond Restaurant, Copper Mountain, **95**

Greek Pizza. The Brick Oven Pizza, Crested Butte, **102**

Pasta della Casa. Mama's Boy, Durango, **117**

Southwestern Fettuccine. Table Mountain Inn, Golden, **168**

RECIPE INDEX

Blackened Chicken Alfredo. Stagecoach, Manitou Springs, **203**

Spinach-Ricotta Pizza. Crystal River Way Station, Marble, **207**

PORK

Grilled Pork Tenderloin with Apple Brandy Mustard Sauce. Cache Cache, Aspen, **7**

Double Cut Pork Chops on Tomato-Apple Chutney with Pickled Figs. Grouse Mountain Grill, Beaver Creek, **30**

Stuffed Cabbage. European Café and Deli, Manitou springs, **196**

Loin of Pork Chop with Cranberry Port Sauce. Village Steakhouse, Snowmass Village, **236**

Baby-Back Ribs with Barbecue Sauce. T. J. Bummer's, Sterling, **259**

SALAD, SAUCE, SOUP AND STEW

Zuppa di Carote "Marco Polo". Carrot Ginger Soup (Hot or Cold). Caffé Amici, Aspen, **11**

Roasted Red Pepper and Corn Chowder. Augustine Grill, Castle Rock, **89**

Provincial Vegetable Soup. The Forest Queen, Crested Butte, **105**

Green Chili. Fairplay Hotel, Fairplay, **134**

Oriental Chicken Salad. Café Grand'mere, La Junta, **190**

Chicken Brunswick Stew. The Stew Pot, Snowmass Village, **232**

Barbecue Sauce. The Mother Lode, South Fork, **239**

Spicy Tomato Tortilla Soup. La Taquería, Winter Park, **296**

Grandma's Beef Stew. Grandmother's Kitchen, Woodland Park, **301**

SEAFOOD

Peppered Ahi Tuna with Tomato Risotto, and Brown Butter-Balsamic Vinaigrette. The Mother Lode, Aspen, **14**

Cioppino. Chefy's, Basalt, **23**

Chipotle Barbecue Tuna with Caramelized Onion. Hearthstone, Breckenridge, **63**

RECIPE INDEX

Cinnamon Spice Rubbed Sea Bass with Pico de Gallo. Mi Casa, Breckenridge, **67**

Salmon sto Fourno. Cyprus Café, Durango, **112**

Pulpos Guisdos. The Loop, Manitou Springs, **199**

Shannon's Shrimp. Butch's Lobster Bar, Snowmass Village, **229**

Steamed Seafood Basket a la Fireside. Aly's Fireside Café, Walsenburg, **285**

VEAL

Sweet Breads "Fawn Brook". The Fawn Brook Inn, Allenspark, **3**

Ossobuco Alla Fiorentina. Pino's, Castle Rock, **92**

VEGETABLE

Peggy's Marinated Cole Slaw. Smokin' Moe's, Winter Park, **299**

WILD GAME

Pan-Seared Medallions of Australian Kangaroo with Sugar Plum Kiwi Compote. The Golden Eagle Inn, Beaver Creek, **27**

Caribou. Adams Street Grill, Breckenridge, **56**

Cornish Game Hens. The Mountain Sage Café, Breckenridge, **70**

Lapin à ma façon. "Rabbit my way". L'Apogee, Steamboat Springs, **249**

Cervena Cold Smoked Roast of Red Deer. The Tyrolean, Vail, **280**

WANT MORE RESTAURANTS, RECIPES AND SPECIAL OFFERS??

If you are enjoying **Colorado Restaurants Off The Beaten Path**, you will want to order a copy of **Colorado Restaurants and Recipes from Small Towns** with MORE restaurants, recipes and special offers (101 of each to be exact). NONE of the restaurants or recipes in either book appear in the other book. That means, that if you have both books, you will have 172 different restaurants from Colorado's small towns and their recipes to choose from!!

Colorado Restaurants and Recipes from Small Towns was a FINALIST FOR THE COLORADO BOOK AWARD! To obtain your copy and SAVE 25% OFF THE RETAIL PRICE, simply fill out the order form on the next page, carefully tear out the page from the book and mail it to the address at the top of the page. You can also order additional copies of this book at a SAVINGS OF $4 PER COPY by using this same form.

HURRY!! There is only a limited supply left of **Colorado Restaurants and Recipes from Small Towns.**

ORDER FORM FOR RESTAURANT GUIDE/COOKBOOKS

SMALL TOWN PUBLICATIONS
P.O. BOX 621275
LITTLETON, CO 80162

NAME _____

ADDRESS _____

_____

Telephone _____

____ Copies of **Colorado Restaurants and Recipes from Small Towns** @ $12 each
(regular price $16 — **SAVE 25%!**) $_____

____ Copies of **Colorado Restaurants Off The Beaten Path** @ $15 each
(regular price $19 — **SAVE $4!**) $_____

       Sub-Total $_____

Sales Tax (4.8% of sub-total) $_____

Packaging and Postage ($2.00 for
1st copy. $.50 for additional copies
up to $6.00 maximum) $_____

       TOTAL (Add last 3 lines) $_____

Please send check to address above. (Sorry, no credit cards). Please allow 10 days for delivery.

NOTE: After December 31, 1998, please call (303) 329-8283 to confirm mailing address.